D1080170

MINI

~ALL MODELS~

GUIDE TO PURCHASE & D.I.Y. RESTORATION

LINDSAY PORTER

Foulis

Haynes

Other Haynes Publishing Group titles of interest to Mini enthusiasts:

BL Mini 1959-69 Owner's Workshop Manual (527)
BL Mini 1969-84 Owner's Workshop Manual (646)
BL Mini Owner's Handbook (390)
Mini Cooper Super Profile by Graham Robson (F445)
Amazing Mini by Peter Filby (F395)
The Works Minis by Peter Browning (F278)
Tuning BL's A-Series Engine (F414)
The BMC/BL Competitions Department – 25 years in Motor Sport (F677)
All of the above should be available from good bookshops. In case of difficulty please write to the publisher.

A FOULIS Motoring Book

First published 1984
Reprinted 1985, 1987, 1988 & 1989

Published by:
Haynes Publishing Group
Sparkford, Yeovil, Somerset BA22 7JJ, England

Haynes Publications Inc.
861 Lawrence Drive, Newbury Park, California 91320 USA

British Library Cataloguing in Publication Data
Porter, Lindsay
   Mini – guide to purchase & DIY restoration.
   1. Morris Mini minor automobile
   629.28'722   TL215.M615

ISBN 0-85429-379-5

Library of Congress catalogue card number 84-48562

Editor: Rod Grainger
Page layout: Tim Rose
Printed, in England, by: J.H. Haynes & Co. Ltd

Contents

Foreword by Paddy Hopkirk

Paddy Hopkirk, one of the greatest British rally drivers of all time, made his name in the Mini.

Born in Belfast in 1933, Paddy's first interest in cars was at the age of 9 when, in a J.A.P.-engined machine, more reminiscent of a bathtub than a car, he tore round an estate near near his home in Whitehouse on the outskirts of Belfast. Later, when studying engineering at Trinity College, Dublin, he bought an Austin Seven and started Rallying in earnest. Four years later, he won the Irish Rally Championship.

Since then, and until his retirement in 1970, Paddy Hopkirk has built up a reputation which was consolidated by his outright win of the Monte Carlo Rally in 1964. In 1966 he 'won' again, only to be disqualified on the most absurd of technicalities and ironically, it was the storm of controversy that broke over his disqualification that helped to make 'Mini' and 'Hopkirk' household names all over Europe. He retired from rallying in 1970, at 37 years of age and took his flair, charisma and sharp competitive edge into the world of business where his motor car accessory company, Mill Accessory Group Ltd continues to thrive and his name and 'Monte' logo can still be seen gracing parts in many an accessory shop. Of course, the accessory boom of the 'sixties, spawned largely by the Mini has long diminished and the Mill Accessory Group has quietly moved into other areas such as luggage racks, petrol cans, dog guards, car ramps and stands and so on.

Paddy writes:

I'm delighted that this book has been written. The Mini has got a very special place in my affections and in fact I tried to buy some of the rally cars when I left, but without much success. Now, people write to me quite regularly saying they've bought one of 'my' old cars. I was given a Mini when I won the Monte but I'm afraid that I don't use one every day anymore, simply because it wouldn't be big enough for all I have to get into a car. Mind you, I did drive a Ford XR3 the other day and the way it went, the way its front wheel drive handled, gave the memory strings a few tugs . . .

In spite of the '66 Monte fiasco, the French thought the Mini was terrific. Lord Snowdon and Princess Margaret used them, they became very much the in-car and so, in fashion conscious Paris, it was much more *chic* to pick up your girlfriend in a Mini than even a Jag. The same applied in London where they were driven by the Sloane Rangers of the time.

There's no doubt that Issigonis was an out-and-out genius to have designed a car that could mean so many things to so many different people. It was revolutionary and started the trend to transverse engine design, yet it did everything as it should. Even after a quarter of a century of Minis, those earlier cars have got real character and I'm pleased that folk are going to be putting them back together again, with the help of this book.

Today's restorers may not have quite as much to do as we gave the Special Tuning boys at Abingdon on occasions, but even so this book will be a fantastic help to every Mini repairer and restorer because it shows how to rebuild just about every part of the car. It deserves to be every bit as successful as the other restoration guides Lindsay Porter has written in this series and I offer it and every Mini restorer my best wishes.

Paddy Hopkirk.

4

Introduction & Acknowledgements

When this book first reached the book shops Mini owners were still celebrating their car's 25th birthday; what an incredible idea! The young-at-heart, fun loving Mini was actually a quarter of the age of the motor car itself and still going strong, scheduled by BL to last to the end of the decade at the very least.

Outwardly the first and latest Minis look very similar and, in fact, the cars' body panels have remained the same or are interchangeable. On the other hand early and late Minis are very different sorts of animals to own. The 1980s car comes fully equipped, conventional and civilised. An early Mini contains lots of little surprises which reflect the obstinate, original character of its designer. Other than with a Mini, sliding windows are not too common and you certainly don't often find what looks like a piece of string to pull the doors shut. And where on earth is the starter button?

But of course it's on the floor between the seats where it operates directly on to the long battery cable which runs beneath the car.

Early Minis, Mini Coopers, Mini Estates and just plain older Minis all give, in their various degrees, individuality, fun and terrific mechanical reliability at the same time presenting the owner with a degree of spares availability, economy and usability unrivalled by any other car of its kind. In short, you have in the Mini the ideal restorer's car.

This book shows the real life problems that were encountered when restoring real life Minis and my thanks are due to the owners of the cars which were photographed in my body shop where the cars were restored. A handful of photographs were supplied by Paul Skilleter and Practical Classics magazine and thanks are due to them too. A number of specialist suppliers have helped with expert advice including SIP (Industrial Products) Ltd, The Welding Centre, BOC Ltd and Murex Welding Products Ltd, Lifesure Insurance Specialists, Finnigans (the makers of Waxoyl) and Sykes-Pickavant Tools.

On the Mini front the Midland Mini Centre kindly helped out when photographs were needed in a hurry, while as an authoritative source of information on what to look for when buying a Mini Keith Dodd of the Mini Spares Cente in London was highly impressive. Keith's Company also sold me most of the Mini parts shown in use in this book while the MIG Welders shown being used throughout were supplied by SIP.

Finally, but not least my wife Shan put in a sterling amount of work in sub-editing, typing and taking a large number of photographs. Without her these restoration guides would scarcely be possible.

Using this book

The layout of this book has been designed to be both attractive and easy to follow during practical work on your car. However, to obtain maximum benefit from the book, it is important to note the following points:

1) Apart from the introductory pages, this book is split into two parts: chapters 1 to 7 dealing with history, buying and practical procedures; appendices 1 to 7 providing supplementary information. Each chapter/ appendix may be sub-divided into sections and even sub-sections. Section headings are in italic type between horizontal lines and sub-section headings are similar, but without horizontal lines.

2) Photograph captions are an integral part of the text (except those in chapters 1 and 2) — therefore the photographs and their captions are arranged to ''read'' in exactly the same way as the normal text. In other words they run down each column and the columns run from left to right of the page.

Each photograph caption carries an alpha-numeric identity, relating it to a specific section. The letters before the caption number are simply the initial letters of key words in the relevant section heading, whilst the caption number shows the position of the particular photograph in the section's picture sequence. Thus photograph/ caption 'DR22' is the 22nd photograph in the section headed ''Door Repairs''.

3) Figures — illustrations which are not photographs — are numbered consecutively throughout the book. Figure captions do not form any part of the text. Therefore Figure 5 is simply the 5th figure in the book.

4) All references to the left or right of the vehicle are from the point of view of somebody standing behind the car looking forwards.

5) Because this book concentrates upon restoration, regular maintenance procedures and normal mechanical repairs of all the car's components, are beyond its scope. It is therefore strongly recommended that one of the Haynes *Mini Owner's Workshop Manuals* should be used as a companion volume.

6) We know it's a boring subject, especially when you really want to get on with a job — but your safety, through the use of correct workshop procedures, must ALWAYS be your foremost consideration. It is essential that you read, and UNDERSTAND, appendix 1 before undertaking any of the practical tasks detailed in this book.

7) Whilst great care is taken to ensure that the information in this book is as accurate as possible, the author, editor or publisher cannot accept any liability for loss, damage or injury caused by errors in, or ommissions from, the information given.

1 Heritage

Mini-Make-up

Nowadays, we in Britain are so used to passing a Mini in the street, parking next to one, hurrying across the road as one tucks sharpishly round the corner or, perhaps jumping into and driving a Mini, that the reaction of the public to the car's introduction in 1959 is a little hard to take on board.

Everyone knew even before the Mini appeared that something 'different' was on the cards and the car's launch became a well orchestrated media event. Sadly, there was a heck of a lot of national cynicism around at the time, and the first reaction of most folk was to guffaw at the very idea: the Mini didn't fit the conservative view of what a car ought to be and it didn't fit many people's image of what the British Motor Corporation ought to be doing.

At that time, BMC were in the running for being the fourth largest car manufacturing company in the world (in contrast to today's sad and sorry position of being the smallest mass-producers in Europe) and their new car *had* to be something special. The first crop of post-war motor cars were ageing, the first petrol crisis (Suez, 1956) had brought a new dimension to the needs of the motoring public and the general level of affluence had risen. Folk could afford more, and manufacturers were rising to the challenge. Most car makers gave people new cars which were simply pretty new wrappings neatly folded around boxes which contained much the same as before. Of course, there were technical improvements to be made but you could hardly describe anything that the contemporary opposition was to offer as a quantum leap forwards. It's probably an over-simplification to say that Ford merely modified the Prefect to make the Anglia; that Renault dressed up the 4CV and called it the Dauphine; or that Triumph rebuilt the Standard 10 as the Herald. Of course, Renault for instance, invested the Dauphine

with real *chic*, (though with diabolical road-holding) and an advertising campaign that now features in marketing history textbooks as a 'classic', but the Renault Dauphine was hardly as new as its image. The Mini, in contrast, came . . . from where?

It's often said that there's nothing new in this world, and to an extent that is perfectly true. Even the Mini, regarded by many as a 'new' breakthrough, was the sum of many individual parts with their own background and development histories. The most venerable part of the car was its engine.

Alec Issigonis, the Mini's designer, was told right from the start that he would have to use the BMC A-series engine as the basis of his new car and time has shown that to have been a wise move. The car was sufficiently innovatory without having to run the risk of using an unproven engine too, and the 848cc version of the A35/Minor engine was a great success from almost every angle. It was a direct development of the unit which had first seen service in 1951 in the Austin A30 and which was itself essentially a smaller version of the 1200cc Austin A40 unit; this was later to become known as the B-series engine and find fame in enlarged form when fitted to the MGA and MGB amongst several other models. The smaller A-series engine was originally of 803cc capacity and was a conventional four-cylinder with a three bearing crankshaft running in thin-wall bearings. One of its most notable features was its highly efficient cylinder head, designed by Harry Weslake, an independent consultant, who discovered that a heart-shaped combustion area with a protruding peninsula between inlet and exhaust valves permitted gases to swirl and so promoted more complete and efficient combustion of the mixture. The engine was used in the Austin A30 and Morris Minor until 1956 when it was enlarged to 948cc and the cars renamed Austin A35 and Morris 1000 respectively. Actually, the engine was redeveloped rather than simply enlarged, its bores being siamesed (i.e: losing the water jackets that were previously situated between them) and lead-indium crankshaft bearings were accompanied by great improvements in crankshaft and connecting rod strength and bearing sizes.

Having dealt with the engine, let's take a look at the rest of the car where there are ideas that seem to have come from nowhere but the brain of the brilliant designer Alec Issigonis. The gearbox was placed beneath the engine, sharing its engine oil with the unit 'upstairs' because, in all logic, that was the only place it *could* go in order to meet Issigonis' design criteria for the car. A front mounted, transverse engine was a 'must' if maximum passenger space was to be made available and an in-line configuration gave an intolerably poor steering lock. (In fact, it could be that Issigonis was influenced by the stillborn Alan Lanburn economy car of 1952 with engine-over-gearbox transverse layout — after

all, Issigonis corresponded with Lanburn when the idea was offered to Alvis where Issigonis was working at the time.)

The tiny wheels, which seemed especially small by comparison with the chariot-sized wheels fitted to other contemporary cars, such as the 'sit-up-and-beg' Ford Popular, were deemed necessary to give the required amount of additional passenger space inside the car while the partnership with rubber suspensions provided the ideal foil to the problems of excessive harshness which small wheels can produce on rough roads. Rubber suspension proved ideal for the Mini for a number of other reasons, too. The car was so light, weighing in at only around 1300 pounds, that the addition of four occupants could easily add 50% to the all-up weight! Any conventional springing system designed to put up with that sort of loading would have been unduly stiff at low load levels, or would have possessed the length of suspension travel of the lean-happy Citroen 2CV, which Issigonis clearly did not want. Rubber, however, has the useful quality of becoming progressively stiffer as it is depressed, which fitted the bill perfectly. In addition, of course, the small amount of room taken up by the suspension gave another space-saving bonus.

The Mini's ten-inch wheels were all its own and were developed by Dunlop after Issigonis approached them with his requirements. It is said that Dunlop's researches actually began with an examination of an *eight* inch wheel, but it was found that such a small size left insufficient room for brakes. Even the idea of a ten-inch wheel broke with all tradition and meant that new ground had to be covered in its design. Of course, bubble cars had used wheels of this size but only in conjunction with skinny tyres, poor performance and light loadings. There were some initial problems with ensuring that the tyres remained located on the wheel but these were overcome by increasing the depth of the rim. Issigonis' thinking with regard to

small wheels was not an over-night revelation but the end result of progressive thinking in that direction. When Issigonis designed the Morris Minor just after the Second World War, he stood it on 14 inch wheels, while the contemporary Morris Eight used 17 inch diameter wheels and even the 'baby' Fiat of the day, the 'Topolino', used 15 inch wheels. When the time came to design the Mini, his daring innovation on the Minor had become the norm and another leap of imagination was required.

The point that evolution played its part in the design of the Mini is worth making here. Even the rubber suspension idea had been around for some time and, indeed, Issigonis had used it as early as 1939 in his hillclimb car the 'Lightweight Special' (although in a different form) and Alex Moulton, another notable innovator of the age, had developed the basic thinking behind the suspension (before, incidentally, going on to market his own 'mini', the Moulton Special small-wheeled bicycle with its own rubber suspension system).

The final piece in the technological jigsaw was the acquisition of a suitable type of constant velocity joint to drive the wheels. The problem with the traditional Hookes type of c.v. joint, as any owners of an early 2CV will appreciate, is that the 'velocity' imparted is less than 'constant', especially at lower speeds and full lock; in fact it was felt that this type of joint would give an unacceptable degree of snatch and feedback through the steering wheel. Hardy Spicer were commissioned to examine the problem and found a joint which was already in very low volume production and used in connection with submarine conning tower control gear. It had been designed as far back as 1926 by a Czech called Hans Rzeppa, and now its moment had come.

Strangely, in examining each of these key innovations one by one: the transverse engine, transmission in the sump, 10 inch wheels, small tyres and wheels, rubber suspension and true constant velocity joints, one does not gain a true impression of the impact of the whole car, not even when you consider the strides made in space, utilisation, weight saving and so on. The reason is that the Mini was conceived by Alec Issigonis as a total concept and that the components are only its necessary building blocks. The car as a whole adds up to much more than the sum of its parts, impressive though they may be. In the end, it's what the Mini did and continues to do for ordinary folk that makes it so extraordinary. The individual ideas just *had* to be made to work in order that the original concept could function.

Man Behind The Mini

The days are now gone when the inspiration, let alone the design effort behind an individual car can be ascribed to one man. The Chapmans, Herbert Austins, W.O. Bentleys and the Healeys of today are now cut down to anonymity in the motor car world where the financial safety of the manufacturer must be the prime consideration. Alec Issigonis must rank among the greatest of all innovators being responsible for not one but two 'landmark' motor cars and with ideas enough for more.

Alec Issigonis was born in Smyrna (now Izmir) in 1906 as a British subject, with a German mother and in line to inherit the family business. When Germany occupied his homeland during the First World War, young Alec lived under house arrest while the Germans commissioned his grandfather's factory. After the war, his family was forced to flee and abandon all they had as Greece and Turkey fought one of their periodic wars over possession of disputed territory. At 15, Issigonis arrived in England and attended Battersea Technical College where he gained a grounding in basic

engineering in spite of a glaring and self-confessed weakness in maths.

In 1928, he began work in a London drawing office draughting a design for an automatic clutch. Humber showed an interest in the clutch but in the end rejected it and 'head hunted' Issigonis instead. In 1936, Issigonis made the significant move to Morris at Cowley, his pre-Second World War work there culminating in his design for the MG YA front suspension which was not actually put into use until after the cessation of hostilities but which was good enough to find favour with a line of cars including the MGA and then, in refined form, the MGB.

After spending the war years allowing his fertile mind to range over a wide variety of military vehicle applications, Issigonis' first moments of wide acclaim came with his design for the new small Morris, the post-war Morris Minor. In its way, the Minor was a revolutionary car: it was the first small British car to be equipped with independent torsion-bar front suspension, it was fitted with wheels that were considered daringly small for the time and its cornering was nothing short of sensational when compared with that of its contemporaries. Unfortunately, the Minor's engine and gearbox failed to match the performance potential of the rest of the car until the Austin Morris merger into the British Motor Corporation in November 1951 made the cross-fertilisation of an Austin engine into the Morris Minor a possibility. (Although most would agree that the A-series engine still left the Minor underpowered until it was enlarged to 948cc in 1956.) Issigonis had fitted the sidevalve pre-war Morris 8 engine from Hobson's choice, although he had produced exciting plans for an all-new flat four engine for the Minor that Morris simply couldn't afford to develop.

However, during 1951/52, Issigonis produced an experimental front-wheel-drive Minor with engine, clutch and gearbox transversely all in a line and a final

drive beneath. Issigonis never drove the prototype but it was completed and used as an everyday car by Jack Daniels, one of the Minor development team. Daniels was later to claim that this prototype Minor played a key role in the conception of the Mini because not only was its handling outstandingly good but also, so the story goes, it was parked outside Leonard Lord's office window every day!

Shortly after the BMC merger, Issigonis moved temporarily away from BMC and joined Alvis where he designed a sports saloon with almost frightening specification. It was to be capable of over 110mph and boasted a 3.5-litre V8 engine, a two-speed gearbox with overdrive on each gear and — significantly — hydrolastic-type suspension.

In November 1955 Lord lured Issigonis back into the BMC fold with the promise that he could start again where he left off with the Minor and have a free hand in designing an all-new small car which would rejuvenate BMC's ageing model line-up. Issigonis gathered around himself a small team including, once again, Jack Daniels. Issigonis already had a number of established concepts about what a small car should have as its major attributes, such as front wheel drive (he had a long-standing regard for the Citroen *Traction Avant*), small, space-saving wheels and wheelarches, rack and pinion steering, front-heaviness and a general high regard for function rather than fashion. With that much established, Issigonis began, unconventionally but typically, by considering the ergonomic requirements of four passengers, finding the space needed by them and designing a bodyshell to fit.

In the Ancient Greek, there are no words to differentiate between 'Art' and 'Craft'; they were considered to be one and the same thing. Issigonis, the modern Greek, was a man capable of drawings of great artistic merit which although far removed in appearance were every bit as effective as 'technical' drawings. The fact that Issigonis was capable of truly creative thought and yet was an engineer with the technical insight and determination to make things work in a highly successful manner, went some way towards proving the ancients right. Being right and looking right were, to Issigonis, one and the same thing: a rare view in our modern, dualistic society.

Mini Roots

Where did the concept behind the Mini and its name come from? Leonard Lord who had been in charge at Austin since November 1945 announced in 1947 that Austin were to build their first post-war medium sized cars to replace the sit-up-and-beg old-timers they were still churning out. As R.J. Wyatt in his book *Austin 1905-1952* points out: 'As early as January 1947 Lord had told shareholders that he was not yet proposing to make a *Mini* car [my italics]; that description seems first to have been applied to a small economy vehicle much earlier than has generally been imagined. He could not really have called the A40 a Mini any more than Nuffield could have used the name for his famous Morris Minor. A car had to be very much smaller to be termed Mini and it had to be revolutionary enough to become a cult before any title would stick.'

So the Mini *car* concept was known to be voiced by Leonard Lord some twelve years before the launch of *the* Mini, but that was not all. In 1951, Austin launched the A30, a baby car in the pre-war Austin Seven mould but with far more advanced features. The engine was a development of the Austin Dorset and Devon engine but generally reduced in size, the smaller engine becoming known as the A-series engine and the larger, the B-series. Wyatt, again, says of the car's development: 'Many components and arrangements were tried, including two-cylinder and four-cylinder engines, front and rear engine locations and just about

every known variation of power unit and suspension system. The basic problem was to be able to carry four people and luggage in the smallest body possible at the minimum cost.' Once again, Leonard Lord was the motivating force behind the car and while it failed to match Issigonis' Minor (produced by the arch rivals at Morris, of course) in terms of steering, cornering and in the utilisation of space, it was a somewhat more compact car. It ended up as a car which was conventional in all respects, except that it was Austin's first chassisless car, but it is interesting to note that so many innovations were considered, almost certainly at the behest of Lord.

Later, of course, it was Leonard Lord who brought Issigonis into BMC to design the Mini, and there is no doubting that the initial push towards the ideas revolution that became the Mini actually started with the widely disliked but undoubtedly successful Leonard Lord.

It has already been noted that Issigonis set about designing the car around the needs of the occupants – he came up with the requirement that, less engine and boot space, the car required a minimum of 105 inches (2670mm) in length, 50 inches (1270mm) in width and 52 inches (1320mm) in height – and that several leaps of the imagination were required to make the package come together but perhaps nothing was more unconventional than his view that the gearbox could be placed beneath the engine, in an extended sump and share the engine's oil. (Incidentally, Mini gearboxes seem to last just as well as others, so why the need for 'special', more expensive oils. Are they simply more profitable for the oil companies?)

In the event, there was just one small feature of the car that was partly spoiled because of Alec Issigonis' famous stubbornness. He deemed that radios in cars were a 'bad thing' and so there was never any provision for locating a radio in the Mini's dashboard area. Mind you, if it had not been for the

stubborn determination of Sir Alec Issigonis (as he later became) the little car, with all its advances and their attendant problems would undoubtedly never have existed . . .

The first Mini prototype was fitted with a 948cc engine, as used in the contemporary Austin A35s and A40s (the Farina type, not the bulbous, earlier A40s) and the Morris Minor and the car was significantly quicker than any other saloon using this unit. It was built with the 'front' of the engine facing the right-hand side of the car and this meant that the exhaust pipe had either to snake its way around or pass underneath the engine and also that the carburettor, situated behind the front grille was prone to icing-up whilst the distributor was cramped inaccessibly between engine and bulkhead. A decision was made to turn the engine around which meant, of course, that the crankshaft was turning the 'wrong' way (unless owners had been prepared to put up with four reverse gears and one forward!) and so an idle or 'drop' gear was used which meant a 4% drop in efficiency due to the energy taken out of the system by the additional gear. The reversed engine made the carb the now all-but inaccessible component, while storing up trouble for the ignition system: in any case the change to Morris' favourite carburettor, the S.U. and away from Austin's Zenith downdraught probably did as much as anything to solve the icing-up problem. Another future problem identified at this stage was that rear-end lightness caused lack of braking efficiency and locked-up rear brakes: the battery was moved into the boot in an effort to minimise the problem while the addition of a rear brake limiter in the hydraulic system also helped.

Other alterations that took place between the construction of the sheet-metal 'Orange-Box' prototype and the pre-production versions were that engine size was reduced to 848cc from the 948cc of the standard unit, by the relatively simple expedient of reducing the stroke from 76mm to 68.2mm. The

The Mini's construction is unusual in that its front end is a self-contained structure . . .

car was made two inches wider and it was decided to mount most of the front-end mechanical components into a separate, detachable subframe and the rear components, such as they were, into another independent subframe. The Longbridge assembly plant was designed to build cars with engines offered up from beneath and even though a new assembly line was built for the Mini, the tradition was continued, only this time engine, gearbox, final drive, front wheels and brakes, steering and suspension all came to up to meet the car in one unit.

Launch and Development

For what was virtually an all-new car, the Mini was designed and developed in incredibly short order and it now seems surprising that there were not more technical problems with the car than proved to be the case. However, there *were* problems, including those of oil getting onto the clutch and leaking floorpans (the official and completely lame excuse was that final pre-production road testing was carried out during a particularly dry spell!). In fact, the car's 'newness' and its faults, which were often blown up out of all proportion by the contemporary press, meant

that initial sales were disappointing, many potential buyers showing great interest in the car but in the end prefering to stick with the known qualities of the Minor or A40. In addition, the dealers were not entirely enamoured with the car. As Jeff Daniels says in his book, *British Leyland: The Truth About The Cars*, 'It was not the car the dealers wanted. Their spares and service departments took justified fright at some of the Mini's complications. It was a cheap car, which made for low margins. Its early problems of unreliability swallowed a lot of time in warranty paperwork. None of that mattered. Lord had faith in Issigonis . . .' In spite of all this, the show was on the road and the dealers, who had been given both Austin and Morris versions of the car, built at Longbridge in Birmingham and Cowley near Oxford in deference to their still-jealously guarded pre-BMC status, were later to cry all the way to the bank as the Mini sold and sold, giving them a continuing turnover on cars, parts, accessories and servicing. Moreover, in spite of the oft-repeated claim that BMC/B.L. made a trading loss on the sale of Minis, the benefit that accrued from economies of scale in many shared components must have been enormous.

The Mini's price-new caused some comment when it was launched (although the legendary below-£500 price tag is not confirmed by *The Motor* whose 1959 road test showed a price of £537. 6s. 8d., nor by *Glass's Guide*

of the day which gives a launch basic price of £506). Even so, only the old 'upright' Ford Popular (which was dropped in price by Ford from £444 in 1957 and '58 to £419 in 1959 to help clear their decks for the 'New Popular') was cheaper among small cars, and for that you still got an unmistakeably pre-war car! The more modern looking (but mechanically ordinary) 'New' Ford Popular was still £2 dearer than the Mini, the tiny Fiat 500 was priced at £525 and everything else, from Minor and A40 to Standard 8 and the Ford Anglia 105E ranged in the £603 to £665 price bracket. If the Mini seemed cheap in 1959, what of the 1963 price move which *dropped* the Mini's price to a mere £455 and left it below the £500 mark until 1967? And yet, in retrospect, it may not have been only its low cost that turned the Mini into a big seller. Its extremely poor sales figures for 1959 can be discounted because of the fact that the car was not launched until the summer and because it is unlikely that production would have got properly under way. In 1960 the Mini sold a little over 100,000 units world-wide, in 1961 the figure was 150,000 + and by 1962, the figure had jumped to the over 200,000 level which was to become the minimum for almost a couple of decades. As people overcame their natural caution and came to accept the Mini as a normal piece of street furniture, they became more likely to buy it. In addition, the rich and famous had taken to the Mini like a new toy and created the image that the Mini was *tres chic*. Certainly once they had overcome their inhibitions, no one could have failed to have been impressed by the little car.

The Motor was impressed at launch, saying: 'Characteristics which have often been thought utterly incompatible are combined amazingly well in the new 848cc Austin Seven. It is an exceptionally low-priced car which costs little to run, and its overall dimensions are extremely compact. Yet it carries four adults with space to spare, potters with conventional multi-cylinder smoothness or accelerates briskly up to a top speed of well over 70mph, rides comfortably and handles with exceptional precision'.

After it had had time to think the Mini over, *The Motor* published another road test, this time of the other Mini twin, the Mini-Minor. Apart from a small criticism of the size of the rear view mirror and the only semi-adequacy of the brakes, this mid-1960 road test was just as enthusiastic about the little car, pointing out that in spite of the Mini's lack of inches, 'far from needing to feel slightly apologetic about his rate of progress in a modern main-road traffic stream, the Mini-Minor owner is far more likely to be irked by bigger cars getting in his way.'

The Motor rounded off grandly: 'In short, this 850cc BMC design is an outstanding example of advanced theory being proved to the hilt in practice, and it is doubly satisfying to find such a car emanating from a British factory at so modest a price.'

In May 1960 came the first of the many Mini variants when the Mini-van was launched. Utilising a longer wheelbase than the car but with almost identical mechanical specification, the Mini-van was one of the cheapest ways to whizz around, if you could put up with the lack of rear quarter visibility, a very high level of interior noise and the very real chance of being 'nicked' for exceeding 40mph in a goods vehicle which, as the author found to his cost, was likely to elicit a fine of £5 or more from the local Justice. BMC made available for the van an excellent folding rear seat conversion which, when folded down, reduced the carrying capacity not at all and, in conjunction with a pair of side windows, the Mini-van became a passenger vehicle capable of being piloted at speeds up to the legal maximum before the boys in blue took an interest. Unfortunately, you were then supposed to pay some of the purchase tax which had not been paid when the van had been a new £360 commercial vehicle.

In March of the same year, the Austin Mini Countryman was announced. It was a tiny estate car based upon the van but with the spare wheel where the van's fuel tank went and with a saloon type tank. In the style of the Minor Traveller, the Mini had wooden 'shooting brake' embellishments at the rear, but unlike the Minor's they were stuck on and not a part of the vehicle's structure. The all-steel version of the Countryman was not made available in the U.K. until October 1962 but it eventually replaced the 'Woodie' version. Later, in September, the Morris Mini Traveller version was announced. Early in 1961, the Pick-up was introduced and proved to have great sales potential, especially in rural areas. All of the Commercial vehicles had a higher rear ride height, made so by the use of longer rear suspension trumpets.

Later in 1961, in October, a new Mini duo was launched called the Wolseley Hornet and the Riley Elf. Both front and rear of the car were revised while the whole appeal was somewhat more 'up-market', a trend which became even more apparent when leather replaced leathercloth for the wearing surfaces of the seats in 1962.

In September 1961, one of the most significant of all Mini developments took place when the first Cooper was introduced. The story of the Cooper is covered in another section of this book but the impact of the Cooper went beyond the requirements of those who wanted to embarrass owners of much larger cars; it led to successes on the international rally circuits on a hitherto almost unprecedented scale and it will be realised that it is no coincidence that from this point onwards, Mini sales figures really took off.

The Mini Clubman, introduced in May 1969, was an attempt to give the Mini a new look 'on the cheap'. Several design studies had been carried out at Longbridge for a Mini replacement, including one with an overhead camshaft, all-aluminium engine of excellent promise, but all were scrapped on the grounds of cost and because of the presence of weak management prone to making a string of decisions of the sort which led to the eclipse of BMC and then BL as a major force. (Incidentally, the belief that the unions were responsible for the strangulation of BL, although fostered with glee by the Fleet Street comic-strip newspapers, is proved to be a myth by those such as Graham Turner and Jeff Daniels who have both carried out in-depth analysis of the company. Obviously, the unions *reaction* to bad management was deplorable and unhelpful although perhaps inevitable under the circumstances . . .) In any case, the virtual demise of BL (as successor to BMC) meant that the only affordable long term development of the Mini turned into the Metro and that, as everyone knows, was destined to accompany the Mini and not supplant it. So, it could be argued that the Mini has kept on plugging along for almost a quarter of all the history of the motor car simply because the company that made it was too weak and too poor to replace it: a veritable silver lining if ever there was one!

Quirks and Cocktails

By designing the Mini in such a way that almost all of its mechanical components were attached to two removable subframes, Issigonis unconciously gave a lead to builders of odd-balls and specials of all types. Moreover, the Mini was such a bare little package that the minute it became fashionable it also became prone to being customised in all sorts of both tasteful, and tasteless, ways. Much of the blame, or the credit depending on how you look at it, must go to BMC themselves who, in their usual attempt to please all their dealers, produced 'badge engineered' Riley and Wolseley Minis, each with up-market appointments and revised appearance. The idea caught on and Harold Radford Ltd., suppliers of quality coachwork to the limousine-owning gentry, seized upon the Mini-Cooper with the idea of turning it into a Mini-Rolls-Royce. Although fitted with deep-pile Wilton carpet, an elaborate fascia, claustrophobically large leather seats and electric windows, the quality of craftsmanship was by no means up to coach-built standards, a fact which did not prevent the sometimes outrageously expensive little gimmicks from selling so well that other coachbuilders such as Wood and Picket and Crayford with their convertible Mini, were prevented from getting in on the act.

Another Mini conversion that caused a sensation in the mid-'sixties was the Mini-Sprint, which was a 'de-seamed' Mini with a roofline that was actually lowered by 1.5 inches to give the appearance of a rather squashed but very purposeful little car.

One of the strangest looking of alternative Minis was developed and produced by BMC themselves with the idea of military applications. Called the Mini-Moke, it consisted of an open-topped platform chassis and although it was given the thumbs down by the Generals, the Moke was regarded as a very 'swinging' mode of transport in an era when being 'with it' and 'a dedicated follower of fashion' as The Kinks would sing, mattered more than anything. An almost Moke-like variant that reached pre-production levels (and possibly around 40 were actually built) was the code-named Austin ANT (or 'Alec's New Toy', as one wag had it). The Ant was a four-wheel-drive Mini 1100 built as a chassis-cab unit with a variety of rear-end options in the style of the Land-Rover. With permanent f.w.d. and a transfer box to a tiny, square rear differential and with bags of potential versatility, the Ant could surely, have been a world-beater (and still perhaps, could!). The logic now seems clear enough: country dwellers who loved the Pick-up for its economy and utility, now aspire towards many of the existing four-wheel-drive vehicles because of the guaranteed mobility that they give and would surely have flocked to

the Ant. However, while there are still a tiny number in use today, production of the Ant was not to be.

Perhaps the Innocenti Minis should not be considered 'quirky' at all: in the late 'fifties and early 'sixties, BMC set up a number of satellite plants in several different parts of the world. From 1961, the Innocenti plant in Milan, Italy built Austins under licence and then, in 1965, began to build the Mini. In 1972, Leyland took direct control of the one-time motor scooter factory and then, two years later, launched the Innocenti Mini 90 (1000cc) and the 120 (1275cc). The two new cars were far more stylish than the standard offering both inside and out and featured a hatchback rear door. The body panels were actually made in the U.K. but the car never saw the light of day in Britain, largely because Leyland cut their Innocenti losses and ran, leaving De Tomaso to continue production of the car in spite of its high production costs and inadequate rear seat headroom.

Fitting new bodies to Minis was by no means left to the big manufacturers and many, many kit car makers have offered bodies to take the Mini's front and rear subframe unit, although most were hampered in their attempt to be sleek and stylish by the Mini's tall engine so that even the more successful cars, such as the highly priced Midas, suffered an ugly bonnet line. One of the greatest ironies was that owners of a micro-car which pre-dated the Mini's transverse engine, front-wheel-drive layout, the Berkeley, often threw out their unreliable motorcycle-based engine and transmission units and carved out a location for the Mini front end assembly to be fitted. In practice, none of these alternatives was as successful as the original car — but many were more spectacular!

Production Notes

Only saloons were built at Cowley

near Oxford. Most were Morrises but there were also some Austins. Fewer than 250,000 Minis were built at Cowley and only up until 1969. All others were built at Longbridge, Birmingham.

Non-saloon bodies were all sourced at the Castle Bromwich, Birmingham plant.

All Elfs and Hornets were built at Longbridge.

Mini-Coopers

The Morris Minor had always driven better than it went and, as a result, a number of tuning companies set about providing the early Minor with its missing get-up-and-go. The Mini was similarly possessed of cornering, handling and road-holding that were far and away better than needed for the performance generated by its engine and, once again, performance goodies became available to bridge the gap. This time, tuning was not restricted to a wealthy or eccentric few; *everyone* seemed to want to get in on the act. The engine itself had been around for quite a time and had also been widely used in Formula Junior circuit racing, so the supply was ready for the take-off in demand. The basic 848cc Mini engine, however, was not without its problems. Timing gear was very short-lived at higher engine speeds and clutches were prone to oiling up while engine torque would cause engine mountings to fracture. In addition, the authoritative late Clive Trickey claimed that in spite of its technical brilliance, the early Mini 'possessed one of the worst gearboxes and most inefficient set of brakes ever contrived.' Last but not least, the camshaft, which ran directly in the block without the aid of bearings, could seize and wreck the engine when it was being used in the most enthusiastic manner. Clearly, forcing higher output from an engine with these inherent problems was not exactly conducive

13

to promoting long and efficient engine life.

It took almost two years and a wonderful leap of faith for BMC to launch a purpose-built go-faster Mini called the Mini-Cooper, named after the highly thought of Formula Junior racer John Cooper who had brought almost unparalleled excellence to the racing development of A-series engines. As well as being able to draw upon the experiences of Cooper, BMC had gained enormous and invaluable experience from their own race and rally departments at Abingdon, which had competed in the Mini almost from the word 'go'.

Pat Moss and Stuart Turner (then a pair of unknowns) were the first to win an event in the Mini, clearing the field by ten minutes in a local Knowldale Car Club event, but other events in 1959 served only to point up reliability problems, especially with oiled-up clutches. 1960 and 1961 saw the Mini being rallied in a range of international events but with few successes of any kind except a class win in the 1960 Geneva Rally. The reasons for the car's lack of success lay in its still-developing standards of reliability, the relatively small amount of emphasis being given to it by Abingdon but, most of all, its underpowered engine.

Many private individuals as well as those who took it to the race circuits tried tuning the basic car but then found even more weaknesses. Its phenomenal cornering ability was more than early wheels could stand and under competition use many of them cracked, the brakes were not up to the job of stopping the car from higher speeds and shock absorbers failed rapidly. Under the stresses imposed by the tuners, early Mini cranks were prone to breakage at higher revs and timing gear was extremely short lived. The camshaft, running directly in the block without the normal benefit of white metal bearings, would seize when spun at high speeds which, naturally enough, generally led to a completely wrecked engine.

Then, the enthusiasm being felt for the Mini's outrageously effective handling and the needs of the works rally team were both met in one fell swoop when the first Mini-Cooper was announced in September 1961.

The car worked far more efficiently than the standard Mini could ever hope to, and an early success was chalked up when Pat Moss and Ann Wisdom won the Coupe des Dames in the 1962 Monte Carlo. Then in the Tulip Rally of the same year the same team secured a class win to be followed home by no fewer than seven other Minis!

The Mini-Cooper's improved performance leaned heavily on Formula Junior racing car practice, in which branch of the sport there were already hundreds of engines all based on the Mini (or A-series) unit. As some of these engines were actually churning out 90bhp without calamitous results the new Mini's 55bhp looked quite modest until you realise that it was actually a 50% increase over the standard car! The increase in performance came about by leaving the bore more or less as it was (there was a minute reduction in fact, so that the engine size was kept below the 1000cc rallying class limit) while a new stroke dimension of 81.28mm was used. It was announced at the time that the longer stroke engine was part of a process of 'rationalisation' of BMC's engines, but in fact it was not used again until the 1275cc engine appeared in the 1974 Cooper 'S', after which of course, it became a very common stroke size in the many 1275cc engines used in a whole range of cars. However, in 1961 it was an oddity and made the car look extremely long-stroked, although in practice, the long stroke helped to keep the engine flexible and at 1500rpm (which represents 22.5 miles per hour in top gear) the car was actually developing no less than 87% of its maximum torque (or 'pulling power') of 54.5lb.ft. What this meant in practical terms was that the car's flexibility was such that it had as much pulling power when trickling along in slow moving traffic as when screaming flat-out down a dual-carriageway, making it

a very versatile car indeed.

Issigonis himself took a personal interest in the development of the Cooper and entrusted most of the highly acclaimed Cooper 'S' development work to consultant Daniel Richmond. It has been said that Issigonis treated Richmond patronizingly and that Richmond accepted this treatment from Issigonis. The designer put what would normally be regarded as intolerable demands on the man (as he did to anyone who would allow him to) and virtually every time, Richmond came up trumps, time and again working through the right to have a piece of testing or experimentation ready for Issigonis the next morning.

Improvements in the camshaft, inlet valves and combustion chambers (the Sprite and Midget 948cc engine's head was used here) were combined with the use of twin 1¼ SU carburettors, and a multi branch exhaust manifold to boost output, while the crank webs were strengthened, lead bronze was used to line big ends and main bearings and the block itself was also strengthened. A torsional vibration damper was fitted to the nose of the crank to drastically reduce the risk of crank breakage. In short, the engine was almost totally redeveloped! A remote gearchange was fitted and the gear cogs were 'pinched' from the Sprite and Midget range to close up the gear ratios.

Special tyres with nylon casings were developed by Dunlop for the new car and disc brakes were fitted to the front. In use, these early cars' disc brakes can be something of a joke and BMC virtually admitted as much by fitting a servo-type brake booster to the new car. The Cooper was trimmed and soundproofed to a higher standard than the basic Mini (which was *very* basic!) and a range of 'Super' Minis was launched at the same time offering most of the Cooper's trim improvements.

The achievements of the 997 Mini-Cooper were apparently few but, quite apart from launching the Cooper concept in a blaze of sensational publicity, the new car coincided with the era in which the Abingdon-based works rally team gathered around it a group of drivers who were to become world famous for their rallying exploits. Pat Moss (to become Pat Moss-Carlsson), sister of Stirling Moss, became famous in her own right but left to join Ford in 1962; however Rauno Aaltonen, Timo Makinen and Paddy Hopkirk became household names as successful Mini rally drivers and each, in their turn, was to win the greatest prize, that of the Monte Carlo Rally, in years to come.

In May 1963, the 1071cc Cooper 'S' was announced, based upon a big-bore Cooper conversion and leaning even more heavily upon Formula Junior racing practice. With a 'unique' bore size and several fairly exotic engine modifications, the engine was a little 'flier' and added further to the Cooper's reputation and competition successes. However, the car was produced only for a year or so and only 4,000 units were built which makes the 1071 something of a 'homologation special' ie a car which was produced in sufficient numbers to allow it to compete as a 'production' car. In January 1964 the basic 997 Cooper was superseded by the 998 Cooper which, although barely different in engine capacity, meant that the innards of the engine were held in common with many other basic production engines, and, in fact, the 998 Cooper engine was developed from the Riley Elf/Wolseley Hornet units, themselves made more powerful in order to drive their heavier bodies.

Eight months into its production run, the Cooper was given hydrolastic suspension in common with all other Minis. Although the 998 engine is a less 'exotic' unit than the 997, *Motor's* road tests show that it had improved performance as well as increased spares availability, giving a maximum speed of 88.7mph (85.2) and a 0-60mph time of 14.8 secs (17.2), the earlier car's figures shown in brackets. The 998 Cooper provided the bedrock of

Cooper Sales, selling steadily until November 1969.

More spectacular happenings were taking place with the Cooper 'S' models. The 1071 block had taken a great deal of development, the bores having been moved in the block which was also given extra stiffness. As a result, the Cooper 'S' developments both used the same basic block but with different strokes. The 970 'S' used a minute stroke length of 61.91mm (the shortest stroke used on any A-series engine; shorter by a considerable margin than the 1952 803cc engine) while the 1275cc engine reverted to the long stroke of the 997 engine, albeit with increased crank journal length. Of the two, the 970 'S' was relatively short-lived and was discontinued in January 1965 after a production life of only ten months, while the 1275 'S' outlived all the other Coopers and saw production from March 1964 through to July 1971 and in numerical terms sold in numbers which were second only to the 998 Cooper.

The 998 Cooper had status attached to its name but the 1275 'S' had something more; it was engineered to an altogether different standard. While the 998 was a 'go-faster' Mini, the 1275 'S' was a car with genuine top-flight competition potential in road-going form. This point was made most famously when, in 1966, the Mini-Cooper 'S' 'won' the Monte Carlo Rally for the third successive time, only to be denied by an incredibly over-zealous display of partisanship when the scrutineers literally tore the winning car apart to try to find something non-standard about it, to triumphantly proclaim that the headlamps were not precisely in conformity with the rally regulations. To answer the French press' xenophobic reaction that the English were 'cheats' (proving only that much of the French press is as extreme as our own in this respect), a Cooper 'S' was borrowed from a local main dealer's showroom and compared up a steep hillclimb course with Paddy Hopkirk's own 'winning' car. The event was overseen by *L'Equipe*, one of the

more suspicious sporting papers, and even they had to own that 'once and for all, in all important respects the cars that really won the Monte Carlo Rally were genuinely the same as you can buy', as Peter Browning, then Competitions Manager at Abingdon, wrote in his book *The Works Minis*.

After its 1964, 65 and 67 'official' Monte Carlo wins and the host of wins in international rallying, on the track and on the grass circuits, the Mini inevitably started to become less competitive as a new generation of quicker cars came along, produced largely by continental manufacturers.

Then, in 1968, came the British Leyland merger under the 'super-Salesman' Donald Stokes. One of the first decisions made by the new management was that Minis should be competed on the track rather than on rally circuits; circuit racing being a far cheaper branch of the sport. Rallying was to continue in a much reduced form but only in those countries where a direct sales benefit was perceived. The all-conquering rally team was disbanded and an air of undisguised pessimism set in among those at the Competitions Department. Their feelings of doom were quickly seen to be well founded when the department was closed down completely in mid-1970.

In 1969, the Mini 1275 GT had been announced. It was a car with 'go-faster' appeal but with little of the engineered excellence of the Cooper 'S' but at a cost of £868 compared with the £942 of the real McCoy. The 1275 GT was based on the inherently slower Clubman bodyshell and was quite a lot less powerful than the 'S', being fitted with a single-carburettor Austin 1300-type engine although in common with the 'S' it did have disc brakes and a rev-counter. In spite of the fact that the GT was clearly a shadow of the car that the Cooper had been and an unworthy successor, the demise of the Cooper 'S' was announced in July 1971, the final car undoubtedly having been built some time earlier.

Edwardes and on . . .

British Leyland lurched through the 1970s in a dreadful state: reviled at home and abroad for having a poor product range which was shoddily produced, over-manned at the virtual insistence of Government and lacking in the basic managerial skills or labour relations to get itself out of the mess.

Then the paroxysms ran themselves out and British Leyland began to change from a dying giant to a much smaller and thinner, but nevertheless surviving entity. The first event to arrest the illness was the true onset of the world recession. This forced Leyland to act or go under very quickly and it made it easier to lay off workers without total condemnation, because so many other companies were having to do the same. The fact that Britain's recession was so much deeper than that of most of our neighbours also helped inasmuch as the unions, previously dominated by extremist leaders, became more afraid of job losses and so initiated fewer stoppages.

This trend was exploited to the full by a new Chairman at British Leyland, a diminutive South African by the name of Michael Edwardes. When he joined BL from the highly successful Chloride group in 1978, Edwardes' motives were difficult to understand. If he had been looking for a challenge then he had certainly found one! Never a man to court popularity for its own sake, Edwardes won the respect of his management team and, just as importantly, the general public to such a degree that even though he left the company after a relatively short four year tenure, people began to speak well of the attempts by the various companies within BL to pull themselves together and build a model range with quality standards to satisfy almost everyone.

Through all the traumas, the upheavals and the re-adjustments sailed the evergreen Mini. Throughout the 1970s, the Mini was

retained because no one at the top had the will or the *nous* to push through its successor. When the new generation Mini did come, the old Mini was retained while the new Mini-Metro made its own impact upon the motoring world. If the Mini was retained simply as an insurance policy, then it has truly passed that stage. Virtually all of its development costs have been amortised long ago, leaving it as a profitable income earner. It has been able to share in the newly efficient engine adapted for the Metro and in its generally improved levels of quietness. Of course, mounted on rubber suspension, the latest Minis are little more comfortable in terms of ride than those that went before, but the small sensation of 12-inch wheels and disc brakes fitted from mid-1984

did improve ride quality just a little.

Apart from the relatively crude Citroen 2CV, the Mini still has no real competitors and word has it from Longbridge that it will go on, and on . . . at least until 1989 when safety regulations may outlaw its external body seams and protruding door handles, unless special dispensation can be obtained. Certainly the current Austin-Rover management have no plans to drop the Mini but instead celebrated its 25th Anniversary in 1984, the year in which appropriately, this book was completed. Long Live Mini!

H1.   Seen often at the time of the Mini's launch, this cutaway of the original Mini was much used to demonstrate the remarkable space efficiency of the then-new car.

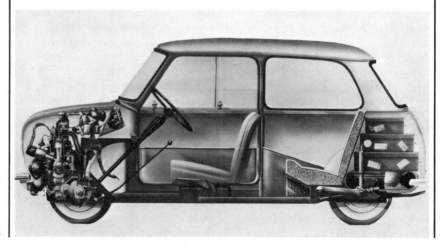

H2.   Alec Issigonis, the Mini's creator, poses with the very first Mini, and other landmark cars from his brilliant career, at his retirement party in 1971.

H3.   Minis were campaigned right from the start, but it was not until the 'S' came along that the successes came flooding in. GRX 5D came 'third' in the famous 1966 Monte Carlo, with its disqualification fiasco, and in general was not one of the most successful 'works' Minis, although it is said to be one of only eleven 'works' cars still in existence.

H4.   GRX 5D's engine bay has been restored to a high standard whilst maintaining complete originality. Its twin 1 ½ in. SU's are most impressive!

17

H5. Perhaps the cockpit of GRX 5D is its most impressive sight, with stopwatches and primitive time/distance computer at the ready. Note what appears to be the radiator expansion tank located by the navigator's feet!

H6. One of the legendary Cooper 'S' models — this time in unadulterated form. This is a 1967 MkII Austin.

H7. Austin engineer from the Mini's salad days and stalwart of the Austin-Healey Club, John Wheatley stands proudly by his 998cc 1969 Cooper which he and his wife Heather have cared for lovingly since they bought it new. Inset is the bonnet badge.

WOLSELEY *Hornet* **Mk II** *with Hydrolastic Suspension*

H8. & H9.   Two well-known Mini derivatives were the Riley Elf and Wolseley Hornet pictured here – the Wolseley Hornet MkII as it appeared in BMC's sales brochure of the period.

The Elf and Hornet possessed the benefit of a larger boot, but the tailfins are not universally liked today. Both models were painted in colours traditional for their marque name rather than in standard Mini colours.

H10. & H11.   The Mini Moke represented a real burst of eccentricity for BMC. It never found favour with serious users, but those who found the Mini an attractive little gimmick when it first came out, found the Moke irresistible. It seemed to consist of a platform chassis and bulkhead, mechanical components and very little else. Its image evoked fashion, fun and sun, even in central London where the white Moke was photographed. After production ceased in the UK, it continued in Australia and then it was said production was to be continued in Spain from 1984 on.

H12. Another spin-off from the Mini. Farmers always loved the Pick-up: what a shame that BL don't produce anything like it today! Note that MkI Mini doors, hinges and sliding glass were used throughout the Pick-up's production life. Upholstery could be had in any colour as long as it was black.

H13. The Mini Van is also a tremendously useful workhorse. It is still used as a surprisingly tough workhorse with a carrying volume that easily exceeds that of the Metro van.

H14. The Mini Clubman represented an attempt to move the Mini's image up a notch at the cost of redesigning the front end only. In spite of the fact that the internal, structural components of the under-bonnet area were redesigned, engine accessibility is not significantly improved. The shape of the Clubman, particularly the saloon, has always been widely criticised because, it is said, the cars look front-heavy and out of proportion. Clubman front-end body parts are a lot more expensive than standard Mini panels.

H15.   The Mini 1275 GT was supposed to take over where the Cooper left off, but while it did have excellent performance it never had the charisma of the Cooper. This particular car is fitted with optional Dunlop Denovo 'run flat' tyres and wheels: an idea that didn't work too well in practice as the tyres produced a lot of road noise and tended to wear rapidly.

H16. & H17.   Of course it has been possible to buy the Mini in its original shape since 1959. Here are the two enduring stalwarts of the range, a 1975 Mini 850 and a 1981 Mini 1000. These pictures illustrate how little the basic Mini changed over the years, the most obvious external changes being confined to the 'disappearance' of door hinges and the revised grille shape which became standard on late models.

H18. & H19.   The attractive Mini 1100 Special of 1979 — complete with stripey cloth seats. This is just one of a number of Limited Edition Minis which have appeared over the years.

H20.   The Mini range of 1981 — including the super-economical and popular City model.

H21.   This goes some way towards illustrating just how many Mini models there have been over the years. Happily, most of these original badges are still available from Mini specialists.

2 Buying

Over the years, buyers' guides galore have appeared in the motoring magazines on what to look for when buying a Mini, but in the past couple of years something has changed that they all overlooked: Minis are not *just* second-hand cars any more: they're unique, timeless classic cars which still manage to do the job for which they were intended. And on top of all that, during the quarter century or so it has been in production, enough variations of the Mini have been produced to satisfy just about everyone! No one of them can be considered a 'Best Buy' Mini – it really depends what you want but if a car's potential resale value is of importance to you, it's well worth noting that different Minis with exactly the same current second-hand value can have widely different potential when it comes to re-selling in a few years time.

Probably the most rapidly appreciating Minis are the Radford and Wood & Pickett Mini-Coopers while 1071 and 1275 'S' models follow a little way behind.

Surprisingly close behind are prime examples of the very earliest cars with some interest being shown overseas in these now rare cars.

The Moke has a high financial standing because of the eccentric flair which owners like to think it gives them – those who want a Moke feel they *must* have one, which pushes them to pay strong money for the spartan little beasts – while a scarcity of Mokes on the open market also helps keep prices high. Of course, the scarcest of all Minis are the works race and rally cars and the few that are not known about could take some finding. In any case, owners of these cars frequently forget that they are similar to the woodman's axe which, after twenty year's use was still as good as new: three new heads and five new handles had kept it that way!

At the opposite end of the utility scale, Mini Pick-ups are likely to become more valued than might be expected and that is almost certain to happen to the 'Woody' Travellers and Countrymans,

especially since the wooden components are available from specialists such as the London-based Mini Spares Centre to go along with all the standard body panels which are, of course, still in plentiful supply. Riley Elfs and Wolseley Hornets were idiosyncratic little Minis that gave semi-opulence to the bare package but of course there are body differences which could make the restoration or repair of these cars more difficult. Good examples are bound to appreciate. The Mini 1275 GT is also likely to hold onto its value better than a comparable 'standard' Mini of the same era but it is certain to fare less well than the Coopers because it is widely known to be inferior to the 1275 Cooper 'S', even by those who know little of its technical spec.

Limited Editions of many cars have attained a higher value than others of the same age and type and the 25th Anniversary Limited Edition Mini is likely to be no exception. However, most modern Minis are bought for their value as frugal, easy to own little motor cars and purely from that angle, the owner may be prepared to put up with their loss of value through depreciation so that he or she can reap the benefits of the extra soundproofing and rustproofing of the later cars, the highly efficient A-Plus engine that comes straight from the Metro development programme and the larger wheels and better braking from 1984-on.

Take Your Pick

When it comes down to it, most people interested in buying a Mini will want to own it for reasons other than what it might fetch in a few years time. The character of the car is far more important, and really that is just how it should be!

If you fancy the idea of buying a Mini, take a careful look at the various options on offer and don't expect a 1964 Mini to have anything like as much to offer as your neighbour's Mini Mayfair in which you were recently given a lift! It's useful to study the specifications and production modifications listed in the appendices, but it is also worthwhile trying to put the little car's variants and its stages of development into groups:

Collector's Minis. Into this category must come all those Minis that owners would think twice about using as everyday cars. The very early Minis probably come into this grouping now because, even though the body panels are little more difficult to repair than later Minis, the correct original trim, badging and many of the mechanical parts are now hard if not impossible to find. Also, if the car is an original example with low mileage, not many owners would want to spoil its record at this late stage. Exactly the same can be said about the specially-bodied or trimmed Minis such as Mini-Sprint (the lowered roof line cars), Radford and Wood & Pickett – the

bodywork is easy to replace but replacements for badges and trim would have to be made on a one-off basis. On the other hand, while the lack of brakes, noise and harshness of the early standard cars would be a deterrent to the everyday user, especially if any distance has to be covered, the upper class Minis were invariably built around the nippier Cooper starting point and their add-on opulence can make them very pleasant little motor cars to drive.

The other major collector's piece is the Moke but then, if you're idiosyncratic enough to want a Moke, you may even want to drive it every day and put up with being frozen half to death for two thirds of the year. Incidentally, the early Mini most likely to become a treasured rarity is the 1959 Austin Seven and Morris Minor with lights inside the rear pockets. The Austin's interior trim was 'improved' from December 1959 and the Morris from February 1960, so if you want a bit of extra kudos, try to get one of the first twenty-odd thousand of these cars (see Appendices for chassis/body numbers where available).

Quick Minis. The choice here is actually wider than would at first appear because, as well as all the Cooper and Cooper 'S' models, there are the GTs and also the thousands and thousands of Minis that owners have made go faster by tuning or by the simple expedient of fitting one of the larger engines. If you become interested in a Mini with extra speed appeal, the first areas to check are those associated with the quality of the work. It is easy to slot a bigger engine and transmission assembly, a set of wheel spacers and spats onto a Mini, and then add a body stripe but is that enough? Check, for instance that the brakes match the engine (the combination of early single-cylinder front brakes and a 1275cc engine, perhaps with an M.G. Midget head and cam is a frightening idea) but ensure also that the engine is in good condition and not just a scrapyard wonder and that the basic structure of the car is sound. Make sure that the tyres are

up to the job along with the braking system as a whole and check that the wheels, which may be old and flawed or that wider steel wheels which may be of good quality but which just might have been converted from narrow size by a 'backyard' set-up, are in good condition. The Mini 1275GT is by no means a slouch and it suffers badly simply because it is rubbished by those who were upset about the demise of the Cooper. Take a look at the cars' performance figures and decide for yourself whether the GT is quick enough for you!

All Coopers are thought of as extremely rapid little motor cars but anyone who takes that expectation into the driving seat just could be disappointed. It all depends on what you are used to driving! In its day, the Cooper *was* a very rapid motor car, especially in terms of the early 'sixties, but a standard 997 or 998 Cooper (their engines were very different but performance was similar) seems not terribly exciting by today's stop-watch standards. On the other hand, the noise and the fury, the close proximity of the outside world and the thrill of not knowing whether the early disc brakes will eventually drag you to a reluctant halt all make Mini Coopering exciting in a different sort of way. The 'S' models added some real bite and snap, of course, and the largest engined car has both enough torque and sufficient 'kick' to make driving as easy or as thrilling as you could wish.

Trim parts are virtually unobtainable for any of these cars, (and for *any* Mini more than just a few years old) and while 998 Cooper engine components are no trouble to come by, since much of the engine is common with the standard 998 unit, parts for any of the other cars can present problems. Again, this is an area where the 1275GT scores because most of the Cooper 'S's specially engineered components were abolished from the GT making it easier to obtain standard components.

Custom Minis. The world of customised cars is one all of its own, but the Mini has always been a firm favourite for customising for fairly obvious reasons. First of all, there are just so many of them around that coming across an old, cheap car suitable for customising is easy and second, the concentrations of all the components into two subframes means that all sorts of permutations on the theme become possible. You can buy a 'Porsche' lookalike body shell which takes the Mini powertrain at the rear end while some brave souls have been known to make their own long-bed, six wheel Mini Pick-up by adding extra suspension units to the rear. There are simply too many specials and kit-cars around to advise on what to buy and what not to buy but I can make a few general points. When looking over a customised Mini, bear in mind that it probably started off as a basket case and that there were probably several bucket loads of body filler used, especially if the bodywork has been resculptured. The car *may* have been customised by someone with very high standards and scruples. And then again . . . In general, the greater the length of time since the car was finished, the better its chances of lasting, since rust bubbles its way back through filler in a matter of months. If the paint is hardly dry, unless you have evidence to suggest that the job has been well done, leave it alone!

Another piece of advice applies to both custom and kit cars: drive the car for as far as you possibly can before making your mind up. It's not for nothing that the big manufacturers spend millions on getting the details of their cars right, and without their resources, any car that is homespun is *bound* to have disadvantages. If it's just that the rear view is obstructed by a spoiler, or you bang your knees when getting in and out, only you can decide whether you can live with that kind of fault. On the other hand, if the only way in is through the sunroof, or you have to part dismantle the dash to get third gear, you may decide that the penalty is too high. But seriously, do check

that you *can* live with the car and especially that it is **safe to drive!**

The third piece of advice affects all fibreglass cars, or cars with fibreglass panels. The design of a fibreglass car is extremely sophisticated, mainly because the material is extremely poor at taking localised stresses. Check the points where the body meets the frame and also check all hinge points for stress cracking, which will be impossible to repair properly without major surgery. Check that panels are not de-laminating (look at the edges and check that they are not separating into distinct leaves) especially where the glass is bonded to steel: it can easily unbond itself if the steel was not properly prepared in the first place. Check that flat panels don't have splits or cracks either in star shapes or in the shape of wave marks. In either case, fairly dramatic remedial work is needed; filler repairs are not enough because they usually last only a couple of days. Check that steel box sections enclosed in fibreglass are not suffering from the effects of corrosion as the task of replacement can be mind-boggling!

Having pointed out all the problems, it must be said that Mini specials are undoubtedly more fun than conventional Minis and some, such as the Midas (which is both more expensive and more ugly in the author's eyes than any Metro), are surprisingly sophisticated packages. You get what you pay for, and if you want to be both 'different' and sophisticated, you pay even more!

Utility Minis. I could include the estate versions here and even the Moke, which was originally intended to have a military purpose but never made it, but it is best to include just the dear old Mini Van and the Pick-up. The Pick-up has always been loved by farmers who use it for lugging the odd few bales of hay or a piglet or two during the day and for tootling down to, and weaving back from, the local at night! In fact, a thousand and one tradesmen who have wanted to chuck a few tools and materials in

the back, from farriers to tyre depots have found the Pick-up a godsend. Nowadays, it is just as likely to have a private owner, perhaps a DIY fanatic or someone who repairs cars and wants a way of carrying unwieldy body panels. And whatever you use it for it can be a great advantage to have a separate cab, away from the dirt and the tools that give van drivers a slap in the neck if they brake too hard and so perhaps it's having a 'front-room' that makes the Pick-up feel a little superior to the Mini Van.

Ever since it was launched, the Mini Van has given incredibly cheap transport to people who otherwise could not have afforded it. In the days before VAT they were tax-free and thus even cheaper, so in those days there was probably more private use than nowadays. The author and his wife bought a Mini Van when they restored their first house, and carried vast quantities of materials in it at weights that made nonsense of the recommendations, the law or even, one is embarrassed to say, safety requirements. But through it all, the Van never missed a beat! Vans are much noisier than Pick-ups but the performance of both is virtually up to (or down to, depending on engine size) saloon car standards.

Improvements to the Minis' fixtures and fittings were not usually applied to the Van and as a result it never gained wind-up windows or hidden hinges. Spares are no problem for either (although non-genuine and thus inexpensive front panels are not easy to find; they differ there from the cars) but you can expect Pick-up rear-end panels to be the first to go out of stock and not be replaced. On the other hand, the Pick-up may even become some sort of collector's car, who knows?

Everyday Minis. Naturally enough, the biggest selection of Minis available is for those who want an everyday car. Working backwards in time, the latest spec. Mini is as you would expect, the most satisfactory available from the point of view of everyday use and it is worth noting that from mid

1984-on, all Minis have been on 12 inch wheels with disc brakes at the front. This cured a long term problem which occured with Minis on 10 inch wheels and dual-circuit brakes which were very prone to mysterious pulling to one side to a common and annoying degree. However, aside from the 'specials' which Austin-Rover have offered to help promote the car such as the smart looking Mini 'Sprite' and the 25th Anniversary cars, Mini production in the 'eighties has been based around two models: a plush Mini with deep pile carpets and various other fixtures and fittings such as the Mayfair and a basic Mini such as the City. Brand new, the Mini continues to be one of the very best buys around and certainly, if you don't want the crudity of the 2CV, the suspect quality of the subsidised Korean and East European imports and if you don't mind a car that is not as highly developed as, say, the Metro, you can save a lot of money by buying a new Mini.

Looking back in time, the basic Mini shape stretches right the way over the horizon, there being few changes that have made an incredible difference to the quality of the car, except perhaps the move towards more quietness that began in the very early 'eighties. In August 1969, the nearest thing to a sea change took place when hydrolastic suspension was dropped in favour of the traditional rubber cone suspension (the ride certainly became a little harder again but cornering was improved) and wind-up windows were fitted to doors with concealed hinges. In September 1968, an all-synchro gearbox had been fitted. Hydrolastic suspension had itself been phased in around late 1964 and it was September 1964 that saw the advent of the improved twin-cylinder front brakes, but here we're getting into collectors' country again!

The Mini Clubman was announced in saloon and estate versions in May 1969 and used hydrolastic suspension until June 1971 which is hardly logical in view of the changes which took place to the standard car! In spite of the larger front-end, there are hardly any bonuses to be gained in engine access but fuel consumption and top speed are slightly worse than with the traditional Mini. The main plus points, leaving aside *any* judgement on the aesthetics of the car, are that the dash had face-level vents (which are actually prone to chucking the occasional handful of road grit and dead flies into your face along with the cooling breeze) and the Clubman was the only Mini to make the faster 1098cc engine available, as used in so many other BMC/BL cars. The Clubman estate had simulated wood strips on the side but in all other respects was like the all-metal Traveller/Countryman.

Mini Estates are worth a mention all on their own because from many angles they are the ideal all-rounders. Their van floorpan gives a longer wheelbase which in turn presents passengers with a less joggly ride, the rear side windows open really wide which can be a joy on hot days while when closed they give excellent all-round vision and, of course, estates present the huge advantage of being able to carry household loads, camping gear, dogs or whatever else you want to pile in! Disadvantages are minimal: the rear doors obstruct rear vision a little; they can (but don't necessarily) rattle and, in the long term, rear end repair parts may just be harder to find than for the car, although in view of the numbers of estates and vans made, that might be an over-pessimistic view. Remember to check the sliding window channels and the surrounding area for oasis of fungus and rot in the surrounding metal, make sure that all the trim is in place on the Clubman Estate (some of it is becoming impossible to buy) and look very carefully at the delightful half-timbering on the ash trimmed estates (available September 1960 to October/November 1969). If the timber is soft and spongy when pushed with something hard it is rotten and will need replacement. Specialist suppliers such as the Mini Spares Centre stock new timbers but, while they are not structural like those on the Morris Minor, they can still be hard work to fit successfully.

Where to Look

With so many millions of Minis having been built, finding one is going to be no problem at all, but if you really fancy a particular model, finding the *right* one could be tricky! The group of Minis which I called 'Collectors' Minis' include the earliest and rarest of the cars and for these, the best way of finding an example would be by poring over the classified advertisements in magazines such as *Practical Classics* and *Thoroughbred & Classic Cars* and those in the weekly advertising papers such as *Exchange & Mart*. Local press adverts could be worth examining too and even a tour of local scrapyards might turn up a 'find' or, if nothing else, sources of cheap parts. However, the best source for the enthusiast who is really serious about the early cars is the Mini Owners' Club whose founder Chris Cheal provides a really helpful and cheerful service to Mini owners — but do play the game and join the Club first! The coachtrimmed Minis don't appear very often at all, but adverts in the same branches of the specialist press or in the Mini Cooper Owners' Club magazine throw the occasional car up. Mokes also appear occasionally in the same publications but here a better bet would be to visit someone who specialises in Mokes — again sift through the same two 'classic' magazines or look at the classified ads in the *Sunday Telegraph* where Mokes occasionally appear.

Custom Minis are advertised in *Exchange & Mart* and also in the specialist magazines which cater for these quirky cars and the address of kit car makers can be found in a magazine called *Kit Cars*.

Quick Minis, such as Coopers, are advertised fairly frequently in the sources already mentioned but here the problem is in finding the right car in the right condition and you could find yourself spoiled by the wrong kind of choice. Again, joining the right club could be more than useful. The local press is undoubtedly the best place to look for 'souped-up' Minis, together with the classifieds in magazines such as *Car & Car Conversions*.

Everyday Minis are widely available in the local papers, local garages and almost everywhere you might choose to look, but here are two unconventional ways of finding the right Mini that you may not have considered and both can invoke big cash savings although each carries its own risks.

Try visiting your local 'trade' auctions to see what they have on offer. Anyone can go to an auction and the savings can be huge — often in the order of 30% or more over showroom prices. Go once, just to see how it all works: take someone with you who really knows about cars, unless you're fully confident in your own ability, because the guarantee is as minimal as you could imagine (only on major components and usually for one hour! — just long enough for the traffic jam to clear at the end of the auction, so there's no real chance of a road-test). *Don't* get carried away by the bidding! Set yourself an upper limit and stick to it; bidding is not a game to be 'won' or 'lost'.

If you want to buy a new Mini, you may wish to consider importing one. You can do this yourself or buy from one of the firms who specialise in car imports. In either case, the savings can be impressive although you must make certain that you get the original purchase invoice with the car's chassis number on it or Austin-Rover will not recognise the first service or warranty. On the other hand, the savings can be huge because of the far lower cost of new cars in some continental countries and this may outweigh all the disadvantages.

Making Sure

Checking over a prospective purchase not only can be, but *should* be, very time consuming if the right car is to be bought rather than a glossed-over heap of trouble. What follows is an elimination sequence in three separate parts, each one taking longer and being more thorough than the first, this approach having the virtue of saving the purchaser both time and embarrassment. It is always easier to withdraw at an early stage than after an hour spent checking the car over with the aid of the owner's comments and mugs of coffee! Thus Stage A aims to eliminate the obvious 'nails' without having to probe too deeply. Stage B takes matters somewhat further for cars that pass the first stage while Stage C is the 'dirty hands' stage, the one you don't get into on a snowy February evening unless you are really serious!

Tool Box

Old, warm clothes (if the ground is cold). An old mat or board if the ground is wet. A bright torch. A pair of ramps. A small hammer. A screwdriver or metal probe. This book and a notepad. Pencil. A bottle, trolley or scissors jack. Axle stands.

Safety

Safety should be carefully considered and any necessary steps taken. In particular, do not rely on a handbrake holding a car on a slope or ramps. NEVER crawl under a car supported by a jack only.

Using the Checklist

This checklist was designed by the author and is based upon experience gained at his body shop, The Classic Restoration Centre, and is compiled with the help of Keith Dodd at Mini Spares Centre Ltd. It

is designed to show step-by-step instructions for virtually all the checks to be made on a car offered for sale. After each, the fault indicated is shown in brackets, eg the instruction: 'Look along wings, door bottoms, wheel arches and sills from the front and rear of the car' is followed by the fault, shown in brackets, as (Ripples indicate filler presence/crash damage. £££). The pound sterling signs require some explanation. They are intended to give a guide to the cost of rectifying the fault. £ indicates that the cost is likely to be less than the cost of a new tyre. £££ stands for the cost of a new set of tyres, or more, while ££ means that the cost is likely to be between the two. The cost guide relates to the cost of the component/s only — allow more if you have the work done for you and therefore have to pay for labour also.

When examining a car you are advised to take this book and a notepad with you. As each item is checked a record can be kept in the notebook. You may wish to record a running cost total for necessary repairs as faults are discovered — this could be a useful bargaining tool at the end of your examination.

It is strongly recommended that the repair and restoration sections of this book and also the *Haynes Mini Owners Workshop Manual* are examined so that the reader is fully familiar with every component being examined.

Stage A — First Impressions

This is the stage where you can gain an impression of a car you are interested in virtually at-a-glance and almost without ringing the front door bell or attracting the salesman's attention!
1)   Does the bonnet fit the front wings and front panel evenly all the

way around? (Poor fit could indicate poorly adjusted bonnet but could, equally indicate very poorly carried out repair work to front end. Remedy? Remove welded on panels and start again! £££ +)

2) Look along wings, door bottoms and wheel arches from both front and rear of the car, catching the light along the panels as far as possible. (Ripples indicate presence of filler or fibreglass panels. £££)

3) Hold a magnet against tops of front wings, front and rear, scuttle tops at outer edges, door bottoms, quarter panels all along their bottom edges and base of boot lid. Magnet won't 'stick' if panels are full of filler. (Heavy use of filler could represent nothing but thin air underneath. ££ to £££ for materials)

4) Glance inside the car. Is the trim all of matching colours and all of the same type and/or is it badly ripped. Glance at the headlining, too. (Early headlining and most trim more than just a few years old is almost totally unobtainable at any price, except second-hand and then only if you are very lucky. £££ +)

5) Take a look at the tyres. Peculiar wear patterns on the front could simply mean that the track needs adjustment (£ + cost of new tyres) but odd wear patterns at the rear can be more worrying. (Worn radius arm bearings — new bearings require special tools and work has to be carried out by a main dealer. ££. Rusty rear subframe and/or mountings causing the subframe to move around, indicates severely corroded vehicle. £££ +)

6) If a car is advertised as 'low mileage' or 'unrestored', check the numerals on the mileometer to ensure that they line up ('clocked' mileometers rarely do so) check pedal rubbers for wear, door hinges for up and down movement when the door is opened a little. Check for overspraying, new underseal or any signs of welding that could indicate crash damage or rust damage repair. (Potentially £££ + as genuine cars could be worth a lot more, in the case of 'classic' Minis while later cars' mechanical components could be worn out.)

Stage B – Clean hands

If a car doesn't match up to requirements after Stage A, don't be tempted — reject it there and then or, if the car is rare, and you especially want it, attempt to make dramatic adjustments to the asking price. Stage B involves taking a closer look rather than the almost cursory glance you have made and decreases the risk of making a mistake without even getting your hands dirty!

Check thoroughly for body corrosion in all the places shown below. Body rot is by far the most expensive work to have carried out properly and the most time-consuming if you do it yourself. Use a magnet to ensure that no filler is present — magnets will only stick to steel. Work carefully and methodically, jotting down your findings in the order shown here. Remember that the £ signs apply only to parts replacement but where parts are more difficult than average to replace or even unobtainable, there will be a comment accompanying the £ sign.

Bodywork

1) Front apron below bumper and grille panel (behind chrome on all but Van/Pick-up) above bumper — it's all one. (Kerb thumping or other accident damage, corrosion in apron and near wings. ££ for 'factory' panel. Corrosion unlikely to be confined to this panel.

2) Front wing headlamp area. (Corrosion. £ for standard wing but ££ for Clubman.)

3) Front wing around scuttle top, outer end of scuttle top, area beneath windscreen rubber. (Corrosion in the form of blisters or heavy filler use. £-££ for panels but fairly complex repairs required, including hidden inner areas.)

4) A-panels, especially at top and bottom (Corrosion and superficial repairs to external-hinge models. £ and very simple repair on concealed-hinge models. ££ and

moderately complicated on earlier cars.)

5) Door bottoms, door skins and door tops just beneath sliding channels on early cars and all commercials. Check both from outside and inside door. (Corrosion — new door skin £ but fairly complex to fit if door channel supports have rotted too.)

6) Look for rippling or blistering in the bottom curve at the front of each rear wheel arch. (Corrosion, filler repaired. Distortion from corrosion in other areas leading to flexing here. £££ for new side panel complete but ££ for non-genuine quarter panel. The former is very complex to fit.)

7) Boot lid at its base. (Corrosion or distortion caused when wire boot lid stays break allowing the panel to bend backwards on its hinges. ££. New boot lids are expensive, the early types may be unobtainable new.) Check that the correct type is fitted.

8) Boot lid hinge panel. (Corrosion. Relatively simple repair. £)

9) Rear valence, below bumper. (Corrosion. Relatively simple repair but usually indicates further hidden corrosion which can be more complex.)

10) Sills and doorsteps. The top outer section is separate from the lower outer section with another inner sill separate again. These are replaced with ease but may not necessarily in the past, have been replaced with skill. Check ends of door step and outer sill for evidence of crude fitting flushed over with filler. Check outer sill for coatings of fresh underseal — what is it covering up? Lift carpets from inner sill and check vertical face and front end adjacent to floor. Examine jacking point, inside sill. Is it in position or has it collapsed? (Corrosion and poor fitting. £ to ££ dependent upon number of parts needed. Collapsed jacking point indicates bad internal corrosion to jacking point, crossmember, sill structure. ££ and a lot of hassle!)

NB Whilst removing carpets to check inner sills, are carpets soaking wet? (Floor plugs missing or leaking windscreen rubbers. £. Severe corrosion letting water in − not uncommon. ££ to £££ +)

11)   Guttering and windscreen openings. Both can rot out and be extremely difficult to repair without a high level of body repair skill. Probe any suspect areas of blistering or rust with thin-bladed screwdriver, especially the front of the gutters and both front and rear screen surrounds, particularly at the lower outer corners.

12)   Open door. Lift up and down and note any sloppy movement. (Hinge wear on externally hinged cars. £ with easy-to-fit hinge pin kits. £ to ££ on later cars where new hinges are needed. Corrosion in A-post panel on early cars − see 4. Severe door corrosion or hinge pillar corrosion on later cars. Possibly £££ because severe corrosion indicated.

13)   Vertical seam and chrome mouldings. (Rust, discoloration or a disinclination for wheel arch trims to stay put. New mouldings £ each or even £ for all four vertical mouldings.)

14)   General. Mini Wings and other replacement panels *can* be fitted with pop-rivets or self-tapping screws but this is highly dangerous in a car which depends upon the soundness of every part of the shell for its whole strength. Check carefully. Look especially under mouldings and beneath bumpers. Check for too many layers of steel in a seam. Too many could indicate a rotten panel bodged by having a new one slapped over the top of it − the replacement panel firms make them to do just that! (£££ because an apparently sound car can turn out to be a wreck in disguise.)

Interior

1)   Examine front and rear seats, rear of front seats, side trim panels and all other cloth or vinyl upholstery. (Worn, thin or ripped trim. From ££ to £££ + to have retrimming carried out by specialist. Most fabrics and textures are unlikely to be available in the exact original pattern).

2)   Check dash. (Torn or missing trim. £ if available, or from a scrapyard. DIY multi-instrument dashboard and correct instruments missing. Probably ££ plus a long search for the right bits, dependent upon model. *NB* Check Coopers and 'S' speedometers to make sure the correct one is fitted as they are virtually irreplaceable.)

3)   Check cleanliness and condition of headlining. (If dirty, could clean up at virtually no cost. Replacement from ££-upwards dependent on whether new headlining available ex-stock or has to be custom made.)

4)   Examine steering wheel, gear knob, floor starter button (v. early cars) and all other knobs, lamps and switches for correct fittings. (Cost unpredictable but presence of all correct parts makes car worth more. Replacements can be virtually impossible to find.)

5)   Check seatbelts (if fitted) for good, clean condition and for operation of buckles. Check that they seem to be the right ones for the age of the car. Test inertia reel seat belts by tugging sharply − should 'catch'. (£ + each but early types may not be replaceable.)

6)   Check that seats slide and lock into position and that reclining seats, where fitted, operate satisfactorily. (Stiff, unlubricated mechanisms £ or less. Replacement seat or frame repair £ to ££)

7)   Where winding windows fitted, wind windows up and down. Where sliding windows fitted, including rear side windows in Traveller/Countryman/Estate, glass should slide freely although with some friction and no up-and-down movement. All glasses should close and lock. Faulty operation could be lack of lubrication on wind-up windows, or worn mechanism. £. Sliding window channels rot out and need periodic replacement £ to ££ dependent upon number required. Catches break fairly easily on some models. £, if available.)

8)   Check door seals. (Damage and fraying. Easy to replace but surprisingly expensive. £)

Mechanical

Ask owner to start engine. Let it idle − thorough warming up takes quite a while on the road but is necessary to gain a complete picture. This will help.

1)   Pull and push steering wheel and attempt to lift and lower at right angles to steering column. (Clonking indicates wear in column bush, £, loose column to body connections, loose steering wheel nut, loose column to rack clamp.)

2)   Open bonnet. There were many, many changes to underbonnet spec mostly of minor nature. Check 'your' model of car for non-standard air cleaners, rocker cover, oil cooler, servo etc. (If originality is important and parts are wrong or missing, anything from £ to £££, if parts available.)

3)   If oil cooler is fitted check for leaks. (Replacement £ +)

4)   Check engine/engine bay for general cleanliness and presence of oil. (Leaking gaskets, lack of detail care, blocked breather system on later cars with some emission control.)

5)   Listen to engine. (Expect tappets to be generally louder on 1275cc engines. Others should be quieter.) Bottom-end rumble, timing chain tinkle − non-adjustable − should not be audible. (Worn engine: timing chain and sprockets ££; worn crank £££ + for full rebuild + spares problems for Cooper 997 and 'S' models.)

6)   Is paint peeling around clutch/brake cylinders? (Carelessly spilt fluid strips paint. £ + time.)

STOP ENGINE AND LEAVE FOR A FEW MINUTES.

7)   Remove radiator cap SLOWLY with a large rag and beware of spurting, scalding water. (If steam hisses and water bubbles and boils as cap is removed, replace it and leave to cool down. Note that excess pressure of this sort in the cooling system usually indicates head gasket problems − see below.) *NB* for models with expansion tanks the coolant in the tank is not a good indicator of the

cooling system as a whole. Check for orange colour inside cooling system, check for oil on top of water either in form of droplets or oil film on top of water or as a brown 'gunge' of emulsified oil. Remove dipstick and check for water droplets in oil. Before replacing radiator cap, restart engine and let it tick over for a couple of minutes and look for air bubbles. Replace radiator cap. (Orange water indicates rust and a long time since water has been changed or topped-up with good quality antifreeze. Poor maintenance − from £ to £££ in long term. Oil in water, water in oil or air bubbles in cooling system indicates head problems − not unusual with 1275. Probably £££ if head damaged or if overheating has caused associated problems.)

8) Look at exhaust pipe whilst someone revs the engine and then let the revs drop quite sharply. (Whispy steam or droplets of water *could* be cold-start condensation on a cold day − no problem − but could mean blown head gasket: check again after road test if unsure. (Potentially £££.) Beware of clouds of blue smoke, or clouds or large puffs of black smoke. (Blue smoke indicates severe piston ring/valve guide wear ££-£££ + , or worn out servo seals, when servo fitted ££.) (Black smoke indicates over rich carb setting £)

9) Inspect external radiator fins as closely as you can. Newer cars appear to have greater problems with rad. oxidation than older cars. (Exchange radiator ££)

10) Examine subframe mounting nuts/bolts/and tab washers where fitted and engine mountings for scratch marks and signs of previous removal. (Previous engine removal is not necessarily a bad thing but it would be interesting to know why it was undertaken, what had gone wrong and who carried out the work.)

Road Test

If you are driving ensure that you have adequate insurance cover − otherwise carry out as many as possible of the following tests with

the owner driving.

1) Start up. Is the starter noisy on engagement? Does oil pressure light fail to go out? (Worn starter dog £. Faulty oil pressure sender unit £. Worn engine £££)

2) Is it difficult to engage first gear? *NB* Later cars with rod-linkage remote control can baulk a little, especially when new when they can baulk quite badly for a few thousand miles. (Worn clutch and/or worn gear selector mechanism ££)

3) Start away. Clutch should be light and rather sharp. Is there any clutch judder? (Could be oil on clutch, failed oil seal ££.) Could be failed stabilizer rods £. See 5 below.)

4) Drive at 30mph. Brake steadily to a halt.
Single line brake hydraulics:
A. Does car 'pull' to one side? (Oil or hydraulic fluid contamination on drum brakes £. Worn pads, shoes or wheel cylinders £. Seized disc brake calipers £ to ££)
B. Do brakes rub, grind or squeal? (Worn pads or shoes £. But more if discs or drum ruined.)
Dual line brake hydraulics up to 1984
Does car pull to one side and then possibly to the other on repeated brake application? (The 'mystery' ailment! £+ and much time bleeding system, replacing brake shoes and swapping them from one side to the other.)

5) Drive at 30mph in 3rd gear. Press, then release accelerator four or five times in succession. Listen for transmission or other clonks. (Could be worn drive shaft couplings ££, worn differential £££. More likely worn engine stabilizer rods or rubbers. £. *NB* Top engine-to-bulkhead bushes most likely to 1973, but from 1973-on, one of three varieties fitted underneath engine. All £)

6) Drive at 40mph. Lift off accelerator. Listen for differential whine. (Worn differential. If unbearable £ second-hand to £££) Also . . .

7) . . . accelerate hard in 1st gear to around 4000rpm (fairly high revs), then lift off. Repeat a couple of times. Listen for engine knocking.

(Worn engine big end bearings £££.) Also . . .

8) . . . does gearbox jump out of gear? (Worn internal selector mechanism ££)

9) Drive as in 7 and 8 above, but lift off in second gear then repeat the exercise in third and then fourth, road conditions permitting. Does the 'box jump out of gear? Try again, as far as is safe and practicable though going to lower revs with reverse gear. (Jumping out indicates worn selector mechanism. ££)

10) Drive at 40-45mph (or more if conditions will allow it with the bigger engined cars) in 4th gear. Change into 3rd gear. Does gearbox 'crunch'? (Worn synchromesh. At least £££ or £££ for recon gearbox.)

11) Drive at 25-35mph in 3rd gear. Change into 2nd gear. Does gearbox 'crunch'? (Worn synchromesh. At least £ or £££ for recon gearbox.)

12) Do front or rear wheels flutter or shake at speed − felt as vibration inside the car? (Wheels out of balance or faulty tyre, £)
NB In general, Mini gearboxes should select all gears cleanly and easily up and down the box even at higher speeds. Early three-speed synchro (none on 1st gear) boxes are noisier in 1st and reverse but if in doubt, it's safest to assume the worst!

13) Check that road conditions are suitable. With handbrake button depressed, pull the handbrake on whilst travelling at 20mph or so. Don't risk a skid! (Car pulls to one side − faulty wheel backplate mechanism, oiled-up brake shoes or seized or badly adjusted cable on one side, £. Car hardly slows down − faults on both sides, £ per fault, plus time.)

14) At low speed brake and listen for 'clonks'. (From front end: loose brake calipers: retighten! Brake pads moving within calipers: no problem providing everything else is sound − disc braked cars only, of course. Worn steering ball joints or suspension top/bottom ball joints, £ each. Suspension tie-rod pins worn − weld up, drill out and re-pin, £. Engine stabilizer bushes worn, £

each.) (From rear end: rear suspension radius arm bearings worn, ££ each.)

Boot/Trunk Inspection

1) Is the spare tyre inflated and with a good tread and is the wheel buckled or bent anywhere around the rim? (Replacement tyre, £ obviously! Replacement wheel, £)
2) Are the jack and wheel brace available and does the jack work? (Replacement, £)
3) Is there a key for the boot lock and has the lock seized? (Replacement key if correct number can be discovered or new lock assembly, £)
4) Is the boot trim all in place, in those models where it should be in place and is it serviceable? (Replacements may not be easily got hold of.)

Stage C – Dirty Hands!

This is the stage at which the car is now being seriously considered and the following list of checks are designed to make sure, as far as possible, that there are no hidden faults big enough to ruin the whole thing. It might also help to throw up a few minor faults to use as bargaining points with the seller! While Stage A took only a few minutes and Stage B took a while longer, Stage C involves a lot more time, effort and inconvenience but if you want to be *sure*, it's the most vital stage of all.
Safety: Ensure that the wheels are chocked when using jacks or ramps. NEVER go under a car supported by only a jack.
If you want to make absolutely sure that every single potential corrosion area has been examined, refer to the bodywork repair section of this book where all the rust areas are exposed in all their gory detail.
1) Jack up each wheel in turn. Spin wheel and listen for roughness in wheel bearings. (Imminent wheel bearing failure. £-££)

2) Lift both front wheels off the ground and secure the car with axle stands. Have the steering wheel held by an assistant and attempt to pull the track arm back and forth hard. (Play in the rack and/or pinion. Exchange steering rack, ££.) Now see if there is any sideways movement in each end of the rack. (Play there means bush needs renewing £, but expensive to have work carried out at a garage.) Tell assistant to release steering wheel and pull the rack from lock-to-lock. (Tight spots or patches of roughness means an exchange rack is needed, ££.) Pull the rack and check that the U-bolts holding it in place are not coming loose – also shown up by clonking in the footwell when on the road. *NB* Steering rack removal is not a particularly easy or pleasant job.
3) Grasp each front wheel while they are off the ground and attempt to rock it top to bottom to feel for play. (Play in swivels: £ to replace. Play present but no wear in swivels: problems in wheel bearing/hub area. New wheel bearings £. New hubs and flanges ££)
4) Grasp each front wheel and attempt to rock it side-to-side, with steering wheel held by assistant. (Play in wheel bearings – see above. Play in track-rod end, £)
5) Grasp each rear wheel, jacked up off the ground, and attempt to rock it in both directions. (Wheel bearing repair, £)
6) Still with the rear wheel off the ground, put a large jemmy or other suitable bar between the front of the rear wheel arch and the radius arm. (Any sideways movement shows wear in the bronze bush – quite a common fault through lack of maintenance. Repair is not a DIY job because special tools are essential, ££)
7) From underneath car, examine backplates and insides of wheels for brake fluid leaks – compare visual clues with your knowledge of the system's efficiency on the road.
8) Using a thin-bladed screwdriver, probe beneath the car looking for corrosion. Check especially: outer sills; outer edges, front and rear of floors; rear

subframe including flat surfaces on bottom and vertical webs above them; heelboard area into which rear subframe sits and all subframe mounting points; front subframe, especially on its front rail to check for accident damage. (Damage or corrosion in any of these areas apart from sills is costly to have repaired but of course much less so if the approach shown in this book is followed.) Check base of battery box for corrosion, too.
9) *Vans, Pick-ups and Estates:* Check underslung fuel tank for leaks. Sniff for petrol and look for the tell-tale dark staining of a creeping petrol leak.
10) From inside car, remove front carpets to check for corrosion in front of floor; remove rear seat base to check for rot in rear floor/rear heelboard area (rather serious) and lift trim out of rear oddment pockets, each side of the rear seat. (Bases rot out and access for repair is very difficult.)
11) From inside boot, remove floor trim, spare wheel and any other debris. Check battery box area again and also remainder of boot floor, especially up against the rear panel and the two rear outer corners. (Battery box £, boot floor ££, both plus time.)
12) Front inside front wings, check for corrosion/filler in and around headlamp bowls and also check the rear of the front panel. (Headlamp bowl £. Front wing £ to ££. Front panel ££. All parts only.)
13) Check engine for oil leaks. *NB* There will almost inevitably be some other than on a new or newly rebuilt engine. However, some Mini seals are very time consuming to replace and involve removing the whole engine/gearbox assembly. The main trouble spots are listed below with a 1 to 5 scale of difficulty encountered in changing them. The highest number indicates that the whole unit has to come out, the lowest means that the part involved comes away very easily while the numbers in between are obvious! Check drive shaft seals where they enter the differential (Difficulty rating: 2½.)
Check differential to gearbox seal.

(Difficulty rating: 5.)
Check engine to gearbox gasket. (Difficulty rating: 5.)
Check casting of gearbox to which left-hand engine mounting is bolted (Difficulty rating: 5.)
Check primary drive to gearbox casing. (Difficulty rating: 5.)
Check oil filter housing. (Difficulty rating: 1 ½.)
Check oil leak through bottom of clutch bellhousing. (Indicates leaking oil seal behind clutch. Difficulty rating: 3 ½.)
Check oil cooler and pipework. (Difficulty rating: 2.)
Check rocker box cover. (Difficulty rating: 1.)
Check engine side plates (where fitted) beneath manifolds. (Difficulty rating: 3.)
Check timing chain cover to engine seal. (Difficulty rating: 2 ½.)
Check timing chain cover front oil seal. (Difficulty rating: 2 ½.)
14)   Look for evidence of grease around grease points and seals, especially around front swivels and rear radius arms. No sign of grease = lack of servicing – potentially £££)
15)   Check condition of exhaust system, exhaust mountings and steel long-centre-branch manifolds, where fitted. (Replacement ££)
16)   Check surfaces of brake discs (where fitted) for deep scoring. (Replacement where available, or reground discs, £ to ££)

Twin carburettor cars.

17)   From under the bonnet, reach beneath the air filter, grasp the throttle shaft and attempt to shake it at each end. (Excessive movement results in uncontrollable idle and vacuum leaks. Exchange or replacement carbs, ££)
18)   Grope around in the driver's footwell and determine how much play exists in the clutch pedal. (If more than 1 inch or so, the clevis pin in the pedal/master cylinder pushrod is worn, £)
NB Springs should be attached to both pedals. (Move the pedal from side to side. More than slight movement indicates worn pedal

bushes or the bolt holding the pedals is loose, £)
19)   From above and beneath the car, check engine bay flitch plates for corrosion but more especially for evidence of crash damage such as distortion or rippling. (Potentially £££ + to put right.)
20)   Check insides of A-panels on exterior-hinged cars for corrosion or 'bodging' especially at tops and bottoms. Use the inquisitive screwdriver to winkle through the mud. (Replacement of A-panel, ££)
21)   Finally, have the owner drive the car down the road for a mile or so while you follow behind in another car. Look for slight 'crabwise' progress, *ie* front wheels not perfectly in line with rear and whole car slightly sideways on. (Crash damaged Minis are occasionally perfectly repaired all but for a twisted body shell which is not noticed until too late. DON'T BUY CAR – ALMOST CERTAINLY BEYOND ECONOMIC REPAIR!) N.B. 'Crabwise' condition can be caused by badly worn rear radius arm bearings allowing rear wheels to 'steer' rear of car to one side. Check them both thoroughly before jumping to the worst-case conclusion.

Minis put under the microscope
by Keith Dodd of the Mini Spares Centre, London

My association with the Leyland network began at the same time as the first Cooper 'S' and 998 Coopers were made and I have been with them right up to the present day with my own company Mini Spares Centre, London. I formed this company in 1975 when I realised that a specialist company was needed by the hardy Cooper owners, because most Leyland dealers were cutting their stocks of a then obsolete model, and at the same time partsmen were just baffled by so many variants and

change-points. My company has now progressed so much that, as BL are finishing with stock or tooling for new parts has been scrapped, we are producing important parts ourselves to help keep the cars on the road.

The cost of renovating a Cooper or 'S' is very high and I can only comment that a well renovated or good original car is actually cheaper to buy than the cost of having a total renovation carried out for you. This can especially be the case with such examples as the Radford, Mini Sprint, Crayford convertible type or Wood & Pickett, which were all unique in equipment and design. When buying, beware of renovated cars which look good, especially if newly sprayed, because they could be hiding many problems; there are a lot of poorly rebuilt examples about. If the paintwork looks original, you will at least see the rusted areas and know what work lies ahead.

For people contemplating buying a Mini, they face a unique proposition: no other car in production for over 25 years offers itself as either a collector's car, an everyday runabout or literally an old banger whilst still being a modern day car of classless beauty. In fact, pop stars, politicians, millionaires and first time car owners all feel suitably at home in the driving seat.

The Mini's basic attributes are super manoeuvrability in tight spaces, with impeccable roadholding, a reliable and nippy power unit providing exceptional economy and a great abundance of replacement spare parts.

The first problem is deciding on what you require from the car. Do you want:
1)   A Cooper type as an appreciating collectors item?
2)   A means of cheap to run transport or the family's second car?
3)   Your only car individually prepared with car cosmetics and extra engine power, making the car a status symbol?
4)   Or simply the choice of a small easy to drive car either as an old banger for cheapness or a late good quality vehicle to last indefinitely?

The second problem is finding a good quality model of your choice. This is more difficult because the Mini can generally be driven on through years of abuse and still seem to run perfectly, but on inspection can reveal many problems that can lead from simple jobs to expensive or specialist repair.

Buying a Cooper or 'S' — Identification at a glance

Buying a Cooper or Cooper 'S' really needs a chapter on its own, because so many Coopers have been taken apart unceremoniously and put back together. If you wish to buy a true Cooper the following change points in their history should be a useful guide but check that the log book substantiates chassis and engine numbers. If numbers do not appear to tie-up beware! — many people think they have Coopers but in fact only have the correct running gear and badges, or a normal Cooper with 'S' badges and running gear.

The Mini Cooper was introduced in 1961 with a 997cc engine, dry suspension and rather ineffective disc brakes which had very small pads and a non-synchro 1st gear. Their calipers were uprated in March 1963 using a larger pad but the same 7 inch disc. These were an improvement but still probably not as effective as ordinary drum brakes using two cylinders per front wheel (the type fitted from 1970-on being the best bet with larger bore wheel cylinders). In early 1964 the 997cc engine was replaced by the more robust 998cc engine and later that year hydrolastic suspension was fitted on all Coopers and the 'S'. At the beginning of 1966 the factory fitted a safety boss to the door where the end of the exterior handle exposed itself to oncoming objects (such as pedestrians!). The handles were also beefed up in size.

In 1967 the MK II was introduced with a larger rear window and square rear lamps, a new grille and trim changes. In late 1968 the all-synchro gearbox was fitted and, externally, the only way of telling is to look at the front of the transmission case for the casting number '22G 1128', which is quite visible. This casting number was used on every all-synchro gearbox up to the introduction of the rod change box which was never used on any Cooper or 'S' as it was introduced in 1973.

In 1970 quite a few Cooper MK IIIs were built, but gradually dropped in favour of the 1275GT which was also in production. The MK III Minis and Coopers all had wind-up windows and external door hinges, enlarged side windows and on all Coopers were of the opening variety, as opposed to the 850 standard Mini whch had fixed non-opening windows. The interior trim was also changed. The last Cooper 'S' went down the track on the 9th February 1971.

All MK I Coopers should have corner bars on the overriders. All Cooper MK Is and IIs had chrome door surrounds. Both these parts, including trim, are no longer available from BL. The Cooper 'S' was in line with the Cooper in most respects, except for some trim and body colours and running gear, engine, roadwheels, hubcaps and twin tanks. All Cooper and 'S' models were fitted as standard with two × 1 ¼ inch SU carbs and a large oval filter casing containing two round filters.

The first 'S', March 1963, was fitted with a 1071cc engine but was superseded by the 970 and 1275cc versions in March 1964, the 1071 actually finishing in late 1964. The 'S' models were all similar in appearance but had the following engine numbers: 9F followed by 3 or 4 more letters which denoted the characteristics of the engine and cubic capacity. Only the MK III 1275s had a 12H engine number but beware — so did nearly all 1300 engines! The sure way of telling is that all genuine Cooper 'S' engines had tappet chest cover plates on the rear of the unit, whereas ordinary 1300 blocks had no tappet inspection covers: just a solid wall block. All 'S' blocks had the dished type of core plug, 1 11/16 inch wide,

while the 1300 block had the 1 5/16 inch type fitted. The 997/8 Cooper had the domed type, 1 5/8 inch wide. The 997 block had the legend '1000cc' cast in the block while the 998 had just a casting number.

The MK III 'S' chassis number was XADI but the car itself was similar in appearance to the ordinary Mini so check logbooks carefully. The 'S' also received the four synchro gearbox casing number '22G 1128' in 1968 and used the Hardy Spicer universal joint instead of rubber couplings. This coupling set-up was also used on the Cooper 'S' from mid-1966 when most units carried the 'B' type gears of the three synchro box. The gearbox casting (number 22G 333) and the parts are now very hard to find and expensive too, when they can be found. The parts from the four synchro 'S' box which had the same casing number as other vehicles fitted with all synchro first are not too expensive and are all readily obtainable. In actual fact the only difference in the gears between the 'S' and a Mini 1000 is the laygear which has '22G 1040' stamped on it and the 1st motion shaft which has 18 teeth, helically cut.

The Cooper 'S' models all had much superior braking systems to the Coopers, with larger 7 ½ inch discs, uprated calipers and general strengthening of the steering arms and larger CV joints and of course Timken tapered bearings. The actual track of the car was also about 2 inches wider which meant the use of rear brake drums with a built in spacer of about 1 inch. Leyland did make Goldseal engines for the Coopers so if the engine number is not 9F type you are welcome to check with Mini Spares Centre for originality. There were a few 'S' MK IIIs built at Abingdon by the Special Tuning department which had special engine numbers and chassis numbers, after BL ceased production and if one of these cars could be found and identified . . .

In late 1975 the Clubman was fitted with 1100cc engine and some limited edition varieties were available. The parts for this engine are almost identical to the long running Austin/Morris 1100 model and are reasonably priced and readily available.

Bodywork

Because of the age of some Minis there is obviously quite a body rot problem affecting many areas, some of which are visible, some not. The problem with Mini bodywork is that most of it needs to be welded if renewed; only the doors, bonnet and boot lid unbolt, which means it can be expensive if not repaired by yourself or a helpful friend with access to the correct equipment. The actual panel work and repair sections are probably the cheapest available and this gives the buyer one of the largest selections of genuine or replacement panels available for any car ever made.

The first area to check is the outer and inner sills and door step, which are very cheap replacement panels but quite expensive to fit. This area of rot quite often leads to the floorpan being rotten where it joins the inner sill in both the front and rear floor areas. Once again the panels are not expensive but the fitting can be. Most floorpans include the inner sill section so it does cut out some repair work, but if you're not sure, the Mini Spares Centre will always advise on all bodywork fitment problems.

The second area is the rear valance and boot area, which can be a real problem as rot found here sometimes leads to the rear subframe area. The rear valance can easily be replaced and is not a major stress area like most of the other parts, but on taking the valance off it exposes two rear reinforcement panels which should help stop water from the rear wheels spraying into the valance area but which rot away. These panels are available but any piece of metal can be used, because the valance covers the repair from sight. When removing the rear valance you will notice that there are another two skins: one is the floorpan, the other is the boot

hinge panel and both tend to rot. The hinge panel is available as a spare part and so is a boot repair section but beware — the only complete boot floorpan available is from Leyland and is very expensive and difficult to fit. The repair section available includes the holes where the bumper bolts on and only goes into the boot 9½ inches which just reaches the spare wheel well. There are two small repair panels available for the sides of the boot where it joins the body sides. Cars with this type of boot rot should be especially avoided as it can lead to work on the next subject, the rear subframe.

Because of the car's design, the rear subframe, which is a structural part of the Mini, should be looked at very carefully. If there is any rot in the subframe it will fail the MoT and replacement is an expensive repair in most cases. The frame itself is available quite reasonably as a replacement part, but the genuine item is quite expensive. The problems start on removal of the frame because, although only eight bolts hold it in place, the panelwork holding these tends to rot — but repair sections are available. Removal of the frame usually means replacement of all brake pipes, more usual signs of rust and on changing the suspension arms (radius arms) signs of wear are noticed. The job of refurbishing radius arms requires two bushes to be changed and one of these needs reaming out which is a specialist job. Hydrolastic cars seem to entail a few more problems, needless to say, especially letting out the fluid and pumping up the hydro units; also the metal pipes can easily be damaged on removal. An area best avoided!

The third most important area is the door hinge area on both early models with external hinges and the later internal hinge type with wind-up windows. The MK I and MK II Minis external hinges can indicate visually whether they are cars with rust problems or not. The A panel which holds the front panel part of the hinge has an outer skin and an inner panel with reinforcement plates to hold the weight of the

doors. If the outer panel is badly rusted it has probably rotted the inner panel too. These panels again are not expensive but on removal can reveal further areas of rot to the top of the bulkhead and the corner of the windscreen panel. There is a splash plate from the inner A panel to the bulkhead to stop water and mud from getting to the windscreen panel but this usually rusts away. So watch out because the apparently simple looking A panel repair can lead to extensive work being required especially if the windscreen corner shows signs of rust as well as the A-panel.

On the MK III, wind-up window car, the hinge panel is internal and does not fare very well, particularly if the hinges are stiff as the extra stress put on this panel tends to break it. The A-panel on MK III Minis is only single skinned and on repair usually causes no problem unless all the hinge panel area is rotten. There are various panels available for this repair but only in the hinge area and anything else constitutes buying a door frame, which is expensive, or patching it up. Problems in this area usually mean the door itself has suffered extra damage so check the door window frame which holds the window, where it joins the door skin, as fractures and subsequent bad repairs often occur there.

The fourth part of the bodywork check generally covers all visual parts: wings and front panels can be obtained cheaply but replacing them can be expensive. Also check for badly fitting bonnets as a give away to bad workmanship on front end repairs. All the doors suffer from rot due to drainage and vibration problems; window weatherstrips should be kept in good order, and renewed when necessary even though they are quite expensive. Door skins are cheap but require careful and experienced fitting. Doors are expensive, especially the MK I/II variety as used on the Mini Van. Check the bottom of the door pocket for excessive rot. Body sides tend to rot at the bottom, just ahead of the wheelarch where it joins the sill panel. There are quite cheap repair panels available but once again it entails expensive welding. Boot skins are available as repair panels but the doorskins are not easy to fit. Bootlids are available in steel or fibreglass as a cheaper replacement. Fibreglass bonnets are available but require to be bolted in an alternative method to the steel bonnet because they will not accept the original hinges or bonnet lock mechanism without great difficulty. Complete fibreglass front ends are a cheap method of replacing the front for DIY people with no access to welding equipment. The law does require the fitting of strengthening bars from the front of the subframe to the bulkhead area or inner wings and these are available ready-made.

Only a short mention on trim: NOTE CAREFULLY that none of the old Cooper trim is available and it is difficult to get trim for cars more than five years old. Some specialists can do repairs but the old Cooper brocade trim is definitely finished. The front end section and bumpers for the Mini Clubman are *very* expensive.

Suspension

Check tyres for irregular wear on rear caused by wheel bearings, or radius arm bearings needing renewal or other faults in the suspension which can be quite costly. If the car does not sit the same height on both sides, check the following: if the car is a saloon and built between September 1964 to 1969, the Cooper and Clubman up to 1971 included, the car is likely to be hydrolastic and it usually means a fault has developed in the hydrolastic units, pipe connections or pressure valves. It could be that the car just requires pumping up but often they will not maintain correct height after a week or so. The 'S' units are not available any longer and the correct second-hand units are rare in good condition: also, because there were so many types, they were colour coded for indentification. To convert the car

from hydrolastic to dry is very costly so unless you are sure of the car's history, beware of buying hydrolastic models. If the car has dry suspension it is likely that the rubber cone spring is weak on the end of the suspension trumpet or if the knuckle on the other end is worn, this too could create the same symptoms. (See sections on suspension rebuild for identification.) If the car is very low on one corner, it is usually the knuckle joint that is broken but this is very cheap to buy, whereas the suspension cones can be costly. Use your initiative when bargaining!

Shock absorbers are cheap but worth checking especially on the rear where wear tends not to get noticed as much as the front. Whilst checking the rear shock absorbers, give just a glimpse to make sure the rear wheel arch is sound, especially at the top where the shock absorber mounts. Although not very prone to bad corrosion, they are very expensive to renew.

The front suspension can bring a multitude of problems. While none is too expensive by itself, a number of repairs can mount up to a considerable expense. The tie rods from the lower arms are often bent but can be straightened or replaced cheaply. The upper arm has two roller bearings which do not often get renewed but if stripping the suspension they are worth checking as the cost of renewal is not too high. The lower arms give very few problems, but like the tie rods, have rubber bushes which need checking, again, they are very cheap to renew. The wheel bearings do tend to wear, and can easily damage the drive flanges or the hubs themselves; careful checking is required. The hub also carries swivel pins at the top and bottom which wear through lack of maintenance, but are cheap to repair.

Due to having front-wheel-drive the Mini uses constant velocity joints to get the power to the wheels, whilst still providing enough articulation to allow steering of the car: obviously this high stress area does take considerable punishment.

The joints themselves are expensive, and quite a lot of work is involved in their renewal. The cheap, reconditioned, constant velocity joints available are just not worth having. Usually worn CV joints make a heavy knocking sound on full lock and a general guide is: if it knocks with left steering lock the right-hand unit needs repair and vice-versa. If the car was built after May 1973 it should have inner CV joints where once Minis had rubber couplings: these tend to knock on acceleration or overrun. These are also expensive. Earlier vehicles had rubber couplings which need to be checked as they often break up but at least they're quite inexpensive. The Cooper 'S' from 1966-on and all automatics used a Hardy Spicer type joint on the inboard end of the driveshaft and if badly worn these are expensive to replace but if they knock slightly, they can be repaired by fitting a new UJ quite cheaply.

Brakes

Brakes need to be checked thoroughly on any Mini because at the rear particularly, they are subject to corrosion. Check that handbrake cables move freely on the pivots on the subframe and if the adjusters look rounded-off on the rear brake backplates it could well be because they have seized. The same applies to the front adjusters, although here it is an especially expensive repair to carry out. Brake drums if worn are fairly expensive but discs on the Coopers really *are* very expensive. Calipers, if seized, can cause excessive disc wear so check for caliper pistons in a corroded condition. The caliper pistons and seal kits are obtainable but they're not cheap (the Cooper 997/8 type being very expensive). The ordinary Minis only had one wheel cylinder per wheel up until late 1964 and these are expensive too. The Mini from 1964-on had two wheel cylinders per wheel and these changed to a larger bore size in 1969 and are quite pricey if they all need replacement.

Wheels and tyres

More designs of wheels have been fitted to the Mini than I care to think about, but the following points are worth a mention. Any Mini wheels more than 5.5 inches wide need 165 profile tyres, which are expensive. Rims to 5 inches will accept ordinary 145 profile radial tyres which are more competitively priced. From 1974-on the 1275GT was fitted with 12 inch wheels and no brake servo because it had larger discs and different calipers. Most of these cars had Denovo type wheels and tyres which are not liked by most owners because of their poor roadholding and fast wearing characteristics and extreme expense, so many people change the special Denovo wheels for aftermarket types and ordinary tyres. The 'S' had ventilated type steel wheels originally 3.5 inches wide then, later on, 4.5 inches optionally.

Petrol tanks

The Van and Estate car petrol tank is slung under the rear floor and does suffer from rust and leaks from the seams. Held by six screws, this type of tank can be a problem because of rusted screwheads and so is quite expensive to renew. The Saloon tank is in the boot, and does not suffer as badly as the exterior type, but although easier to renew is very expensive. The Cooper 'S' from 1966 had twin tanks and rarely gives problems with either tank.

Engine and drive train

The power unit is the most varied of all the parts, the engine ranging from 850cc to 1275cc and the gearbox also having many types of gears and final drive ratios.

If you are buying a Cooper or 'S' the only sure way of authenticating engine type, after the normal checks, is to contact Mini Spares Centre for the different engine numbers and change points. On any of the other Minis just make sure that the engine has good oil

pressure: 15 psi on tickover when hot should be the very minimum with about 20-25 psi on the 'S'. During normal running expect about 40 psi on all except the 1300 which should be about 60 psi. The 'S' when cold will often reach 90 psi or more if in good condition, and ideally should not drop below 50-60 psi under normal driving conditions.

Always check for excessive smoke from Mini exhausts: this can be expensive as the remedy can involve new valve guides or piston rings.

Camshafts tend to be very long lasting but cam followers, rockers and timing chains do wear and the latter two cause excessive engine noise. All these can be cured quite cheaply, except for the 'S' type Coopers for which rockers can be expensive even if rebushing. All the others can use the late type sintered rockers that are made without bushes.

The Mini engine, if neglected, does become very oily and although gaskets and seals are cheap the time and effort entailed in correcting these faults can be expensive: the worst case being the sump gasket and the transfer gear and differential casing which means an engine-out job. The gearbox differential seals are also a problem to change. The timing cover seal and gasket are not too much of a problem and although often neglected, the rocker cover and sideplate gaskets are simple.

Rod change gearboxes tend to have an extra leak from where the external rods go into the 'box but are no real problem. A leaking clutch oil seal is usually evidenced by a slipping clutch, but other problems such as worn primary gear which allows oil to seep on to the clutch are much more expensive to repair. The clutch can become an expensive area if all parts need renewal, but thankfully this is not a common fault although chronic clutch judder can be expensive and hard to cure. If the clutch is being overhauled, it's worth checking the ring gear which is expensive to buy but needs specialist fitting: thankfully it is not a common

problem area.

All engine work can be quite expensive, especially on the Cooper 'S' but while parts are all obtainable and individually not too dear, it seems once you start repairing one part it leads on to another — or you notice something else that requires attention! Some of the early Minis and Coopers had oil fed primary gears that leaked and small crank tail shafts that hold the primary gear but if they have lasted *this* long I see no need to worry.

The gearbox, because it sits under the engine, has to have transfer gears from the crank to the gear shafts. These three gears, the primary gear on the crank, the intermediate gear, known as the idler gear, and the lower gear known as the input gear are particularly vulnerable to problems and are expensive to repair. The real problem is the intermediate gear which has a shaft running through its centre which sits in roller bearings at both ends, one end in the gearbox case and the other end in the clutch casing. Because of its floating action it is shimmed by two washers which need to be expertly measured. This gear can be heard on acceleration or driving under load giving a detonating type noise like pinking, or a heavy rattle on tickover. Beware of a car with these noises, because if this area starts breaking up it can wreck the gearbox case and clutch case too.

If the gearbox has any whines or does not engage a gear properly, watch it, because all the bearings forks and shafts do wear fairly rapidly, especially the ones at the input gear end.

Once again check the gearbox casing number which is visible at the front of the finned gearbox. '22G 1128' is the type to look out for up to 1973 or any rod change box because Minis are nicer to drive with the all-synchro box and cheaper and better on availability of parts. The rod change gearbox has two rods going from the gearlever to the gearbox. It is distinguishable when sitting in the car because the reverse gear is selected by lifting the gearlever through the gate where the earlier remote change and long gearstick varieties just slammed through the gate to engage reverse. Automatics, although well designed, are subject to very expensive failure usually through lack of maintenance. The oil, because it feeds engine and gearbox, should be changed very frequently especially in hot weather. Quite nice to drive but beware on an old car because either the torque converter or gearbox often cost more than the car is worth!

The only heart-warming counterpoint to the power unit's problems is that, except for Coopers, the breakers' yards are full of good second-hand parts: but do try to use a specialist breaker who guarantees his units and not just the local car breaker who might sell you a unit nearly as bad, or possibly worse, than your own. [Author's note: even when a guarantee is given, it doesn't mean that the breaker has inspected or tried the part, even though they might claim that it's O.K. After all what have they got to lose? If the part is N.B.G., they will simply dump it after you bring it back. But what have *you* got to lose? Simply the aggro of fitting a complete component just to find that it isn't any good and then having to take it out again with no certainty that the replacement will be any better. Generally, go for the better class of breaker and give the component a partial strip-down examination on the premises if at all possible.] If it's just component parts you need, ads in most weekly and monthly motor magazines can fulfill all your requirements.

Electrics

On buying your car also check the condition of the wiring loom because if it's rotten they are very costly to have repaired and on the older models, such as the Coopers, the wiring looms are not available any more although specialist companies will get you out of trouble. Not only are electric faults expensive, they sometimes lead to despair with niggly little problems

that seem to go on forever and spoil your enjoyment of the car: after all, electrical faults are the most common cause of breakdowns by far.

Buying – in conclusion

Having examined a car to the extent that my car-check guide and Keith Dodd's hints and tips have taken you, it is likely that your hair will be standing on end! It is extremely doubtful that even organisations such as the A.A. check cars over as thoroughly as this when carrying out their pre-purchase inspections for customers and the outcome is almost bound to be that you will come up with a long list of faults. If, on the other hand, the car has virtually none of the faults shown here, you've found a real gem!

The price check symbols will help you to determine the most expensive jobs to be carried out. Remember, a £ symbol indicates that the parts for repair will cost no more than one good quality tyre or even less, a £££ symbol means that the repair materials will cost as much as a set of tyres or more, while ££ means that the cost will be between the two. It is no use giving actual costs here because inflation rapidly makes printed prices meaningless. Note that the symbols refer only to parts in every case where a DIY repair is possible and that labour charges can be very much more, usually by a factor of 3-4 for body parts. In other words, £100 worth of panels can often cost around £300 to £400 to fit, as a *very* rough rule of thumb.

Don't be too put off by your list of faults unless they are really serious ones; the following notes could help to put them into perspective. Body rot and underbody corrosion are far and away the worst enemies of any Mini and its owner. The car is constructed in such a way that all the outer panels are dependent upon one another to supply the

strength of the whole car, so serious corrosion is a significant problem. On the other hand, replacement of the main rot spots is a fairly straightforward affair for anyone with a modicum of welding ability, or the common sense to prepare a car for someone else to weld it. It's not until you get into the region of new flitch panels, roof support members and other advanced areas of rot that things start becoming rather tricky. Any rot found should be viewed on the iceberg principle: for every spot of corrosion found on the outside, things will certainly be ten times worse on the inside and that includes the critical areas mentioned in the check lists.

Nearly all body parts are readily available and will continue to be so for some time, simply because so many Minis were built that it is worthwhile for Austin-Rover Unipart to keep on manufacturing some panels, even for the earlier cars, for which there is a ready market. Also, because of the numbers of Minis around, lots of independent panel makers sell repair panels for just about every rot spot. Some of the panels, as I've pointed out elsewhere, are pretty poor fakes of the real thing but others are invaluable because there are no 'official' equivalents.

Similarly, nearly all mechanical parts are available and, unless the car is a Cooper 997 or 'S' in which case you should check with the specialists as to which bits are to be had, problems with a car's mechanics are among the most tolerable faults, although of course any larger component rebuild can work out very expensive.

The biggest problem with any but the very latest cars is the non-availability of trim. Even there, the large numbers of Minis built give the cloud a silver lining because scrapyards up and down the country all have nests of donor Minis just waiting for the vital transplant need to arise. The rarer or earlier the Mini, though, the less useful this source will be of course. Two other courses of action for the owner who wants to simply use his or her Mini and not actually show it are either to fit later trim brand new, (*very* costly) or second-hand, or to have trim and panels retrimmed by a coach trimmer. The bespoke specialists, used to dealing with conveyances for the gentlefolk charge a very great deal but the local trimmer to whom the motor trade take their repair work is not usually anywhere near so expensive – ask around your local garages for recommended names. The main disadvantage with this last course of action is that colour, texture and grain of materials cannot usually be perfectly matched with the originals.

Of all the cars on the road, there must be none easier to *keep* on the road than the Mini; at least that's a consolation!

'Agreed Value' insurance

Many prospective purchasers of early 'Classic' Mini's are put off because of the threat of inadequate insurance, specifically pertaining to the real retail value of these vehicles.

As appointed members of the Mini Owners Club, Lifesure Limited, 115 Newnham Avenue, Bedford, are able to place early examples of this marque with insurers who specialize in the insurance of classic Mini's used on a limited mileage basis.

The term used for specifying a value at the outset of the insurance is 'Agreed Value', but many insurers refuse to offer this type of policy despite the fact that for classic cars it is very necessary.

Lifesure's Michael Payne explains, 'Agreed Value is a way of ensuring that a particular vehicle's value is recognised and accepted, in effect agreed by the vehicle's insurer. Normally, the insurer will require a written valuation together with a colour photograph from an approved valuer who has either seen the vehicle or been provided with a complete history of it. An Agreed Value safeguards the owner

of the vehicle by ensuring that, should a total loss claim occur, the set figure agreed at the inception of the insurance is paid by the insurer as opposed to the market value of the vehicle which is normally taken from motor trade guides and does not take into account the pedigree and attention that is often lavished upon individual collectors' cars. This form of insurance is no longer restricted to vintage and veteran cars. Many modern classics such as Mini's as well as other models which have been discontinued by the manufacturers, but are in such excellent condition as to set them apart from the ordinary car, may benefit from it.'

B1.   Whether buying for immediate use or not it pays to buy the best you can afford (although not necessarily the most expensive). Buying for restoration is different: once you start a restoration, nearly everything seems to need renewing no matter what the car looks like beforehand, so you might as well look for a complete (but not completely rotted out!) example. This was John Eddom's Cooper before we started. It looked terrific but just look in the Bodywork chapter of this book where you can see what we had to do.

B2.   Along with sills, front wings are among the most common of Mini rot-spots. The hole in the top is an aerial hole but the rust can be seen near the vertical seam, and near the scuttle panel. It's a certainty that when you see this sort of corrosion, the inner panels will be rotten too, especially at the scuttle ends.

B3.   At the other end of the front wings, similar problems can be found especially above the headlamp bowls, around the headlamp rim (there is often nothing there when the headlamp is taken out!) and the seam with the front panel, the front panel itself and the whole of the apron beneath the bumper are all susceptible. If you're looking at a Riley Elf or Wolseley Hornet, make sure that bumpers and fancy trim are all there and in one piece — they're irreplaceable.

⬅

B4.   Original touches are nice to have in early cars. These Issigonis 'string' door pulls may have looked crude in their day but now they're looking rather quaint. People are very fond of 'customising' door trims and dashboards, too. It's a real bonus if you can find one that is original and complete.

B5.   Wheel spats and alloy wheels may or may not be to your liking. If spats are there and you want to keep them check that they are original (eg 1984 Mini Sprite, 1960s Radford Coopers) or period accessories and that they have been well fitted. Regard old alloy wheels with deep suspicion since, in time, the alloy can begin to crystallise and lose its strength with horribly obvious results.

B6.   More fundamental than the exterior corrosion mentioned earlier is corrosion seen in the floor beneath the rear seat. Stresses from the rear subframe are fed into this area, the adjacent heel board/subframe mounting areas are likely to be similarly afflicted and a lot of work could be involved.

B7.   Rot also attacks the base of the storage bins each side of the rear seats. These are provided with a drain hole for letting trapped water out (into the rear footwell!) but it is a favourite spot for corrosion to begin. It can only be spotted with trim out of the way and although it isn't structurally very significant it is difficult to get at and repair.

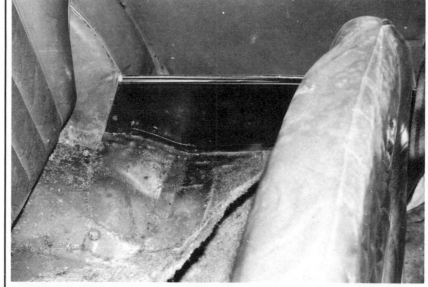

B8.   This Cooper wing appeared sound until the paint was stripped off revealing filler underneath. It is important NEVER to take a car's appearance at face value; check with a magnet to see whether the shiny paint surface covers steel or filler.

B9.   One of the very nastiest places to repair is the roof guttering. Surface rust can be linished off but severe corrosion means that a very difficult repair has to be carried out . . .

B10.   . . . particularly if the rot extends to the upper corner of the door frame as it so often does in really bad cases. Again, check carefully with a magnet to make sure there is no hole obscured by filler.

B11.   Corroded seam cover strips look awful but they can be replaced with nothing more complex than a screwdriver to lift off the old one, a can of aerosol spray to paint the new one and a hammer and block of wood to tap it on. The problems really start when the seam behind it rots out badly . . . Whilst in this area, check the rear screen rubber because the early cars with smaller windscreens used a size of rubber that can no longer be obtained, although specialist glass fitters who take rubbers off a roll rather than in pre-formed shapes claim to have no problems.

B12.   This little 'ear' of trim was fitted towards the rear end of the sill on early cars. It carried a grommet in its centre which was removed for greasing the grease point beneath. In practice, the flimsy bits of steel rotted and BMC agents would then take them off as a matter of course. The presence of these trims in good condition is a good clue to authenticity.

B13.   It is possible to fit the longer Van rear suspension trumpets to cars, and vice versa and the height at the rear of APR suggests that this had happened. Lowering is a simple matter of reducing the length of the trumpet fractionally, an experimental nibble at a time until the desired height is reached.

B14.   Filler under the paint in the area just ahead of the rear wheel arch suggests, nay proves, that here is a rot spot! This is a common area of corrosion and also of distortion when the rear subframe mounts have rotted away, allowing the rear body to flex.

B15. The bottoms of boots, even
the fronts of bonnets on MK II cars
with the chrome strip across the
front are also prone to corrosion.
This was fairly obvious, but rust can
rear its head behind hinges, beneath
window channels and in all sorts of
places where you cannot check
without a stripdown, so be prepared
for the worst − and you will usually
be right!

B16. When is a Cooper not a
Cooper? When the chassis and
engine plates are missing! If engine
number plates are attached, check
to make sure yours is the right one.
If none is attached, there can only
be one reason − it isn't the right
one! Twin carbs, the right
instruments and badges and a white
roof don't prove a thing! (In fact,
many Coopers left the factory with a
black roof or monotone colour
scheme. Note that Tartan Red with
white roof was only used on works
cars and was never a production
colour scheme.

B17. Correct badges in useable
condition (on the right models) are
absolutely essential on older cars
and especially the Coopers,
otherwise you could spend ages
trying to find them. On the other
hand, you might strike lucky
because some specialists are
starting to remanufacture all kinds
of classic car badges: it pays to
check in advance.

B18. When Practical Classics magazine restored their Cooper, they almost overdid the business of starting out with a rough car. It's important for the home restorer to strike a balance between spending more than is necessary on a car that is too good and buying a complete heap that would not justify restoration unless you wanted to build magazine articles out of it!

B19. If you fancy one of the 'extra-specials' such as the Radford Mini Cooper, it becomes absolutely crucial that trim details such as the enamel 'Radford' badges are in place otherwise you could spend a small fortune in having them specially made up on a one-off basis.

B20. On the other hand, Radford 'pinched' a lot of trim from production cars, such as the Riley/Wolseley Minis which at least makes it possible to find new, or more likely, scrapyard replacements if bits are missing.

B21.   The quality of some of the fittings, such as the dashboard on these cars was not all it was cracked up to be. It was distinctly crude compared to genuine coachbuilt cars, so its restoration should hold no particular terrors for the handiman or woman, provided that the formed plastic mouldings are in place. How on earth would you replicate them?

B22.   Undoubtedly the most expensive item in restoring these cars would be the upholstery which was properly done in leather, making a complete interior re-trim reach easily into the four-figure bracket. On all Minis more than just a few years old, condition of trim (and presence of the correct type) is crucial because it is all but irreplaceable (see text).

B23.   One of the more modern Minis is this Mini 'Sprite'. Use of the sports car name, alas, grants it no extra performance whatsoever but, as one of the periodic 'limited edition' Minis, it boasted a few extras such as wheel spats and fancy wheels. This Worcestershire main agent found in the mid-80s that Mini sales were a steady trickle rather than the earlier flow but modern Minis, new, provide one of the cheapest and best-proven ways of getting a new car onto the road.

3 Bodywork

Mini — the ideal restorer's car!

If there is any one car that is the ideal for the novice restorer it has to be the Mini! There are a number of cars whose mechanical components are easier to work on, but the mechanics of a car are by no means the most expensive nor the hardest parts to repair. The Mini's bodywork has several prime values for the restorer: the parts are extremely easy to come by (unlike most other cars more than just a few years old) and are inexpensive to boot, while the car's construction is fairly simple other than in a few specific areas although, as with virtually any other car, welding equipment will be necessary.

As far as parts are concerned, the home restorer and repairer is faced with a three-tier choice. At the lowest level, panels of a non-structural nature (such as bonnet, boot, front and rear aprons) can be repaired with a dash of fibreglass and a scrape of filler, or they can be replaced with some of the huge range of repair panels made by firms like Melbros and Saltofix or, at sometimes twice the cost, original Austin-Rover panels can still be bought (and will continue to be available well into the foreseeable future as Austin-Rover are reported to be planning to continue Mini production until at least the end of the 1980s).

However, having said that 'original' parts are more expensive, their price is only relative. A front wing costs around the price of a new tyre, or less if a non-original part is bought. You only get what you pay for of course, and non-standard parts are often a very poor fit. In fact, in terms of quality of fit (the author has, in the past, questioned which *car* specific non-original panels were made for, their resemblance to the originals needing a great leap of the imagination!) and time saved, the Austin-Rover panels are preferable every time unless the car is being 'bodged' together just to make it sound, or unless the original part is just not available as in the case of the scuttle top panel and one or two other parts.

All of this makes the 'Bodywork' section of this book potentially the most useful to the home restorer, especially since much of the information it contains can be found nowhere else. There is no doubt that sound bodywork is the most crucial area of any car; poor bodywork reduces the life, safety and value of any Mini while restored bodywork makes the car tauter, safer and less of a rattling collander.

Equipment

Of course, the home restorer has to invest in a certain amount of equipment, although most people carrying out a full-scale project will already have acquired much of it. Those who have to buy from scratch can console themselves with the knowledge that the equipment they buy should cost far less than the labour costs of a rebuild plus the fact that they will still own the equipment for future use. Hand tools receive the largest amount of use and it is always well worth investing in the best that are around, as poor tools make a good job well-nigh impossible. Sykes-Pickavant produce a huge range of bodyshop tools and are developing an increased range at lower cost suitable for the DIY repair/restorer. An electric drill is invaluable, of course, but so is a mini-grinder which can be useful at almost every stage for cutting out rusty metal, linishing paint and surface rust away from weld surfaces, dressing welds and dressing the edges of repair panels.

With these basics plus the more obvious hammer, bolster chisel, screwdrivers and spanners, as well as a means of cutting out sheet steel (a good pair of universal tin snips will do for a start) the first-timer could make a start. He or she, would have to fit panels together with self-tapping screws and/or clamps until a 'mobile welder' could be dragged out of *Yellow Pages*, or the bodyshell trailered to professional premises. Several such visits would be necessary as some panels have to be 'closed-off' before others can be welded into place, but the procedure is not impossible. If restoration is to be taken seriously, it will be necessary to learn to weld at some time or other. It is possible to hire electric arc welding equipment in most large towns, although this type of welding equipment is considered to be too fierce for outer body panels by even the most experienced hands. For work on subframes and tack-welding inner panels or door skins, arc-welding can be acceptable. Arc-brazing, which is more versatile but less strong, can also be carried out with an arc welder with the addition of the appropriate accessory.

In the U.K. most Technical Colleges and Evening Institutes run evening classes where beginners can learn the rudiments of gas or arc welding. Gas welding is far more versatile than arc welding at least as far as car bodywork is concerned, but gas bottles are more difficult and more expensive to obtain and are far less safe to store and use. A company called Murex, owned by the Scandinavian welding rod firm ESAB, now market a range of products including 'Portapack' (nothing to do with the author!) welding kits. These are small-scale oxy-acetylene welding kits which the user rents for a renewable seven year period, the bottles being exchangeable at a BOC centre in the normal way. There are a number of other independent concerns producing cheaper alternatives, the foremost among them being The Welding Centre. Their products come closest to matching professional equipment (and, indeed, are often used by professionals where true portability is required) and consist of excellent quality welding and cutting torches run from a replenishable oxygen container and a discardable container of Mapp gas which is almost as hot as acetylene but with none of the storage risks.

Haynes publish a complete manual showing how to carry out every operation in bodywork care and repair. It shows all the tools, all the techniques and a host of projects in which the equipment and skills are put to use. Written by Lindsay Porter, the author of this book, *Haynes Car Bodywork Manual* (available winter 1984) is intended as a complete, easy-to-follow guide to every major and minor aspect of car bodywork repair and includes, of course, major sections on spraying and on all types of welding systems.

One final note regarding panels concerns production differences between earlier and later cars. A-panels differ between those cars with external hinges and those with concealed hinges, but good old Austin-Rover supply both types through their dealer network. Early-type front panels, flitch panels (without the air ducting hole) and boot lid are not currently available and other 'No Longer Available'

parts are bound to arise with the passage of time. It is then up to the owner to decide between searching for the right part through magazine classifieds and club sources, repairing the existing panel, fitting a non-original repair panel or a later alternative (they nearly all fit) or looking for a second-hand alternative. There is plenty of choice and specialists such as the Mini Spares Centre in London can usually help.

E1. The Welding Centre produce a fully portable gas welding set which looks and feels more like a professional welding set than any other of the DIY sets on offer. When used with a cylinder of Mapp gas (bought from many DIY centres) it gives a flame which is very nearly as hot as an acetylene flame. The only drawback is that the torch controls are a bit sensitive and also running costs are higher than for a full scale set, although the advantages of portability and lower purchase cost can more than balance this out.

'Welding with the MIG is a bit like drawing a slow line with a felt-tipped pen.'

E2. MIG welding is, as far as both DIY enthusiast and full professional are concerned, simply the finest type of welding there is. The author's bodyshop uses the SIP Ideal 120N and its bigger brother the 150 and both are as easy to use as drawing a slow line with a felt tipped pen – well almost! As well as being the most straightforward form of welding for the beginner to use, it is also far more economical to run than gas welding and it creates far less distortion. It can also be used for a form of spot welding. Minus points are that it can't be used for heating or bending in the way that gas can and it needs an Argon bottle (Air Products or BOC) or a CO_2 bottle (try the local pub!) to accompany it.

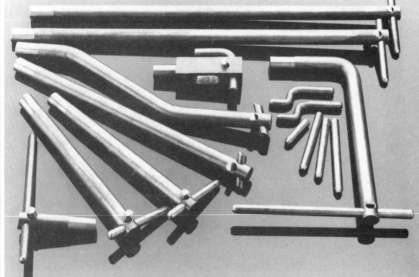

E3. Spot welders work by passing a current through two overlapped pieces of metal, the heat formed actually fusing them together. The only material consumed is electric current. You can reach round obstructions with the spot welder – a particularly useful tool on the Mini with so many external flanges – by using a set of extension arms like these available for the SIP Spotmatic spot welders.

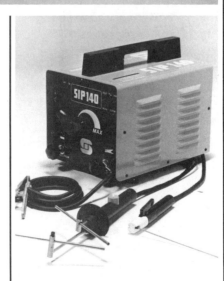

E4. Right down the price scale is the arc welder set which can be bought through national ads and DIY centres at very moderate cost. You have to be a real dab hand to be able to weld thin metals with an arc welder and indeed the conventional wisdom is that you can't do it. Actually, you can sometimes just get away with it if you are extremely careful and just a little accomplished; DC arc welders being easier to handle with thin metals than AC. A carbon arc brazing kit makes working with thinner metals far, far easier, although you are of course restricted to brazing with this part of the kit.

E5.   The Portapack, available jointly from BOC (who supply the gas) and Murex (who provide the hardware) is a fully professional standard of kit available to the DIY user. Portapack presents a convenient source of gas and absolutely first-rate equipment, albeit at a price that reflects such excellence.

E6.   This is one of BOC's many Cylinder Centres where Portapack cylinders can be changed when they have expired. (Find your local centre in the telephone directory.) Portapacks can be purchased here or at many motor factors.

E7.   This tool, made by Sykes-Pickavant is terrific for cutting out sheet steel. Taking up far less room than a guillotine, it can also cut slight curves. It consists of upper and lower cutting wheels which slice through the sheet while also pulling it through the machine.

E8. This is another Sykes-Pickavant tool and this is really invaluable for the home restorer. It pulls the edge of the sheet along between two rollers which form a 'set' or a shoulder in the edge of the steel. This allows you to join two flat pieces of metal with all the smoothness of a butt joint but with all the strength and ease of welding of a lap-joint. Wonderful!

E9. Although a little more expensive, the Sykes-Pickavant sheet metal folder is the only way to create perfectly formed folds in sheet steel. It forms very accurate, very crisp folds and even pulls any light wrinkles out of the sheet while it does it.

Tool Box

At the start of every section, a 'Tool Box' section appears, listing most of the tools and equipment needed to enable you to carry out the work. No list of 'essential' workshop tools is presented here but simply the advice that it is safer and cheaper in the long-run to always buy (or hire) the best tools available.

Safety

At the start of every section is a 'Safety' note. Naturally, safety is the responsibility of each individual restorer or repairer and no responsibility for the effectiveness or otherwise of advice given here nor for any omissions can be accepted by the author — 'Safety' notes are intended to include some useful tips and no more. Some further useful information on workshop practice and general safety measures is given as an appendix — you are strongly advised to read this appendix before starting any of the tasks detailed in this book.

Be sure to disconnect the alternator (if fitted) to avoid risk of damage to it when carrying out electric welding.

Stripdown and examination

Tool Box

Axle stands or ramps; a thin-bladed screwdriver; eye protection; paint stripper; rubber gloves and a scraper; notepad; bags and boxes for strong nuts, screws, small fittings etc; a range of spanners and screwdrivers including an impact screwdriver; releasing fluid and a source of heat for freeing stubborn threads.

Safety

Never use a flame near the fuel tank or fuel lines. Paint stripper is damaging to the skin and eyes — read instructions before use and wear gloves and goggles and protective overalls. Ensure that the car is firmly supported when lifted off the ground — a jack is NOT safe enough. Wear goggles when 'poking' beneath the car and beware of rusty, jagged edges.

The first task in carrying out a restoration of any size is to go round the car and methodically examine it, taking notes of all the problem areas. Of course your instincts tell you to make a start, to strip bits off the car straightaway. Once begun, this idea can be so infectious that you can lose yourself in a haze of releasing fluid fumes and rust dust, the excitement overcoming you until you reach the point of no return — and it's past closing time! Once graceful lines are now a tangled heap of metal on the floor and you haven't a hope in hell of remembering where all the bits came from. Perhaps the reader might see something of an exaggeration in this — but beware: it's not so far from the truth!

SE1. John Eddom's Cooper looked like a super little car and it was certainly in terrific order for its age! However, as well as suffering from a slight front-end bump, both front wings were starting to corrode, sills needed replacement and so did the doorskins and boot hinge panel.

SE4. The headlights were taken off this car at an early stage. On some, the trim ring is held on with a self-tapping screw inserted from beneath while others are sprung on and have to be levered off from beneath with a screwdriver.

SE2. If you aim to carry out a total restoration, you need to reach this sort of state of stripdown before any of the body panels are removed. (See 'Engine Removal' for details of that part of the work). Note that the engine has been removed, leaving the front subframe in place although it is possible to take out the whole front subframe complete with all its mechanical components, by lifting the body off at the front. The major disadvantage of doing things this way is that the car is rendered virtually immobile. The other is that the front subframe helps to keep the front of the car rigid and stable and gives a reference point for fitting new panels. The simplicity of the Mini's front-end construction can be seen here: each front wing is welded to its flitch panel (the engine bay side panels) along its top edge, forming a rigid 'box'. The grille surround and front apron straddle them both and tie them together. At the rear of the engine bay is the top scuttle panel and a partial box to which clutch and brake cylinders are fitted, giving extra rigidity. The front subframe bolts up to the rear of the front apron, to the cross-member at the rear of the engine bay and also to the front of the car's floor.

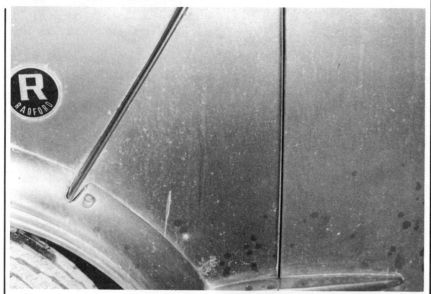

SE3. This car bore the 'R' badge of Radford, the coachbuilders who were responsible for carrying out up-market customising for Minis in the 'sixties. If your car has any special bits or period accessories that you want to keep, take them off and store them with great care. You may remember them as being extremely common but they are certain to be almost irreplaceable now.

SE5. Next the headlamp unit is pushed in against its spring loading and twisted anti-clockwise for about 10mm so that its keyhole slots disengage from the retaining/adjustment screws.

SE5A. Earlier types have these bayonet fitting connectors while later models have plastic plugs and sockets which simply pull apart. Don't forget the separate sidelight bulb which clips into the headlamp unit.

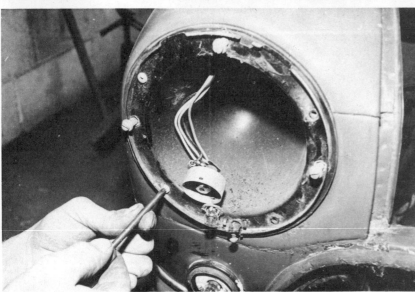

SE6. The headlamp bowl is held to the wing with five self-tapping screws. It is well worth considering the replacement of these headlamp bowls with the non-corrosive plastic type since the steel ones can be a nuisance and do rot out very quickly.

SE7. When taking out the headlamp bowl, disconnect the lamp wires from inside the engine bay and feed them through the grommets in the flitch plates so that the bowl then becomes free.

SE8. You may find that your new wings have no means of holding the headlamp bowl in place. Prize out the plastic 'nuts' into which the self-tapping screws are fitted and keep them safely for future use.

SE9.   The mini grille is held in place
by self-tapping screws, as indicated
by the pointing finger. Some Minis
have knurled nuts for easy finger-
and-thumb grille removal to make
access to the engine simpler.

SE10.   Before unbolting the horn,
try to sort out the knitting basket of
wires in that area. If you can't see
clearly what the colour codes of the
wires are meant to be, tag them
with pieces of masking tape on
which you can write an identifying
code.

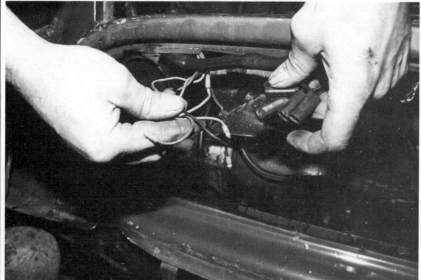

SE11.   The horn just bolts to the
grille panel's centre strut. Simple!

SE12.   After sliding the wiper arms
off their splines (they usually need a
little persuasion with a screwdriver
placed beneath the spline and
twisted to force the arm upwards),
unbolt the nuts which hold the
wiper drive boxes to the scuttle
panel.

SE13. Use a lever to prize the drive mechanism downwards so that the drive splines slide out of the holes in the scuttle panel. If when carrying out this job, you wish you had very long, thin fingers it won't be the last time before this job is finished . . .

SE14. The wiper motor is bolted through the scuttle panel, the three nuts holding it in place being accessible by removing the trim panel from the rear of the parcel shelf. It can be extremely difficult to remove both the motor and the rack attached to it in one go, so refer to the section on 'Windscreen Wiper Motor Removal' in the 'Electrical Components' chapter.

SE15. With the wiper motor out of the way, the complete rack can be removed, too.

SE16. Back in the lighting department, front flashers are removed by first easing out the chrome trim ring from its rubber seating lip with a screwdriver. Old rubber perishes and splits easily.

SE17.   The glass beneath is also seated into a lip of rubber but this usually comes out much more easily.

SE20.   . . . the wires to be disconnected. Scrape the wire with your thumb nail to see if it has perished (it lives in a very vulnerable spot, after all) and to see whether its colour coding is still discernible. Tag with masking tape if necessary.

SE23.   . . . then pull the bullet connectors off the ends of the wire to enable the wires to be pulled back through the rubber. If you intend to retain the lamps, push the bullet connectors back in, or they are sure to get lost.

SE18.   The lamp itself is held in place with three self-tapping screws which, on older Minis, are frequently screwed into thin air!

SE21.   The lamp body pulls out of its rubber sheath, the wires having to be eased back through the holes in the back of the rubber. The body is frequently corroded and often has to be (inexpensively) renewed.

SE24.   Rear lamps are held in place on all models by three bolts with nuts which are removed from inside the boot. Their bullet connectors are also situated in the boot on the floor towards the rear of the car.

SE19.   The lamp body then pulls out, leaving . . .

SE22.   Pull the wire clips out of their holders using a pair of long-nosed pliers . . .

SE25.   Whilst taking the rest of the trim off the car, it is a good idea to examine the bodywork for trouble spots. Remove these seam mouldings by levering them off with a screwdriver. They often corrode out but replacements are not at all expensive.

54

SE26. Plastic side mouldings are even easier to remove but if they are to be retained, be careful not to split them, especially in cold weather. They are so easy to remove that they are rather prone to coming away when the car is in use, and are often held in place at odd points with 'foreign' pop-rivets; drill the heads off where necessary.

SE27. On earlier models, bonnet badges are held in place with spring clips, pushed onto lugs which protrude through the panel. Lever the clips off carefully (the lugs are prone to breakage) . . .

SE28. . . . the badge is then completely free to lift away. Some badges on later models have small pins mounted on their back faces which push into plastic retainers, themselves pushed into the panel. Other badges, such as some of the 'BL' badges, are simply glued on and have to be prised off with a screwdriver, while yet others are held on with nuts and washers.

SE29. Wolseley and Riley Minis as well as some of the 'coachbuilt' Minis have additional trim, such as this around the bottom of the front wings . . .

SE30. . . . and more around the wing to scuttle panel joint. The trim must be carefully *prised* away: it may be virtually irreplaceable so take great care not to damage it.

SE31. Even the clips holding trim like this in place can be surprisingly difficult to get hold of so store such items in a clearly labelled bag. An example of 'No Longer Obtainable' clips are those holding the door trim in place, just below the window, so again, take special care to hang on to them.

➡

SE32. Other small items such as this seal may also be classified as 'NLA', but if they are you can always obtain substitutes from one of the specialist trim suppliers who advertise in magazines such as Thoroughbred and Classic Car *and* Practical Classics.

SE33. The rear bumper bolts through the rear seam but the threads almost always seem to be seized. Try to think ahead and apply plenty of releasing fluid well before the bolts are to be undone.

SE34.   This front bumper was scrap, so we cut into it using a cutting wheel on the mini-grinder (remember to wear goggles!) to gain access. It would be difficult to use a hacksaw here as chrome plating is so hard that it is almost impossibly difficult to saw into.

SE35.   The redundant bumper was flapped upwards to reveal a badly corroded retaining bolt beneath. Good access made undoing it ten times easier.

SE36.   Like the rear bumper, the front was then simply lifted away.

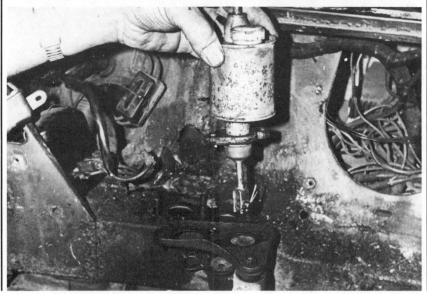

SE37.   Stripping the engine bay is an important task if the under-bonnet area is to be made to look smart. After disconnecting the pedals from inside the car, clutch and brake cylinders unbolt from the cross-member and the engine tie rod can be removed. Note that any hydraulic pipes still in place have had their threaded connectors protected by wrapping masking tape round them.

SE38. On the other side of the cross-member, heater pipes pass through a plate bolted over clutch and brake cylinder holes (put there for markets where the steering wheel is on the other side, of course).

SE39. If you value authenticity, take off the car's chassis number plate and store it in a safe place.

SE40. An almost totally stripped engine bay just before cleaning off with a degreaser. You can now inspect the flitch panels, especially at their front bottom corners, for corrosion and, if you are going all the way with your restoration, paint strip the whole area.

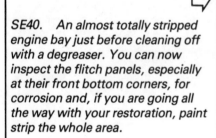

SE41. Inside the car, methods for removal of carpets and most other trim panels are self-evident but there is detailed information on doors, door gear and glass front and rear screens, seats and several other areas in the appropriate sections of this book. In this picture, a leather seat is being lifted out of Pierre Schmit's 'Radford' Cooper: its attachment points are the standard four bolt fixings to the floor cross member.

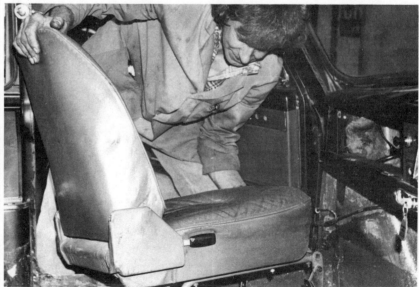

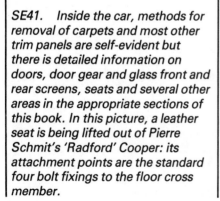

SE42. The door kick plates on this car were held on by four self-tapping screws.

SE43. The windscreen demister ducts are screwed down to the fascia top and are easiest to get at with the screen out of the car. Here one of the three bolts holding the windscreen wiper motor in place (SE11 to 15) has been removed.

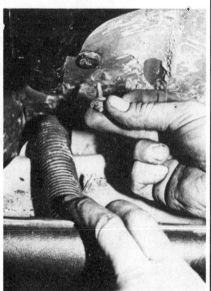

With so many of the car's fixtures and fittings out of the way, it is time to go around the car deciding what needs renewing, replacing or repairing. As a general rule, and based on his experience in his own bodyshop, the author strongly recommends the renewal of panels rather than their repair in every case other than where there is only a very small amount of repair work required. There are several reasons behind this line of thinking (which was actually also found to save customers' money because repairing a panel is almost invariably more time-consuming and more expensive than renewing it): if a panel has begun to rust in one place, it has undoubtedly begun to do so elsewhere, too; the shape and fit of a handmade repair is seldom as good as a mass-produced panel, especially if it is an original part, and; the time taken in repairing a panel and the risk of ruining it can be very demoralising for the home restorer and this is a rather needless risk in the case of the Mini whose body parts are mainly inexpensive to buy.

SE44. Many restorers actually like to strip the bodyshell of paint at this stage so that they can see what really is sound and what is a 'bodge'. Sometimes, beautiful smooth looking surfaces can prove to be works of the fibreglass sculptor's art, with all sorts of horrors behind the filler. When you do come to large lumps of filler, don't attempt to remove it with paint stripper; don an efficient particle mask and power-sand it out.

Fuel tank removal

Before starting work on the bodywork of any car, it is essential that the fuel tank is removed to prevent the risk of a fuel tank explosion. If the fuel tank is to be stored for any length of time, have it steam cleaned to remove all traces of petrol and petrol vapour; it is the vapour from petrol that ignites and explodes, so simply draining the petrol out is not enough. Moreover, in time sediment is prone to collect at the base of the tank and this is likely to find its way to the carburettor, especially after the tank has been disturbed. Having the tank steam cleaned is an excellent way of removing the sediment or the tank could be vigorously flushed out with a hose — but be sure to dry it thoroughly before refitting.

Tool Box

Open-ended spanners for tank removal (saloon); cross-point screwdriver/impact drive (for non-saloon tanks); releasing fluid, ratchet spanners and a power drill for removing rusty nuts (van, estate and pick-up); large safe containers for catching and storing petrol drained from tank.

Safety

Take note of information in the text and appendices on safety hazards. NEVER drain petrol over a pit or anywhere a spark could ignite the vapour (eg near a central heating boiler) — outdoors is best. For obvious reasons, attempting to weld a fuel tank can be lethal and is a task which should always be left to specialists.

Saloons (except Cooper 'S')

FT1. On all saloon models, the fuel tank nestles into the left-hand corner of the boot where it is very well protected against corrosion. On Coopers and other models with De Luxe boot floor trim panels, the trim board has to be lifted away. Early Minis (but not the very earliest) have a drain plug which operates on the same principle as a brake bleed screw, ie the nipple is unscrewed three or four turns, but not completely removed.

Other models have a fuel drain tube which must be completely removed along with the plug before the tank can be taken out. Both of these types have access holes in the bodywork beneath the tank and are reached with a long box spanner. Where there is no facility for draining on the tank itself (ie on the great majority of cars) it will be

necessary to drain the tank through the 'input' pipe to the fuel pump which is mounted on the subframe. Disconnect the pipe from the pump and direct the flow into a container. On cars where there is a mechanical fuel pump, it may be possible to drain the tank through a joint in the pipe, or the tank can be removed with fuel in it by disconnecting the outlet pipe at the tank and very quickly, with the minimum of spillage, fitting a new piece of flexible tubing with its free end held above the level of the petrol tank.

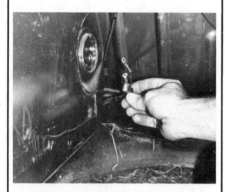

FT2. The wires must be disconnected from the tank sender unit (the battery having already been disconnected) and the breather pipe, which shares a clip with the wires, on the rear bulkhead, must be unclipped.

FT3. The tank is held down by a steel strap which is tensioned by a long bolt. Withdraw the bolt to free the tank.

FT4.   On the outside of the car, the rubber grommet which locates the tank filler can be removed. This is not essential but it does improve tank manoeuvrability.

FT5.   With the fuel pipe to pump disconnected, the tank can now be carefully eased from the car, at the same time easing the fuel and vent pipes through the floor. When refitting, take care that the vent pipe is not kinked or obstructed in any way and, on earlier models fitted with a drain plug, refit, or fit!, a grommet to the drain plug access holes.

Cooper 'S': twin tanks

FT6.   The Cooper 'S' right-hand tank is virtually a mirror image of the left-hand tank except that there is no sender unit and the petrol pipe feeds the left-hand tank, so balancing the petrol levels between both tanks. This balance pipe must be handled carefully as the right-hand tank is removed, otherwise it can easily kink and break. Note that the strap on any of the saloon tanks can be disconnected from the boot floor if preferred.

FT7. If all you're doing is
respraying the bodywork, you can
simply unclip the tank(s) and slide
them out of the way as with these
Cooper 'S' tanks. Do be careful not
to strain pipework or electrical
connections.

Estate, van and pick-up models

These models have their fuel tanks
mounted beneath the rear of the car
(except for early models of Traveller
and Countryman where they are
sited in the same place as the
Saloon) which makes them much
more prone to rusting than their
Saloon counterparts. Also, their
fixing method is more prone to
rusting, so be prepared to have to
battle with tight screws or even to
have to drill the heads off and then
drill what's left of the screws out of
their captive nuts with the tank out
of the way, if the worst comes to
the worst.

Start by raising the rear of the
vehicle off the ground on axle
stands or wheel ramps and drain the
petrol out of the tank bearing in
mind the safety points already
made. The fuel tank outlet pipe and
the sender unit are on the side of the
tank and the outlet pipe must be
disconnected and the sender unit
lead taken off.

Next, place a jack underneath
the tank to take its weight as it is
removed, then take out the six
screws holding it in place. Note that
it may be easier to disconnect the
sender unit wire after the tank has
been lowered a little.

All models

FT8. With the tank out of the car,
drain the last dregs of petrol out of it
and, if it is to be stored for any
length of time, have it steam
cleaned. Obviously, it is far easier to
repaint the tank at this stage.

FT9. If the tank is to be stored for
a short length of time, blank off the
filler aperture using paper and
masking tape, or anything in fact,
that will prevent a spark from falling
into the tank. It also pays to store
the tank in a safe place, preferably
well away from the house and
workshop.

When refitting the tank, make sure
that the rubber sealing ring that fits
around the neck of the filler pipe is
in place, or the hole in the rear floor
will leak water. Also, ensure that the
nylon spacers located at each
retaining screw hole are in position
before refitting the tank.

Sender unit

Early models: the unit is held in place by six screws. Later models: carefully turn the locking ring through 30° then lift ring and sender unit away.

In each case, be careful not to bend the float lever as the float is withdrawn from the tank.

When refitting, always use a new joint gasket and a non-setting jointing compound after first scraping all mating surfaces clean.

Bonnet removal

All Mini bonnets come off in the same way but note that not all 'standard' Mini bonnets are interchangeable. The distance between the hinges differs between earlier and later models although, in extreme circumstances, it would be possible to fit a late bonnet to an early car by drilling out the spot welds on the bonnet hinge mountings and re-welding them in the correct position for the hinges. Before starting to disconnect the bonnet, check that it fits the wings and front panel satisfactorily and if it does, draw a pencil line around the outline of the hinge on the bonnet to assist accurate reassembly later.

BR1. Prop the bonnet open on its stay and slacken the nuts holding the bonnet onto the hinges. It is a good idea to place rags beneath the bonnet corners if the paintwork is to be protected, particularly if you are forced to carry out this job alone.

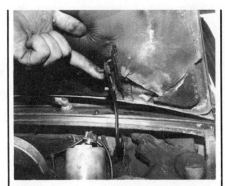

BR2. After removing the nuts, the fixed studs will remain in place in the hinge. Spring the hinge sideways a little to free it from the bonnet mountings.

BR3. The bonnet can then be lifted clear. It is easily managed by one person although it can be useful to have an assistant steady the bonnet as the hinges are disconnected.

Front wing renewal

Even though they are welded and not bolt-on wings, renewing a Mini's front wings must be one of the easiest wing-swaps around. Austin-Rover wings should be fitted in preference to the touch-where-they-fit non-standard panels that can be purchased at a small saving, and you must also anticipate carrying out some repair work to panels surrounding the front wing which may also have corroded, the front panel being particularly susceptible.

Tool Box

Sharp, thin-bladed bolster chisel, air chisel or similar; mini-grinder; goggles; electric drill and bits; variety of welder's clamps and/or self-tapping screws; MIG or oxy-acetylene welding equipment; panel beating hammer; paint for painting underside of new wings; seam sealer and underseal if required.

Safety

Beware sparks from grinder and razor-sharp edges when removing old wing. Use goggles and thick industrial-type gloves. Take all the usual precautions when welding — see appendix at back of this book.

FW1. In the unlikely event that the wing is sound but the headlamp fixing area is corroded, it is possible to purchase 'headlamp rings' to replace the corroded area. Since other areas are certain to be corroded too, this can only be considered a temporary measure.

FW2. One way of removing the front wing from the flitch panel is to drill out the spot welds (it may be necessary to paint strip the area first, so that you can actually see the spot welds) . . .

FW3. . . . While another is to cut the wing away with a sharp bolster chisel just a little way in from the front panel, the top scuttle panel and the A-panel.

FW4. If you decide to do it this way, make certain that the surrounding panels are not cut into — surplus metal can easily be cut or ground away later.

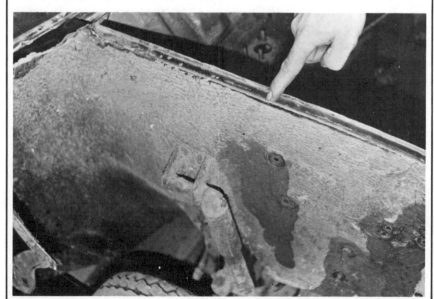

FW5. After removing the wing like this, it is still necessary to drill out the spot welds in order to clean up the seam but access is now much easier, especially for prising open any spot welds that still 'hold' even after being drilled.

FW6. A front panel such as this one on John Eddom's car, may be perfectly sound enough to save but still require some remedial work. A favourite rust spot is the moisture trap behind the indicator lamp.

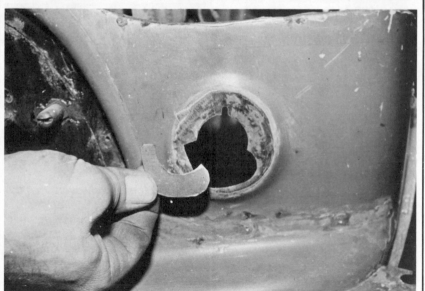

FW7. After filing the rust away until sound metal is reached, a suitable repair patch can be accurately cut out and filed to shape: actually easier than it looks! Start by cutting a square of metal, hold it behind the repair scribe round the opening and cut out to the scribe line. If there are small gaps, it doesn't matter because the welding or brazing will sort them out.

FW8. A Sykes-Pickavant welder's clamp is shown here holding the repair in place so that it can be tacked in several places, holding it firmly in position.

FW9. Then the repair can be seam welded into place before being linished smooth with 36 grit linishing paper on a rubber backing pad mounted on a mini-grinder or drill.

FW10. John Eddom's Mini was suffering from corrosion in the front panel flanges, too, but these were easily replaced. First a piece of card was held along the top of the front panel after the old flange had been cleaned off. From beneath, a pencil line was drawn following the shape of the panel. A card strip template was cut out, transferred to steel and the steel strip, matching the shape of the front panel when viewed from above, was easily bent to the shape of the panel viewed from straight ahead.

FW11. The repair was clamped into place and used as a guide to cut the edge of the flange with a hacksaw. This way is even better than marking out and cutting because it guarantees a perfect fit!

FW12. The new flange was then welded into place with the SIP MIG welder before the weld was cleaned off with the linisher.

FW13. At the rear corner, it was necessary to make a simple but fussy little repair to replace corroded metal. Again, a card template-cum-model of the repair was carefully created first to ensure accuracy.

FW14. The moment of truth for those repairs comes when the wing is offered up. In fact, it would be a foolish worker who failed to offer the wing up to the car after tacking each repair into place to ensure accuracy of fit.

FW15. The new wing is held in place with a number of clamps or, if the welding on is being done elsewhere, it could even be held in place with self-tapping screws. DON'T be lulled into thinking that they will provide a safe, permanent fixing however; they won't and the safety of your Mini depends on having all the bodyshell panels properly welded into place.

FW16. Before carrying out any final fixing, check that the wing is fitted properly all the way round (it will take a little pulling and pushing into place if necessary). Pay special attention to the front panel fit . . .

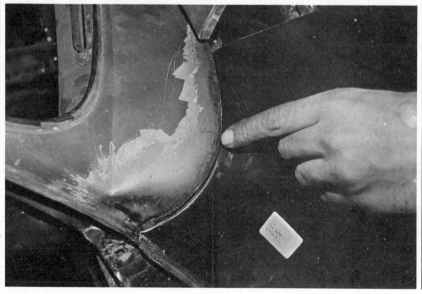

FW17. . . . and to the scuttle-top fit. (See relevant section for repairs to this area if necessary.)

66

FW18. The wing will move fairly freely here to line it up accurately with the flange on the front panel. Don't forget also to sit the bonnet in place to check that all is well with levels and gaps.

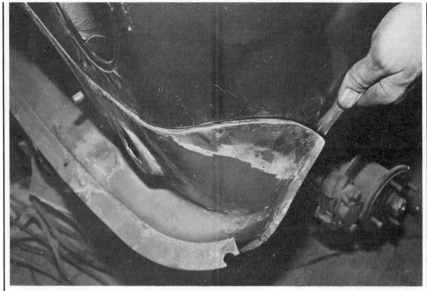

FW19. When you are satisfied that everything fits nicely, drill a series of small holes along the rain channel at the top of the wing. It may be possible to spot-weld it if the car has been stripped right out giving clearance in the engine bay but most people will 'spot' weld using MIG, gas welding or brazing or even carbon-arc brazing: the holes allow the weld or braze to 'spot' the panels together.

FW20. This car was 'spot' welded using the SIP Ideal 120N MIG welder with the spot welding nozzle attached.

FW21. The raised 'buttons' of weld were ground flush using the angle grinder fitted with a grinding wheel.

FW22. Many people forget the small, simple angle plate (made out of thin steel) which fits at the base of the wing-A-panel joint and strengthens it by helping to stop flexing and cracking open.

*FW23.   This is gripped in place
with a self-grip wrench and spot-
welded into position. Note that the
same tool was used for the external
seams although they could have
been button-spot-welded by drilling
through the panel as shown earlier.
The seams underneath the wing can
be seam welded or brazed from
beneath while they are held in place
with a series of self-grip wrenches.*

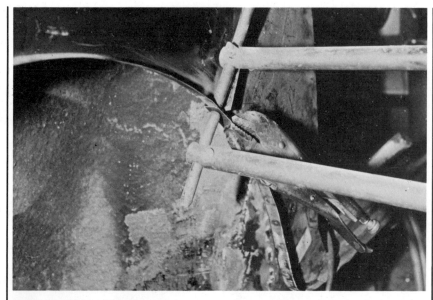

Windscreen and rear screen removal and refitting

Tool Box

Thin-shanked screwdriver or thin
bar of steel; broad-bladed
screwdriver; sharp craft knife;
finisher strip insertion tool;
washing-up liquid to help ease
rubber into place.

Safety

**Deflect the glass as little as you
possibly can to avoid breakage,
the danger of which is self
evident. If you are fitting a
replacement for a previously
broken windscreen note that
tiny particles of glass will have
fallen into the demister ducts.
These MUST be removed and
the heater box must also be
blown out or particles of glass
could blow into the driver's or
passenger's face with obvious
risks of damage to eyes.**

*WS2.   Placing the screwdriver
right behind it, and holding the
screwdriver like mini-handlebars,
the screwdriver is slid along the
rubber which lifts the finisher strip
out without distorting it.*

*WS3.   In both screen rubbers, the
finisher strip covers half the glass,
joining up top and bottom.*

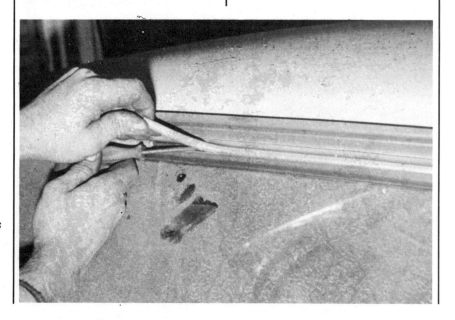

*WS1.   Both front and rear screens
are held in rubbers which are
'spread' tight with chrome-finish
plastic finisher strips. Find the end
of one of the strips and lift it with a
screwdriver.*

WS4.   To get the glass out, ease the rubber from the frame all the way round.

WS5.   Then lever behind the rubber and ease glass and rubber outwards together at one corner. In the case of laminated glass you have to take very great care not to crack it because it's not as flexible as toughened glass.

WS6.   Having got one corner out, ease the glass out of the rubber all the way round. Note how it is necessary to have someone push quite hard against the inside of the screen while all of this is going on.

WS7.   When the glass is out at one end, the screen can be grasped and wriggled out of the rubber at the other end. The edges of the glass are ground smooth, not left sharp like ordinary household glass. Broken pieces are sharp, of course!

WS8.   Exactly the same procedure is followed when removing the rear screen as when removing the front, but remember to disconnect the wires to the window heating element if one is fitted and try hard not to damage the elements as the screen is removed.

WS9.   If the rubber is still in place after glass removal, it just pulls off the frame. If there is any evidence of splitting in the rubber, it must be renewed. MK I rear screen rubbers are not available, but MK II type rubbers can be cut at the top in the middle and made to fit a MK I, or rubber bought off a roll at a windscreen specialist can be used.

WS10.   Be prepared to have to do some cleaning up, painting and perhaps even some cutting out and patching where the rubber has been. It seems to make an ideal breeding ground for rust!

WS11.   When refitting the screen, ease it back in the same way, but pushing from the outside, of course! Get plenty of black, gungy screen sealermastic into the rubber, both in the frame side and in the opening for the glass. Too little and the rubber might leak; too much, and all you have to do is wipe the excess off with paraffin.

WS12.   To get the finisher strip back in place you either need a screwdriver, infinite patience and the luck of the devil to stop you scratching the paint, or one of these, either bought or home-made out of welding wire.

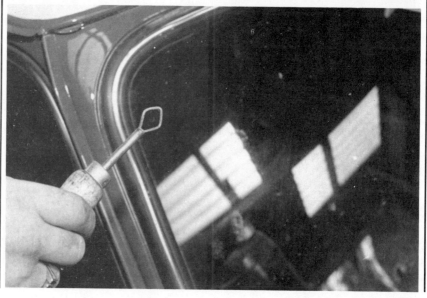

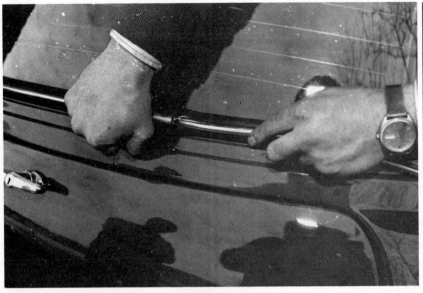

WS13. Here the tool is placed over the finisher, into the rubber and pushed (from left to right in this picture), and hey presto! the finisher is back in place.

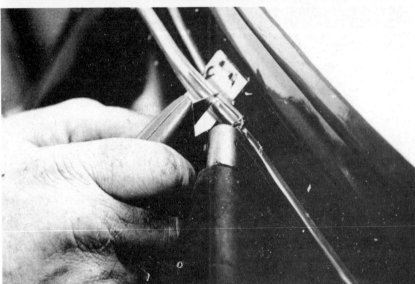

WS14. When you come to the joint, slip a piece of steel or wood under the end of the strip, leave the inserting tool dangling there and cut the finisher off to length with a sharp craft knife, the piece of steel or wood will prevent damage to anything beneath.

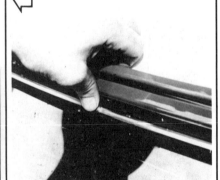

WS15. Ease the inserting tool off the strip and push the end down firmly with your thumb.

WS16. Go round the whole rubber with a screwdriver to finish off, easing out any lips of rubber that remain turned in.

71

Windscreen rail repair

The Mini owner can become aware that there is something wrong with the windscreen rail, or scuttle top panel in a number of ways. One is that the panel bubbles with rust near to where it meets the front wing (and all too often is repaired again, and again, with filler until there is nothing left to fill and all sorts of horrors are perpetrated such as stuffing newspaper into the chasm to support yet another layer of filler); or the wing is cut off to be replaced and it is discovered that there is nothing there to which to attach the top of the wing!; while an even less comfortable discovery is to find water streaming over the driver's right leg every time it rains (Sod's law in operation: you can't move your throttle leg out of the way) or over the passenger's leg, which is actually much funnier of course. The third problem arises because the metal inside the rubber windscreen seal actually rots away letting rain water flow through at will, and a similar problem can affect the rear screen.

Tool Box

Welding equipment, Eclipse (or other brand) pad saw handle, hacksaw, scriber, chisel and hammer.

Safety

Normal safety precautions when handling cut metal edges and when using welding gear should be followed. See Appendix.

WR1.   Viewed from inside the car after stripping out, this view shows how the seam that sits inside the windscreen rubber is prone to corrosion caused by trapped water.

WR2.   The solution with simple corrosion like this is to make a card template of the rusted section, cut out a piece of steel to match, use the steel as a template and cut out the rusty metal before butt-welding the new section into place.

WR3.   Where corrosion is more extensive, as it was on John Eddom's car, a repair panel can be purchased from the Mini Spares Centre to replace the whole of the area. As a non-Austin-Rover part, the fit of the panel we used was not too terrific, but it was certainly an improvement on trying to make up such a complex shape ourselves! The square shown in the picture had been cut out of the repair panel because the original panel was still sound in that area. Note that this full repair can only be carried out with the old wing cut away.

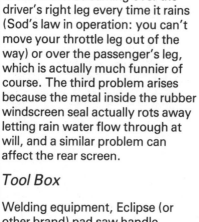

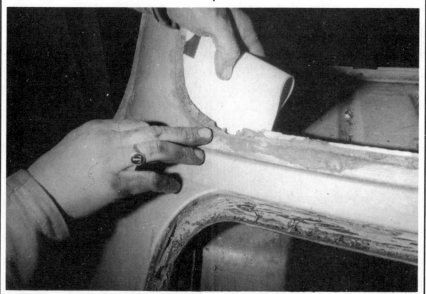

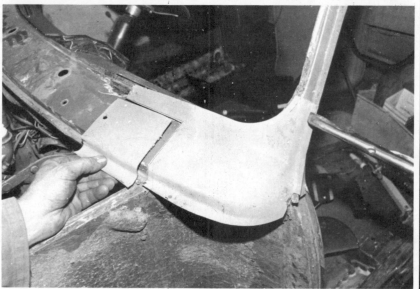

WR4.   Having offered up the panel and clamped it temporarily into place, it was scribed carefully around on the scuttle top . . .

WR5.   . . . and its height scribed onto the windscreen pillar. With a small panel of this sort and because of the necessity for it to fit the windscreen rubber accurately, there was no question of lap-welding it and then 'losing' the overlap with body solder or filler; it was going to have to be butt welded.

WR6.   It was crucial that the area was not distorted and so the old panel was cut out with a hacksaw . . .

WR7.   . . . and where the standard hacksaw would not reach, a piece of broken blade was fitted into an Eclipse padsaw handle and the cut finished off. Incidentally, there will be far less risk of breaking or buckling a flimsy hacksaw blade used in this way if the teeth cut on the upstroke rather than when pushing away from you.

WR8.   Next to the body seam, the steel is far more rigid and so it was possible to use the compressed air operated air chisel but a sharp, thin bladed bolster chisel would have done just as well.

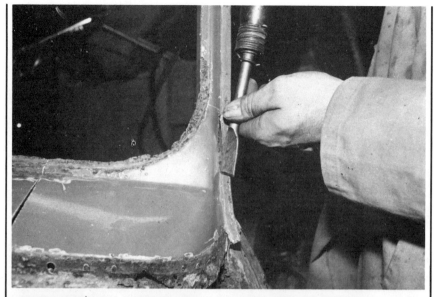

WR9.   Another cut was made along the front edge of the panel, where the front wing fits. At this stage, it wasn't certain whether the closing panel was going to be renewed as well.

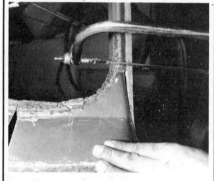

WR11.   Finally, the windscreen pillar was cut through just sufficiently to free the redundant panel . . .

WR13   . . . The top face of the closing plate was found to be on the verge of severe corrosion and, since John's car was having so much done to it, the closing panel was cut off.

WR10.   And then a third chisel cut was made to separate the inner and outer sections of the windscreen rail. Any metal left attached to the inner section can easily be ground off using a mini-grinder.

WR12.   . . . which looked like this!

WR14.   The panel was chiselled all the way round . . .

WR15. . . . leaving the spot-welded flange in place. The flange was also removed with the air chisel, but it could have been taken off by linishing the surface of the flange to find the spot welds and drilling them out. At least, that is the theoretically correct way of doing the job but hunting for spot welds in rusty metal can be impossibly difficult.

WR16. Now that there was improved access, tin snips were used to cut along the line of the repair section where it fitted the windscreen pillar, the vertical cut being made with a hacksaw as before.

WR17. This took out the existing panel a couple of centimetres past the corroded area, which is the only sure way of avoiding further corrosion.

WR18. After carefully tack welding the new panel in place with the MIG welder, ensuring that it was a perfect fit all the way around, the edges were seam welded. Butt welding thin metal is not easy and with the MIG welder it is best to weld a little, pause a little, weld a little and so on. The more advanced SIP MIG welders, those from the Ideal 150 range-on, include a pause control so that this function can be carried out automatically.

WR19. This is the scuttle top and windscreen surround of the Radford Mini Cooper. They were perfectly sound, but the closing panel beneath had rotted out and so had the flange to which the wing is connected.

WR20. The famous cardboard template method of discovering what size of repair patch to use comes into its own once again! The cardboard was drawn around to show the shape and size of repair patch required and a piece of steel was cut out to match the template.

WR21. This is a piece of foam rubber. No, it's not something left over from the carwash, it's one of the pieces that BMC stuffed into the tops and bottoms of windscreen pillars (and in one or two other places) when they built the car. Take it out, it's flammable!

WR22. One non-distorting way of cutting back to sound metal is to grind it back using the mini-grinder. Take a look at earlier pictures to see how the closing panel is removed.

WR23. As you will have seen from earlier pictures, the underside of this area can be covered in surface rust and it's not exactly easily accessible for cleaning off. The most efficient way of doing the job is to use a spot-sand blaster of the type shown here. They are not terribly expensive but they are highly efficient if a little slow especially when used with a small compressor.

WR24. The new wing joint flange was cut out and curved as accurately as possible to the correct shape.

WR25. After tack welding at regular intervals to prevent distortion, the joint was seam welded. Gas was used in preference to MIG here, partly because of the personal prejudices of the welder(!) but partly because old steel often has a trace of corrosion in it which slightly inhibits neat progress with a MIG. The author would have MIG-ed it!

WR26.   The important thing is neatness and accuracy of the work and so, even without the A-panel in place, the front wing was held in position to ensure that the fit was as good as it could be. Actually, this offering-up process was carried out a number of times during the repair process.

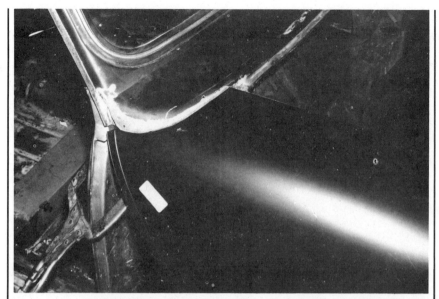

WR27.   Earlier, a closing plate had been made up by the author ready to fit. The rear flange was a bit tricky at the corner (arrowed) but steps were taken to ease its progress. The horizontal part of the panel was marked out from a card template, then the width of the flange added. Where the flange had to go round the corner, it was made half the width of the rest so that there was less metal to stretch. The two straight sides were partly folded first and then, holding the surface of the panel on the top of a square sided round dolly with the flange overhanging, the flange was beaten over. Several 'goes' at turning the flange had to be made before it would go over square because there was more metal there than required and it had to be allowed to 'spread'. If the steel becomes springy during this process, heat it to cherry red and let it cool slowly: this will restore its malleability. Don't be too proud to cut a couple of little 'vee's out; it helps considerably!

WR28.   The closing panel was deliberately made too large, so that it would fit snug against the bottom of the wing mounting flange.

WR29.   On the other side of the car, exactly the same process was followed. The closing panel was first soundly welded to the inner wing with a series of short seam welds.

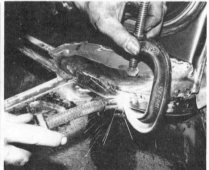

WR30.   Then the front edge was clamped up tight and tack welded.

WR31. As well as clamping, it was necessary to dress the panel up using the hammer, to make a tight fit.

WR32. Next, a continuous seam weld was made all the way along the joint and in conclusion the surplus metal and surplus weld were ground down with the mini grinder. PLEASE NOTE: It is possible to buy Austin-Rover A-panels with the closing plate attached to them. See the section on A-panel renewal for details.

Front door hinge pillar repair

With front wings and A-panels out of the way, the front face of the door pillar almost invariably displays some corrosion behind the line of the A-panel. There do not seem to be any repair panels available for this area but the corrosion is nearly always confined to a flat area of metal.

Tool Box

See 'Front Wing Renewal'.

Safety

See 'Front Wing Renewal' Safety Note and Appendix.

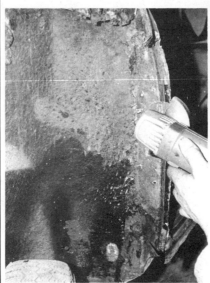

HP1. The first job is to thoroughly linish the area back to bright metal (or dull brown, as the case may be) so that the extent of the damage can clearly be seen.

HP2. Some cars have been liberally coated in underseal in this area and this is best removed by gently heating until it becomes soft, though not so that it goes up in flames, scraping away as much of the underseal as possible then wiping the residue away with a cloth dampened with paraffin or white spirit.

HP3. Here the rusty metal has been cut out and a repair patch has begun to be formed to replace it. The repair can be lap welded or butt welded, depending upon how keen you are to obtain a neat looking finish in a rather hidden area. Also bear in mind that a flush finish will make fitting the A-panel that much simpler.

A-Panel repair

There have been two types of A-panel fitted to Minis: the earlier type, whose replacement is shown here, consists of an inner and an outer panel and between them they support the weight of the door which is attached to them by its external hinges. Later Minis, all of those with concealed hinges, have a single A-panel (ie with no inner, hidden panel) whose fitting is virtually the same as that shown here. Where the rear of the A-panel fits the front of the door pillar it is wrapped around it rather like the edge of a door skin. This wrapping around generally causes the inner flange to corrode away so it is often necessary to make up and weld on a new flange after the old A-panel has been removed.

Some people try to get away with only renewing the outer A-panel on earlier Minis but since it is the inner panel that is constructed to carry most of the weight of the door, that is most certainly a false economy. The following sequence shows how to repair an early type A-panel set up, the later type being rather simpler to fit and not, of course, having any holes for the hinges. The pictures used in this sequence are a selection from those taken in connection with several rebuilds.

Tool Box

Mini-grinder with linishing disc, sharp bolster chisel and hammer, welding equipment (spot welder, if available).

Safety

Normal welding and cutting-out safety procedures should be followed. See Appendix.

AP1.   This is an early type A-panel shown after the front wing has been removed. It is not necessary to remove the front wing in order to renew the A-panels but when they are corroded, the front wings often require renewal too.

AP2.   There's nothing fancy about cutting off an old A-panel; just cut down the panel (both skins at once) near to the edge of the door pillar. Where A-panels have corroded, there is little point in groping behind them with a spanner to remove the doors. Instead, cut the hinges out of the A-panel and unbolt them when they are clear; it's so much easier!

AP3.   The inner A-panel fits against the door pillar so the next step is to remove the remains of the flange. (This is where corrosion takes place: see previous section.)

AP4.   The outer panel, where it fits around the door pillar, can be linished back ready to take the new outer panel.

AP5.   On the left in this shot is the new inner A-panel and on the right the outer panel. Actually, the right-hand panel is for a later car and is identified by its lack of hinge mounting . . .

AP7.   Here a correct outer panel is held in place while a non-Austin-Rover inner panel is offered up. This was a prime case of a non-genuine panel that didn't fit properly: its curved flange, at the bottom, was way beyond that of the outer panel: a problem that would have taken an awful lot of remedying.

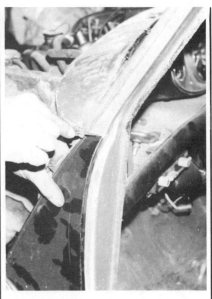

AP9.   Fitting the A-panels involves marking out the height to which the new panel reaches then cutting the old panel to suit.

AP6.   . . . and by the shape at its base, where the earlier panels are curved to match the sweep of the sill.

AP8.   Viewed from inside the wing, an Austin-Rover inner panel showing the broad flange that has to be welded to the door pillar. Note especially the closing plate already in place for fitting to the base of the windscreen rail/scuttle top. The presence of this part alone makes the 'genuine' panel worth having.

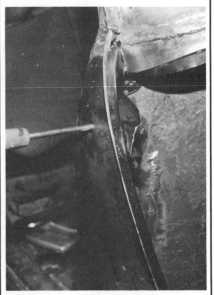

AP10.   Then the outer panel is clamped in place and the inner panel offered up, lining the hinge holes up, before clamping that panel in place, too. Note how the closing panel referred to earlier fits nicely into place.

81

AP11.   Next the door is fitted up and great care taken to align the door so that its gaps are even all the way round, and so that the body lines on the door match those on the rear panel; at the same time the A-panel must be made to fit accurately, too. It is well worth spending some time being certain that all these criteria are met before moving on.

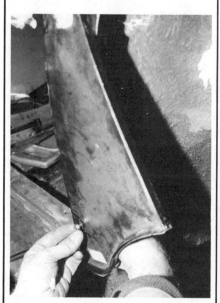

AP12.   Before taking the door off, it is a good idea to tack weld the outer panel in place at top and bottom and then bolt the inner panel to it through the hinge mounting holes to ensure perfect alignment.

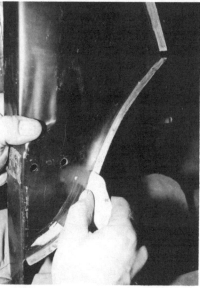

AP13.   At some stage it is well worth cleaning the paint off the parts to be welded together, using a piece of abrasive paper. This is vital if the parts are to be spot-welded, but will give greatly superior welds whatever welding method is used. If the flanges are seam welded or button welded, it will be necessary to linish them smooth with the mini-grinder.

AP14.   The inner panel only seats against the door pillar on two raised mounting points and they too should be thoroughly cleaned of paint if they are to be spot-welded.

AP15.   Anyone can 'spot' weld after a fashion even if they don't possess a spot welder provided that they possess some kind of welding gear. The method is to drill a series of holes in one of the flanges and then to feed braze or weld through each hole in turn to the panel beneath. Don't work from one end to the other, however, as distortion will creep in; instead, space the welds, moving from one area to another.

Front panel renewal & modification

This section gives guidance on how to fit a new front panel which, with the exception that it is part-bolted into place, fits in much the same way as the other front-end panels with internal mating flanges and visible seams. Also shown here, and potentially more interesting, is the method of changing the specification of a brand new, later-type front panel (which is still available) to that of an earlier type (which is not).

Tool Box

Socket set with extension, hammer and dolly, welding equipment, linisher, electric drill (spot welder if available).

Safety

The normal safety procedures for cutting and welding bodywork should be followed. See Appendix.

FP1.   Early Mini front panels were of a slightly different shape to those of later cars. At its ends, the apron at the bottom of the panel, ended in a gentle curve on early cars . . .

FP2.   . . . while on later cars, the ends were notched upwards. Number plate mounting brackets were fitted differently too, as can be seen from this picture of a modern front panel in front of an older Mini.

FP3.   Here the old front panel has been cut away, exposing the front of the subframe and the bolt that holds the front panel to the subframe, one on each side reached through the holes in the front of the apron. In this case, the seam has been cut on the wing side of the flange but of course if the wings were to be retained, the cut would be made on the front panel side and the seam dressed back.

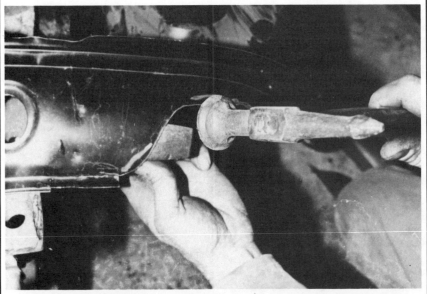

FP4. The wiggly bit of the end of the new-style apron has been carefully cut off here, and the edge is being dressed flat to get rid of its ripples.

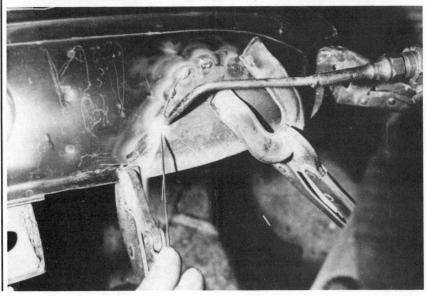

FP5.   The offcut from the new apron was placed over the end of the old panel and used as a template to be scribed around. The end of the old panel was cut out around the scribed line and let into the new panel thus giving a perfect fit but with the old-style appearance instead of the later one. The piece from the old panel was thoroughly sandblasted before fitting to remove every trace of rust.

FP6.   In between tack welds, the edges of both panels were carefully dressed flat to ensure a perfectly consistent level between the two.

FP7.   After welding, the linisher came into play and, fitted with a 36 grit disc on a rubber pad, was used to linish the weld smooth.

FP8. Adopting the same principle of fitting the correct older-style parts to the new panel, the number plate mountings were cut off the old front panel.

FP9.   After drilling out the spot welds holding the 'new' number plate mountings in place and taking them off, the 'old' mountings were sand-blasted, the paint cleaned from the panel where they were to be fitted and then they were clamped into place after ensuring that they were positioned in the right place.

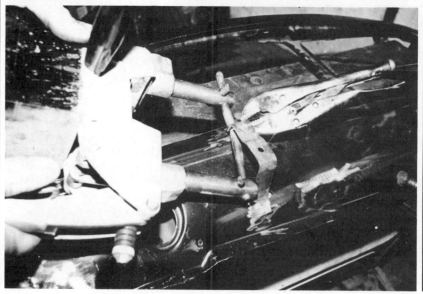

FP10.   It was then simplicity itself to spot-weld the brackets onto the new front panel. In practice, we found that there was still rust intrusion within the steel of the old brackets causing the spot welder to spark and burn the steel, so the brackets were also tack-welded using oxy-acetylene.

When fitting a new panel into place, bear in mind that the bonnet must also be fitted and be seen to fit the front panel correctly before final fixing of a new apron.

Flitch panel renewal

Flitch panels tend to corrode badly starting with the front bottom corner and also the hidden area behind the shock absorber mounting. Full flitch panels are not always available, so make sure that you know what *is* available before hacking steel away. Early and later flitch panels differ in their construction in that the earlier type right-hand panel is blank, whilst later panels have a large hole for the heater fresh air inlet.

Tool Box

Measuring tape, electric drill (for drilling out spot welds), scriber, tin snips, Waxoyl, clamps and/or self-tapping screws, welding equipment, linisher.

Safety

Follow the usual safety procedures when cutting and welding bodywork. See Appendix.

FLP1.   In this case, only a later type flitch panel was available, and even then it was not a full length panel. Here it is shown compared with the original beneath: the large number of detail differences in terms of holes, and blanks is quite apparent.

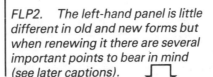

FLP2.   The left-hand panel is little different in old and new forms but when renewing it there are several important points to bear in mind (see later captions).

FLP3.   It is crucially important that the front subframe is left in place whilst any very major front-end surgery is carried out: it gives a reference for their accurate assembly. If the front of the car is structurally weak, it is possible for the subframe to move when all the bodywork has been taken off. Make certain that it hasn't done so by measuring from the subframe crossmember (arrow) to any fixed point on the bulkhead before stripping the bodywork and check it again afterwards.

FLP4.   The new right-hand flitch-panel was modified to 'old' specification by taking the bonnet stay support shown in the foreground, from the old panel to the new and by welding a section of steel into the air intake hole. Obviously, marking out and cutting out have to be carried out very accurately but it's not too difficult if the hole itself is placed over the new steel used as a template and scribed around.

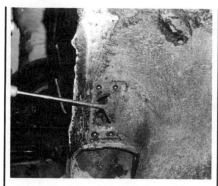

FLP5.   On both sides of the car, flitch plates corrode behind the shock absorber mounting plate. Cutting out and repair is straightforward but make a point of painting and Waxoyling this area after reassembling.

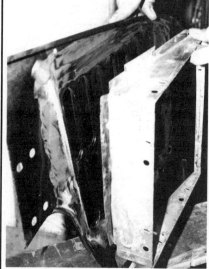

FLP6.   Flitch panels for the left-hand side with the radiator shroud attached were not available at the time we purchased ours. The shroud was taken from the old panel, sand blasted . . .

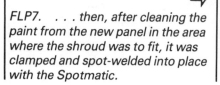

FLP7.   . . . then, after cleaning the paint from the new panel in the area where the shroud was to fit, it was clamped and spot-welded into place with the Spotmatic.

FLP8.   Obviously, it is fairly important to align the shroud accurately so make a point of taking accurate measurements from the old panel before removing it.

FLP9.   This panel is so awkward to get at when on the car that it makes sense to 'flat it' for painting at this stage whilst it is still get-at-able. NOTE that the body number, fitted across the top of the shroud-flitch panel joint has been transferred — an important point regarding originality.

FLP10.   Then, especially if the panel is not to be fitted straightaway, it makes sense to paint it with primer to prevent surface rust forming. When fitting, clamp the flitch panel into place in conjunction with the front panel and front wings to ensure that everything lines up correctly and offer up the bonnet too. There is a lot to be said for tack-welding the entire assembly together, or even holding it together with self-tapping screws and ensuring that it all fits properly before welding it all immovably into place. A Mini with a twisted grin would look pretty silly!

Door stripping, removal and refitting

Mini doors were made in two different major types, at least as far as taking them off and putting them back on again is concerned. Early doors had external hinges with two fixings in the door and two in the A-panel; while later models with concealed hinges are just as simple to remove (or difficult if the bolts have rusted).

Early models tend to suffer from worn hinge pins but it is not then necessary to replace the whole hinge; the Mini specialists can supply hinge pin repair kits to enable the owner to repair his own hinges. Later models can suffer from hinges that snap their pins and their hinge pins can also wear allowing the door to become sloppy when lifted. Concealed-type hinges are only replaceable as a complete unit.

Tool Box

Cross-head screwdriver and impact screwdriver (if available), ring and open-ended AF spanners, flat-point screwdriver, body sealer, contact adhesive.

DR1.   As shown in an earlier section, the easiest way of taking off an early-type door is by cutting the hinges out of the A-panels and then setting to work on the undoubtedly rusty retaining nuts. Not exactly recommended unless you are carrying out A-panel replacement too, of course!

DR2.   Viewed from inside the car, the hinge is held to the door by a cross-head screw at the front . . .

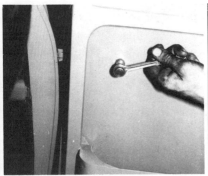

DR3.   . . . and behind the door trim by a nut and washer.

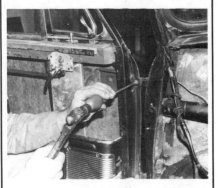

DR4.   It can sometimes be difficult to free the cross-head screw without rounding it off. If it's stiff, try tapping the head of your screwdriver with a hammer or resort to an impact screwdriver. These Radford doors were full of gadgetry and a surprisingly crude assortment of trim supports. All this extra weight was prone to taking its toll on the hinge pins which required relatively frequent renewal.

DR5.   Radford employed leather check straps, while normal early Minis used a rather hilarious piece of what looked like wire coat hanger reject. Both types must be disconnected, of course, before the door is taken off its hinges.

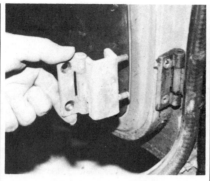

DR6. Later doors, although the same shape, have lots of differences including the fitting system shown here. (See next section for information on stripping these and the older types of door.)

DR7. This shot shows clearly how the later type of hinge fits into the scheme of things. The hinge pin arrangement is larger to take the extra weight of the later types of door.

DR8. Two cross-head screws hold each hinge into captive nuts within the door frame. These screws are likely to be very tight, so take note of the removal tips under Caption DR4.

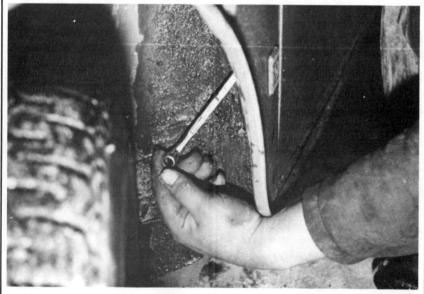

DR9. You have to grovel around under the wing again to free the nuts holding the hinge to the door pillar. If you resort to heat to free off stubborn nuts, move any trim away from the area inside the car, and have someone else keep an eye open for the start of a fire.

DR10. Again, if the whole door is being removed as opposed to one hinge being renewed, the check strap will have to be disconnected. There is absolutely no need to remove the whole thing; just take out the split pin located in the bottom of this clevis pin and tap or pull the pin upwards and out.

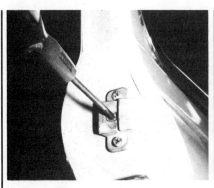

DR11. To adjust the striker plate and guide plate, simply slacken the screws holding each of them in place and slide them into the desired position. You may find, for instance, that you need to readjust the striker plate after fitting new rubber door seals. Ideally, the striker plate should be adjusted so that the rubber seal is just compressed and the door flush with the body while the guide plate will be correctly placed when the gaps around the door are consistent all the way round.

When adjusting the later type of striker plate (see figure 1), it should be placed so that as the door is closed, the striker lock passes through the door lock without fouling. It should also be possible to push the door in slightly against compression of the sealing rubber when the door is closed.

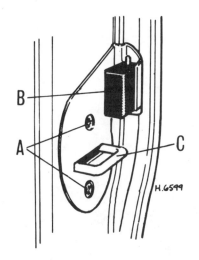

Figure 1. The front door striker plate fitted to late Saloon and Estate models (Sec 14)
A Securing screws   C Striker loop
B Over travel stop

Stripping door trim

Early type

DR12. Start by taking out the trim finishers which simply push into each end of the door pocket.

DR13. Take out the screws that hold the trim into the base of door pocket.

DR14. Take out the card trim, taking care not to rip it.

DR15. Next ease your arm behind the main door trim and push it forwards in the centre so that it bows forwards and comes clear of the door frame at one end.

DR16. Lift that end upwards and lift out the main trim board as shown.

Later type

DR17. Take out the cross-headed screws that hold the window winder knob and the door catch handle (top right). Each handle then pulls off its square shaft.

DR18. Next the door pull handle is removed by taking out the two screws which hold it in place.

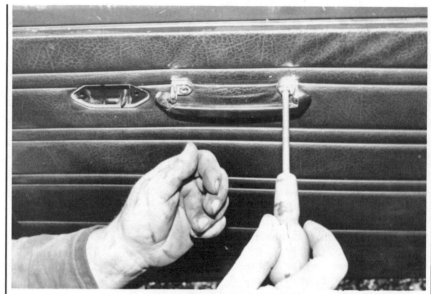

DR19. The trim board is held to the door by a ring of clips which snap into holes in the door frame. Carefully ease a screwdriver behind the trim board and snap the clips out one at a time. Avoid snatching at the clips or they may pull out of the trim board, especially if it has started to age and lose its strength.

DR20. When the two sides and bottom of the trim panel have been snapped away, the top of the panel is eased downwards out of its retaining flap at the top of the door. There should be a waterproof covering behind the trim panel and if this has to be removed, re-glue it into place before refitting the trim panel.

Stripping early doors and later Van and Pick-up doors

See figure 2.

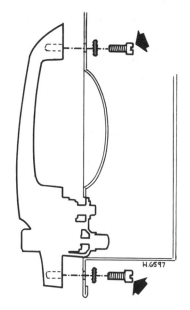

Figure 2. Exploded view of Van, Pick-up and early Saloon models' door lock and handle assembly.

1 Lock handle spindle fixings
2 Lock body retaining screws
3 Interior handle
4 Seal
5 Exterior handle

H.17011

Figure 3. Later type door handle assembly.

See figure 3. With door trim out of the way, later-type door handles are removed by unscrewing the two screws arrowed here. The screws holding the internal handle and lock in place are also clearly visible with the trim out of the way, while the latch assembly is screwed to the rear closing face of the door.

DR21. Start by taking off the screw which holds the lock handle spindle in place. (Fig 2, 1) Use a straight point screwdriver.

DR23. . . . the interior handle (Fig 2, 3) has been eased off the spindle with a screwdriver. Some are held in place with a pinch screw and this is being undone in the photograph.

DR22. The exterior handle can now be removed, but not before . . .

DR24. Keep the oddly sized, oddly threaded retaining screw and its washer safely by putting them straight back into the end of the spindle.

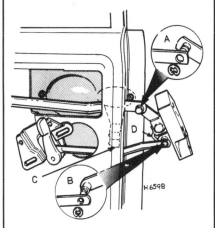

Figure 4. Front door lock removal
A Remote control handle operating rod
B Interior lock operating rod
C Exterior handle lock link
D Latch lock rod

See figure 4. Front door lock removal: note that clips at A and B have to be removed *after* all three mechanisms have been disconnected from the door. With the handle taken off, the lock barrel and push button can be dismantled as follows: 1) Prise off the retaining clip which holds the lock barrel to the handle. 2) Insert the key into the lock and use it to pull out the lock barrel. 3) Undo the screw that fixes the retaining plate to the exterior handle. 4) You can now take out the push button after lifting off the retaining plate, operating link, washer and spring.

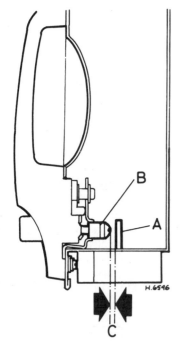

Figure 5.   Door handle push button plunger adjustment
A   Lock release   C = 0.031 to 0.062 in
      lever   (1.0 to 1.5 mm)
B   Plunger cap

Front door glass

Details of how the sliding door glass and channels fit together can best be seen under a later section headed, 'Door glass and channel refitting'.

See Figure 6. Removal of front door glass (later models with rising glass). After taking off the trim panel as described:

See figure 5. On earlier models the plunger cap (B) can be adjusted by screwing in or screwing out to give around 1mm to 1.5mm of free movement before the door lock release lever begins to move.

FDG1.   Carefully ease off the waist rail finisher strips from the top of the door edge, taking care not to damage them as they are lifted away from the clips. (Fig 6, 1 and 2). Wind the window approximately halfway down, so that the two arms of the winder mechanism are as near to being vertical as possible. Now wedge the glass in this position with a piece of wood fitted between the glass and the door frame (Fig 6, 6).

Figure 6. Removal of front door glass
Inset shows regulator arm and position of door glass ready for removal
1   Waist rail finisher   4   Window winder
      (outer)   regulator
2   Waist rail finisher   5   Regulator
      (inner)   securing screws
3   Securing clips for   6   Wedge (to hold
      finishers   glass)

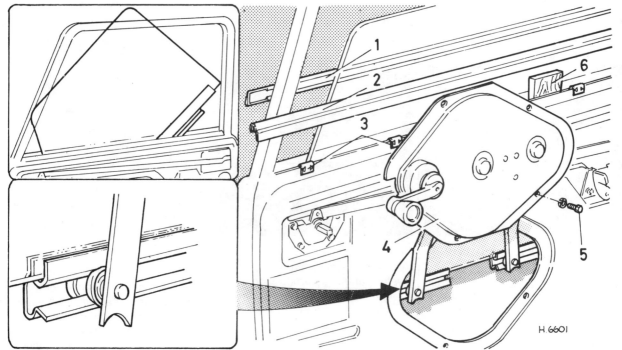

FDG2. Remove the winder mechanism securing screws (Fig 6, 5).

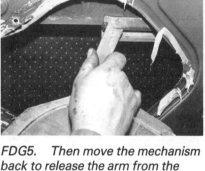

FDG5. Then move the mechanism back to release the arm from the channel and take it away.

FDG3. The regulator is sealed with Mastic and tends to stick. Ease it away with a screwdriver.

FDG6. Support the glass with one hand, remove the wedge and tilt the forward edge down into the door so that the top rear corner of the glass comes inside the window frame. (See Fig 6, top inset).

FDG4. Pull the regulator (Fig 6, 4) away from the door panel enough to move it forwards so that the rear arm comes out of the window channel.

FDG7. The glass can then be lifted out.

When refitting the window, reverse the above sequence, but pay special attention to the following:

a. Make sure that the window is properly located in the frame glazing channels before wedging it in the halfway position.

b. Check that the waist finisher strips are evenly spaced before pushing the finisher strips back on. When fitting the inner finisher, push the front end up against the glazing channel rubber seal before clipping the rest into place.

c. Apply body sealer (available from factors) to the winder mechanism before fitting it back to the door otherwise it will tend to rattle as you drive along. Make sure that the lip on the font edge of the plate is engaged inside the panel.

d. Remember to put any adhesive sealing strips you may have removed back where they came from using a good contact adhesive.

Adjusting bonnet, boot lid and Traveller rear doors

Tool Box

Two $7/16$ inch AF spanners, electric drill, (possibly tin snips, sheet steel and welding equipment).

Safety

If you intend welding near the fuel tank or battery, remove them first. Otherwise follow safety procedures outlined in the Appendix.

Bonnet adjustment

Getting a car's bonnet to align properly is one of the most important steps in making sure that the car's appearance is right. A badly aligned bonnet can make even a beautifully sound car look skewwiff! Details of how to remove and refit the bonnet are shown in the appropriate section, but it is important to note that the bonnet has an up-and-down adjustment at the rear as well as back-and-forwards.

The best way of making sure that the bonnet ends up level is to have the fixing nuts carefully tightened up so that the hinges will *just* move on their bonnet mounting brackets. Then, adjust them so that the rear of the bonnet is too high. Close the bonnet and then press down carefully on each rear bonnet corner in turn until the level is correct. Of course, if you push down too far, you will have to re-open the bonnet and start again.

There is also an adjustment on the front of both early and late-type bonnets: the striker that protrudes down from the front edge of the bonnet can be loosened by undoing the nut that holds it in place (see Figure 7), and then screwing it up or down on its own thread. Sometimes a bonnet becomes twisted, in each case a little brute force and ignorance can be useful. Open the bonnet, grasp the two front corners — and twist it back again!

Boot lid

There is really very little to go wrong with the boot lid unless the check strap breaks and causes damage to the panel, or if heavy loads have been carried with the lid down and taking the weight, in which case the lid can become twisted. The boot lid is shorter than the bonnet and it may be difficult to restore such damage in the way described for the bonnet. In that case, open the lid, put a block of wood under the top corner of the edge that is furthest in, close the lid and push hard on the edge that sticks out. You must be careful to position the wood so that no damage or denting will be caused to the bodywork it is resting on.

From figure 8 it is fairly obvious how the boot lid fits and how the simple lock arrangement and stay are removed. Boot lids are prone to rusting out and also to accident damage, and in either case it can be cheaper to fit a new one or to find a

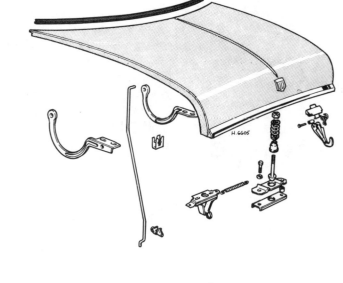

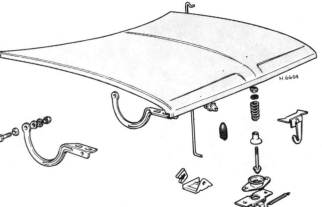

Figure 7. Bonnet hinge and lock assemblies

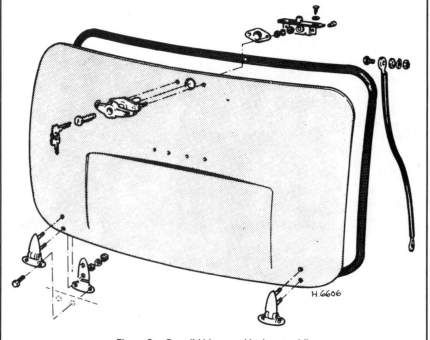

Figure 8. Boot lid hinge and lock assemblies

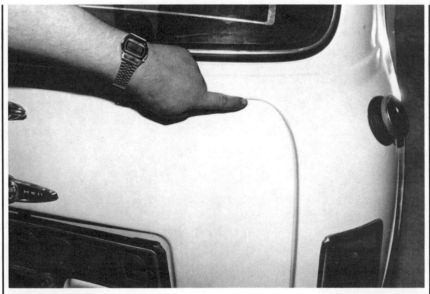

good second-hand panel from the many that languish in scrapyards than to go to the trouble of repairing it. Hinges are prone to pitting and corrosion and they can then be renewed or, unlike the chromed versions on many cars, they could even be cleaned down, filled and re-painted. There is no adjustment available on the boot lid, unless the steps shown in the following photographs are followed.

BLA1.   This car was fitted with a second-hand boot lid which turned out to be too high up in the aperture.

BLA2.   The solution was to undo the hinges, remembering to catch the nuts and washers at the back . . .

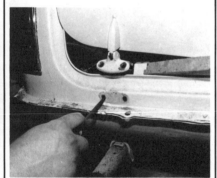

BLA3.   . . . and then file the holes downwards a little way . . .

BLA4.   . . . until the fit of the lid became acceptable, before bolting the hinges back into place.

Traveller and Van rear door adjustment

The rear doors fitted to the Mini Van, Countryman and Traveller cannot be adjusted, which makes it vitally important to correctly set up the supporting repair panels and door skins when they are being fitted. However, if you drop a 'clanger' or non-Austin-Rover parts are used and the holes don't line up correctly, or if you inherit a car or van with badly fitted rear door, here is what to do.

AB1.   The construction and fit of all the Vans and Van-derived passenger Minis, including the early estates with wooden latticework, is identical. This Clubman Estate's rear trim strips shout loudly that 'The doors don't fit!'

AB2 & AB3.   The rear pillar had been welded up (in the wrong place!) after it had rotted out at the base, so there was nothing to be done there short of major surgery which just wasn't justified on this particular Mini.
    The bottom of the left-hand pillar had also been repaired — but filler is not noted for its strength and when the door was open the pillar and side panel were flapping around like a sail in a stiff breeze.
    Before grinding out all the filler, a couple of repair sections were made up to tie the pillar to something solid — the rear door step (see previous shot) and the rear seam.

AB4.   From top and bottom gaps, it was clear that the left-hand door was properly aligned so the bottom right-hand door hinge was deemed to be the culprit. Two bolts pass right through the hinge and the door itself with a soft pad sandwiched between them.

AB5.   Both holes in the door were opened out using a larger drill bit, the actual amount being the subject of trial and error; you obviously don't want to drill out more than is absolutely necessary, so it is as well to be prepared to have several goes at it.

AB6. After the top hinge had been treated the same way (it isn't always necessary to drill out both sets of holes; it all depends where the adjustment is needed), a lever was used to push the door upwards before the hinge bolts were nipped up nice and tight.

AB7. And as a reward, the two rear doors met, once again, in perfect harmony!

Door skin renewal

Renewing a Mini door skin is a common task. This section shows how but, at the risk of sounding repetitive, do be prepared to spend just a little more on 'factory' door skins and make life easier for yourself: they're still available for the early doors with the holes for hinge mounting.

Fitting a new door skin is an ideal introduction to serious bodywork repair for the novice because, although it involves some fairly drastic cutting and some fitting, there should be no problems with achieving a good fit provided that the correct approach is

followed, while the use of a ready-made door skin means that no hand-forming needs to be carried out; all parts are ready-formed when purchased.

Tool Box

Welding or brazing equipment, linisher, industrial gloves, hammer and dolly, cross-point screwdriver, AF spanners, bolster chisel and hammer.

Safety

Linished-off door skins are around the sharpest things you can handle — take great care! Follow normal welding safety procedures — see Appendix.

DSI. Whether the door is still on the car or removed as in this case where John Eddom's Mini Cooper's door skin is being renewed, the first step, if the car is an early one, after removing the door glass (see appropriate section) is to take off the hinges.

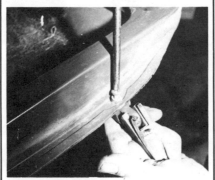

DS2. After spannering off the nut normally concealed behind the trim panel, take out the cross-head screw that passes through the door edge, using a cross-point screwdriver.

DS3. The close proximity of two dissimilar metals and the fact that the hinge acts as a moisture trap encourages corrosion behind the hinge. And you wonder why the door drops!

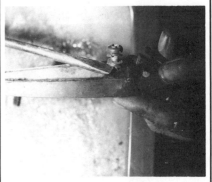

DS4. It's a good idea to put screws and nuts back onto the hinge so that they don't go missing: take extra care of the little spacer washer that sits under the screw head.

DS5. It's a little late for this here, but if you want to be sure that there is no corrosion in your door skins, the paint will have to come off. Here the bottom of the door is being linished . . .

DS6. . . . which reveals, not severe corrosion, but rust holes which are big enough to push a screwdriver into: and they can only get bigger!

DS7. Door skins are held in place by the fact that their edges are folded round the door frame like a flap on a long envelope. However, don't try unfolding it . . .

DS8. . . . the correct method is to grind right through the edge, just as you would slit the top of an envelope.

DS9. Unlike many other door skins, the Mini's folds over the top edge as well as the other three, so this must be ground off too.

DS10. Now you can see why the panel beater, Dave, is wearing thick gloves: the sliver of metal that peels away from the edge is razor sharp. It isn't normally welded down, although it may be 'caught' by weld in a couple of places: break through the weld with a sharp chisel.

DS11. If you haven't managed to cut all the way through the fold with the grinder, open up the steel fold with a thin-bladed bolster chisel. When the old skin is free, just lift it off the door frame but do watch those sharp edges!

DS12. Here's the drain tube that takes water right out of the door. If it is perished, now is the time to renew it. The water runs down through the two ends of the sliding window channel, pointed to by a screwdriver blade here. In Dave's left hand is the tube itself.

DS13. There is a tube on the other side of the door too; it passes into a metal ferrule in the door base. If you have to let in a repair to the bottom of the door, don't forget to build the ferrule in!

DS14. The tube passes through the ferrule and protrudes slightly from the bottom of the door. Make sure that it is clear and not clogged with dirt or bits of rotten window channel.

DS15. John's Mini had a little damage to the bottom of the door pocket which was beaten out from the inside and, of course, this is also the time to carry out any necessary repairs to, or trueing up of, the door frame itself.

DS16. Also take the opportunity to linish the rust from these normally concealed areas, especially the flange around which the edge of the new door skin will be folded. A coat of rust inhibitor is a good idea.

DS17. Take great care to dress the door flange nice and flat all the way along, with a dolly and lightly wielded hammer, before the new skin is fitted. Look down the length of the flange: any ripples will stand out like sore thumbs.

DS18. Place the door on a flat surface and position the new door skin on top of it.

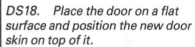

DS19. Make sure that it fits well (some parts of the fold may have to be eased back a little first), be prepared to adjust the shape of the door flange if you haven't trued it up sufficiently. Clamp the panel into place with a couple of self-grip wrenches.

DS20. Make certain that the foremost hinge holes in the early doors line up exactly with the holes in the door frame. A couple of bolts popped through and tightened down would help if getting it right looks difficult. Here, Dave is manoeuvring the door skin with a screwdriver pushed through the holes before clamping it tight.

DS21.   Next, turn the whole lot over . . .

DS23.   Start folding the flange by hammering a section of it over by just a few degrees and certainly no more than a third of the total distance it has to go.

DS25.   Adopt the same softly-softly approach with the top flange too . . .

DS22.   . . . and continue to pull the skin down to the frame using as many clamps as you may have available.

DS24.   Then go all the way along the same section again and hammer the edge over by another third, this time supporting the bottom of the door skin with a flat dolly held flat against the panel.

DS26.   . . . folding it over a step at a time.

DS27.   Here the versatility of a proper panel-beating hammer, such as that offered by Sykes-Pickavant, becomes apparent as the curved shank cross-pein is used to reach into the angled corner of the window opening. You could get over it by holding a shaped piece of wood into the corner and hammering it while someone else holds the dolly.

DS28.   Take special care with the corners, if you try to fold too much in one go in this area, there's a good chance of the flange crinkling. In fact, the reason for folding over a little at a time around the whole frame is because you can easily stretch and then ripple the steel even on the straight bits.

DS29.   Theoretically, a door skin should be sufficiently well held not to need welding or brazing but the belts-and-braces approach is a good idea (especially when you're working on your own car!) particularly since this door skin has to take much of the weight of the door.

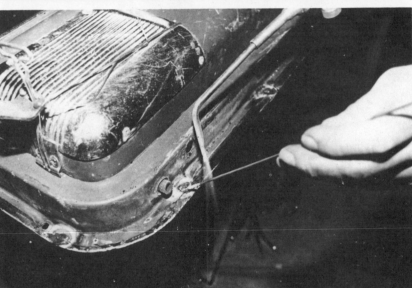

DS30.   Tack weld or braze the folded-over skin at regular intervals . . .

DS31.   . . . not forgetting the top fold which should be welded at its corners to help prevent flexing in the window frame channel. But don't apply more than a few tacks (certainly don't seam-weld) and quench each weld with a soaking wet rag. The last thing you want is heat distortion in the skin panel.

DS32. A true expert won't have made a mark on the door skin with his hammer and dolly. You probably will! Use body solder or filler, according to preference, to smooth out any such dents. Flat the door over inside and out with abrasive paper and paint it with primer. If you don't intend repainting the whole car, it makes sense to hang the door up, well away from any surface which can give off dust as air from the spray gun hits it, and paint the door before refitting which will save an awful lot of masking up.

DS33. If you do buy a non-original panel, be certain that it has all the correct holes, such as these door handle holes, ready stamped and that it is the right panel for your age of Mini (there's no difference between models).

Sill (inner & outer) repair

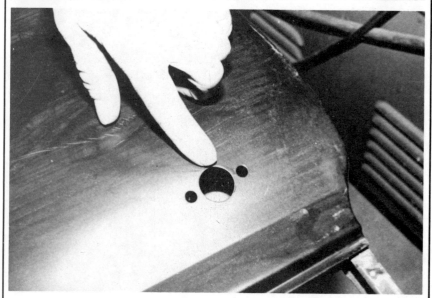

Mini sills are cheap and relatively easy to fit — which is as well in view of the fact that they are as prone to rotting out as any other car's sill sections. Their strength is vitally important in a car like the Mini with its very rigid front and rear subframes because if the sills and floor are weak with rot, there's little to stop the car's relatively heavy front end from making a dramatic entry into the passenger compartment in the event of a front-end crash.

Incidentally, a small number of the very early cars (although not the *very* first) had rigid polyurethane foam injected into their sills and front door pillars. This may have preserved some of these sills intact, which is why the comments made in BMC's 1966 *Mini Workshop Manual* are worth quoting: 'Under the application of heat — for example, in connection with body repairs involving welding — rigid foam

gives off dangerous fumes. A protective air-fed mask incorporating an efficient air filter must be worn, and work must not be carried out in a confined or inadequately ventilated space.'

This sealing was introduced at the following body numbers: Saloon (Austin) 41,416; (Morris) 31,955; Van 10,956; Traveller and Countryman 2,203. Rigid foam sealing was discontinued after car number AA257 62507 and body number L 69999, with the exception of bodies number 70601 to 70630. The numbering system is no more logical than the decision to squirt in the foam in the first place, so it is not possible to calculate how many

vehicles are affected. The advice given here is to open up the sill as shown in the following photos, scrape out every trace of the foam even to the extent of making a steel scraper to reach up inside the door pillar, carry out any welding out of doors with the car's doors open and with an assistant equipped with a fire extinguisher to keep an eye both on you and on the car. Be careful when you confront polyurethane foam; it's extremely toxic stuff when it burns! The Mini's sills consist of three parts: the inner sill, outer sill and door step (or sill top) which only rots out when general corrosion is at a fairly advanced stage.

Tool Box

Bolster chisel and hammer, welding (not brazing) equipment, angle grinder/linisher, zinc rich paint, a number of self-grip clamps (spot welder if available).

Safety

Note the safety comments where rigid foam injected sills are encountered — see text.

MS1.   With the front wing out of the way, you can see here how mud and water has found its way through the base of the corroded door pillar and into the sill itself where it can continue its dastardly work.

MS2.   The corollary of rot in this area is another hole in the front corner of the floor and it could well be that repairs will be needed here, too.

MS3.   Start cutting the old outer sill off by cutting from front to rear just beneath the seam between sill and door step.

MS4.   Then cut down the front edge of the sill to the car floor. Take a look at the new sill if you're not sure how far to cut.

MS5.   Similarly, cut the rear of the sill away, keeping inboard of the steel you want to cut out: you can always cut or grind more metal off later, when you offer the new sill up to fit it in place.

MS6. With the top and sides of the sill cut away, use foot-power to push the old sill downwards: it's easier than pushing by hand and involves far less risk of cutting yourself on the razor-sharp steel.

MS7. You may very well find that there are several layers of sill to take away. The cheap'n'nasty way of repairing a Mini sill is to slap another sill over the top of the old one without taking the latter off. This guarantees rapid corrosion of the new panel but, as some garages say, it lines more work up for them in the future!

MS8. Before replacing the sill, check that the jacking point is sound. It seems that no repair sections are available for this part, so the best approach is to make your own using a piece of square-section tubing of the appropriate size (try it on the jack to see if it fits). The jacking point is situated on an extension of the crossmember, which passes under the seats: this crossmember may also need attention. In this case, the small closing panel that shuts off the end of the crossmember had rotted out and had to be replaced with a piece of 18 gauge steel cut to size.

MS9. Inner sills often corrode, too. This one had a single, small patch of corrosion that was cut out before letting in a new piece using a lap joint.

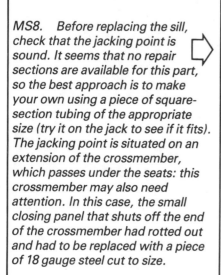

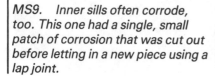

MS10. When John Eddom's car was repaired, a new inner sill was fitted using a non-original panel (an Austin-Rover part was not available) and therefore the old inner sill was cut out to suit.

MS11. As usual, there was a fit problem, although this one was by no means severe and consisted simply of a need to re-fold the flange at the point where the inner sill met the inner wing.

MS12. On the other side of the car, exactly the same problem was encountered. It was overcome by tapping the re-formed flange into place with the sill offered up. That way, it was bound to take on the shape of the inner wing. The inner wing was then tack-welded in place.

MS13. Where no provision is made for the seatbelt mounting in a repair panel, the old one must be cut out of the old panel and soundly welded into place. It's for this sort of reason that it is not a good idea to scrap the old panels until you have completely finished the job; you never know what you might need from them.

MS14. Before fitting the new outer sill, it is important to clean up the flange on the door step so that the new sill can be soundly welded to it. As always, linishing with a 36-grit disc is the most efficient way.

MS15. Also make a point of painting all enclosed surfaces before sealing them off. Even if some of the paint does burn off with the welder, most stays on.

MS16. The new sill has to be correctly positioned over the jacking point bracket. Note how the square tube has been cut off to the correct angle to match that of the sill. The sill is reinforced in this area to support the box section behind. You can weld the sill to the jacking point for extra rigidity and/or drill through the sill where it mates against the flanges on the end of the box-section and button weld it on there. ⇨

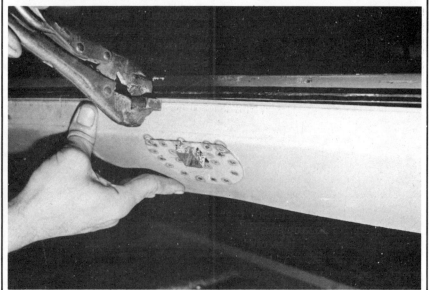

MS17. Using an array of clamps, the sill to door-step seam can now be welded. The panel beater is using a SIP Spotmatic here, but button welds (drill holes in the top panel, weld through) could equally be used. The sill ends have to be seam welded.

MS18. When using the spot-welder, it is important that the tips are kept clean, that they meet in line with one another and that the two pieces of steel are clean and have been closely clamped together.

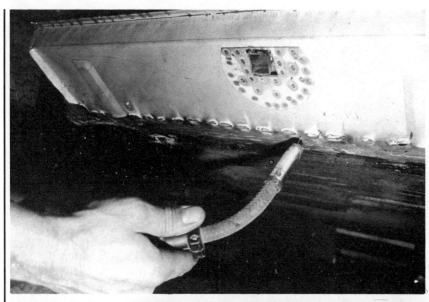

MS19. The outer sill is finally welded along its joint with the inner sill. This is why the inner sill was only tack-welded in the first place, so that it can be readjusted if necessary.

MS20. Remember that the inner sill had to be fitted up first? The outer sill was welded to it from underneath, and now you're certain that the inner sill was, after all, correctly positioned, you can go back and carry out whatever welding is necessary to finally locate it. Note here how a line of short seam welds is being used along the top of this joint.

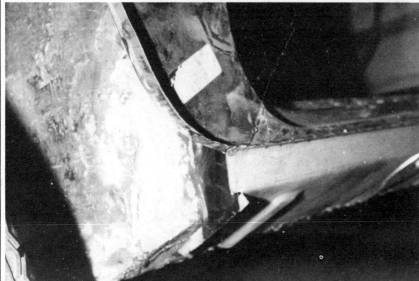

MS21. Most of the sills' problems were caused in the first place by mud and water getting into their ends, so make a point of cutting out any corroded metal from this area and replating it with new metal to close it off completely.

MS22. As a final task, go over the whole repair with a linishing disc or grinding wheel and tidy up any raised runs of weld.

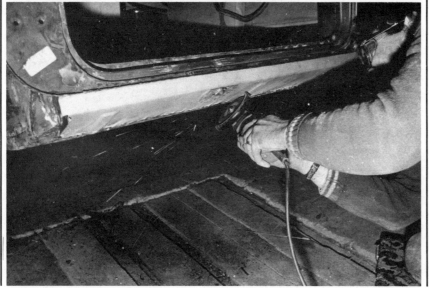

Whenever fitting new sills, especially if the 'door step' (sill top) has to be replaced, always offer up with the door in place and check very carefully for accurate fit after tack welding and before final welding into place. If the rest of the car is severely corroded, ensure also that the door aperture has not distorted before welding the sill up.

Cheap'n'cheerful inner sill repair

Sometimes, when a Mini is used as a hack vehicle with very low value, it's not worth putting in the sort of effort that a restorer would put into his or her car. If this cheap'n'cheerful philosophy were to be carried out in areas where safety hazards might result, there would be no excuse for it, but in this case the result is a car which is much stronger than before with minimal effort and outlay. Purists may not like it but purists are clearly either wealthy or live on a good bus route!

MS25.   When you have reached the root of the trouble, chop out the corroded metal with a sharp bolster chisel. This isn't considered essential by many of the shadier garages and, in the short term, it doesn't make the repair any stronger, but leaving the rust in place means that the repair will rot out again in no time at all.

MS27.   Then finish off by welding all the way round before refitting the seat and trim. Repairs like this won't win any prizes but they could get you out of trouble if your car is starting to become unsound and it isn't economically sensible to spend real money on it.

MS23.   The first step is to assess the damage. After pulling back the carpets and taking out the seats, sand through the surface of the damaged area, particularly if it has been camouflaged with filler or fibreglass. If repair patches have been fitted previously, they will have to come off so that you can really see how much will need doing.

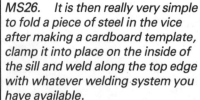

MS26.   It is then really very simple to fold a piece of steel in the vice after making a cardboard template, clamp it into place on the inside of the sill and weld along the top edge with whatever welding system you have available.

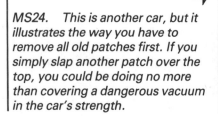

MS24.   This is another car, but it illustrates the way you have to remove all old patches first. If you simply slap another patch over the top, you could be doing no more than covering a dangerous vacuum in the car's strength.

Quarter Panel (Rear Side) Replacement (and rear oddment bin replacement)

The rear quarter panel rots out particularly badly along its base and especially adjacent to the wheel arch. Occasionally, in really severe cases, it also corrodes along the bottom of the quarter light area. This section shows how to fit a 'non-genuine' quarter panel but, for even more drastic cases of rust, there is an Austin-Rover complete body half panel available.

Tool Box

Sharp bolster chisel, drill mounted or purpose built linisher, gas or MIG welding equipment, (spot welder is useful but not essential).

Safety

Follow the usual bodywork safety procedures — see Appendix.

QP3.   As shown in the buying section, the bottom of the bin is prone to rotting out. With the quarter panel in place, its repair is a tortuous affair but access is so easy with panel out of the way that it makes sense to repair it at the slightest sign of rust. The original bin had a drain hole in the bottom that let water out of the bin all right — but into the rear footwell! You may want to carry out your own improvement here.

QP1.   Cut the old panel away just a little inboard from the seams, then grind back to where you intend fitting the new panel. In this case the panel came with the correct flanges for fitting to the Mini's vertical body flanges.

QP2.   The bin on either side of the rear seats silts up with a wide assortment of flammable materials over the years — reduce the fire risk by vacuuming it out.

QP4.   The top of the new panel can easily be spot or seam welded . . .

QP5.   . . . but if you're carrying out this bin repair with the side panel in place (which is actually more likely of course) you just have to resign yourself to having to work at an awkward angle.

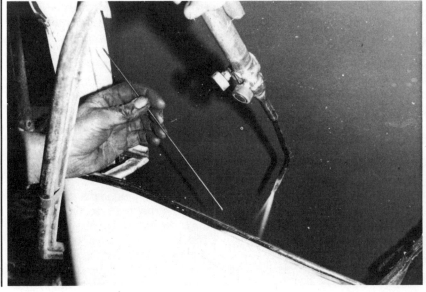

QP6. Before attempting to fit the new panel, clean all seams and joint areas with the linisher.

QP8. Make sure that the panel will line up when it is clamped into place all the way round and weld the flanges into position.

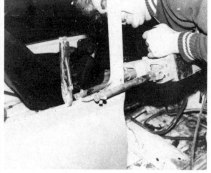

QP9. You can buy extension arms for the Spotmatic spot welder, as you can with most makes and these make it possible to reap the benefits of spot welding even though there are all sorts of obstructions in the way.

QP7. Offer up the new panel and be prepared to spend some time making all the flanges join up accurately. Most of these panels are made for Minis with wind-up windows. Their doors are square at their lower outer corners, and naturally the quarter panel is shaped to fit. Be prepared to carry out some modification here if yours is an earlier car.

QP10. You can get away with spot welding most of the way round. If you don't possess a spot welder, drill holes in the new flange, weld through the holes with your gas or MIG welder, then grind the seam flat again so that the trim strip wil clip back on.

QP11. Where the new panel fitted the front and rear pillars, the panel was held very tight to the old one where it overlapped it and then brazed rather than welded, flowing the braze into the radius of the joint. The braze was washed off with soapy water to remove any traces of flux which could cause reaction under the paint at some future date.

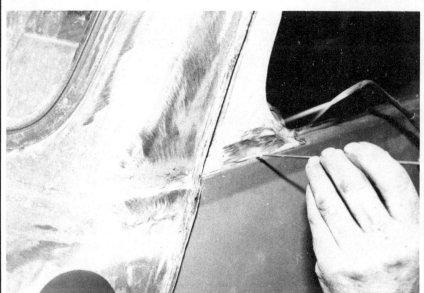

Battery box repair

Tool Box

Linisher, sharp bolster chisel, welding equipment, pop-rivets or self-tapping screws, zinc-rich paint or underseal.

Safety

Never weld in this area with the fuel tank in place and remember to take the battery right out of the boot — it gives off explosive hydrogen.

BB1.   Issigonis put the battery in the boot to help even out weight distribution, so it is said. (But where under the bonnet would you have put it?) Apart from the odd spanner falling across the terminals and causing an impromptu firework display there are no problems, that is until the battery box rots out. The battery box is doubly vulnerable to corrosion, being attacked by the presence of corrosive acid fumes and also from water that can collect in its base. If it rots, cut it out and fit one of the repair panels made by a number of manufacturers. *TAKE OUT THE FUEL TANK BEFORE WELDING IN THIS AREA.*

BB2.   The first step is to cut the old box out. It can be cut out with a chisel, or the top corner could be ground away as when a doorskin is removed, or the flange could be paint-stripped and the spotwelds found and drilled out — the choice is yours!

BB3.   This battery box was chiselled out, so the next step was to grind the old flange away.

BB4.   The new box was dropped into place, but it was found that the flange didn't sit down properly in one corner. A saw cut was made with the box in situ, as shown, down to the level of the boot floor.

BB5.   Then the flange was tapped down to the level of the boot floor as far along each side as necessary. Incidentally, try to choose one of the zinc coated battery boxes, such as the one we used here on John Eddom's car: they last longer.

BB6.   With the flange nicely fitting the contour of the floor, a series of 0.125 inch (1/8 in.) holes were drilled all the way round . . .

BB7.   . . . and the box flange was pop-rivetted down. If this had been a cut-price repair, that might have been enough, especially since you would then not have to take the fuel tank out — and the battery box is scarcely a structural member.

BB8.   We chose to use the SIP MIG to run a series of short seam welds all the way around which, incidentally, is another good reason for having thoroughly cleaned up the metal around where the old flange was situated.

BB9.   To neaten-up appearances, the welds were ground down . . .

Safety

Beware of welding in this area with the fuel tank or battery (which gives off explosive hydrogen) in place. Follow safety notes given in appendix.

BB10.   . . . and the joint sealed off all the way around. Leaving no more risk of dropping the battery in the road behind you . . .

Boot hinge panel repair

Again, a non-Austin-Rover part was used here, because none was available. However, it's a straightforward part and fitting is pretty simple, too. **REMEMBER TO REMOVE THE FUEL TANK BEFORE CARRYING OUT ANY WELDING IN THIS AREA!**

Tool Box

AF spanners; hacksaw; scriber; angle grinder.

BH1.   A rusty boot lid hinge panel starts to show the worst signs of corrosion at the rear body seam to which it is joined. The rot then spreads upwards and into the panel itself and could lead to a flapping boot lid. To get at it, the rear bumper, which bolts through the rear seam, has to be removed.

BH2.   Take off the boot lid and the hinges, place the new panel over the old and mark off the point where the old piece has to be cut away. If it helps, you can bolt the hinges through both panels at once to ensure accurate alignment.

BH3.   Next, cut away the old panel, using a hacksaw to make the vertical cuts while the seam top, which will probably be flaking off, is probably best dressed back with the mini-grinder.

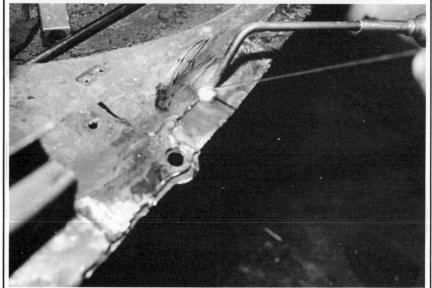

BH4.   It's like opening a sandwich! There are three layers at the seam — the boot hinge panel, the boot floor and the rear apron — and here the outer edge of the boot floor — the jam in the sandwich — is being plated to renew the rotten metal that has been cut out of it.

BH5.   The new panel can now be tack welded or brazed into place. Actually, tack brazing is useful because it allows you to make adjustments later by softening the braze with the welding torch allowing you to move the panel a bit. Save final welding into place until the boot lid has been offered up and gaps checked, bearing in mind that there is virtually no adjustment available from this type of hinge.

Front subframe removal

As you may have noted from earlier comments, it is a good idea to leave both subframes in place while major body surgery takes place, and this applies particularly to the front subframe which forms a reference point for the structure and shape of the front-end bodywork.

If the subframe is being detached with the engine still in place, outline details are given in the following section on what must be removed, but for more detailed information turn to the section on engine removal. If the Mini is fitted with Hydrolastic suspension (it is quickly identified by the presence of a rear spring in the rear wheel arch) the system will have to be drained first and since the hydrolastic fluid is held under high pressure and letting off the pressure at home can be exceedingly dangerous, it will have to be done at the local Austin-Rover agent. (You *can* drive the car home afterwards − but travel slowly and take some extra padding with you!)

Tool Box

High axle stands or trestles, full set of spanners, screwdrivers and other mechanic's hand tools.

Safety

Chief danger comes from working under a car held up high. Make certain it is stable, especially when putting a lot of effort into wrenching bolts undone. Equally, be careful when lowering subframes. Get help − they can be surprisingly heavy. Don't ever attempt to de-pressurise Hydrolastic suspension yourself without the correct equipment. Your local dealer will do it for a very modest charge.

FS1.   This front subframe (which came out of the Practical Classics magazine's Mini) is being checked for evidence of denting or distortion by Terry Bramall. Situated right behind the front panels, it's an early casualty in a front-end smash, so check it carefully for kinks with a straight edge and dimensionally after making reference to Figure 8. The front subframe can be removed with the engine in place or the engine can be taken out separately. If the engine is removed by itself, it must come out upwards through the engine-bay − see section on engine removal − but if both engine and subframe are to come out together, there are again two options . . .

FS2.   . . . the car can be raised up high on trestles and the engine/subframe assembly lowered down using a block and tackle (the buckets in this shot are simply to stop the chains damaging the car's bodywork) or, after everything is dismantled, the engine/subframe can be left on the ground and the front bodywork lifted off, either using a block and tackle, carefully placed so as not to damage or distort the body, or four strong people can lift the front of the car and 'wheelbarrow' it away backwards.

FS3.   As well as the list of engine-linked disconnections that have to be made (see the end of this section for a résumé), other components such as the shock absorbers, shown here, have to be disconnected. The track rod ends must be undone, too (see 'Front suspension rebuild' section for further details).

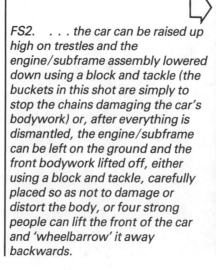

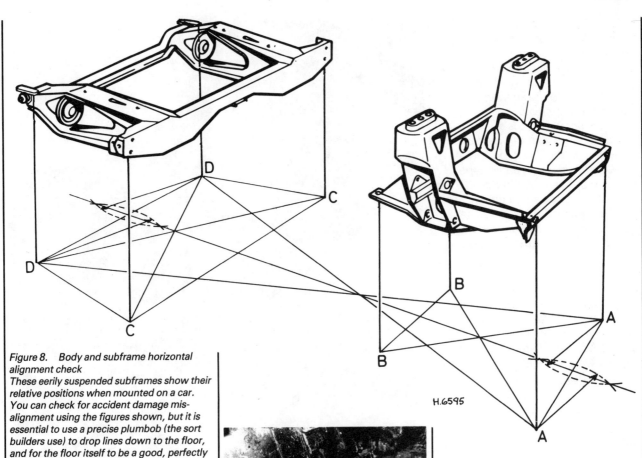

Figure 8. Body and subframe horizontal alignment check

These eerily suspended subframes show their relative positions when mounted on a car. You can check for accident damage misalignment using the figures shown, but it is essential to use a precise plumbob (the sort builders use) to drop lines down to the floor, and for the floor itself to be a good, perfectly level and smooth surface.

AA Width between centres of the front subframe mounting bolts — 26.0 in (660.4 mm)

BB Width between centres of the front subframe rear mounting bolts — 16.25 in (412.75 mm)

CC Width between centres of the rear subframe front mounting block lower bolts — 50.5 in 1282.7 mm)

DD Width between centres of the rear subframe rear mounting block bolts — 38.5 in (977.9 mm)

H.6595

FS5. The rearmost subframe mounting bolts are found at the front of the floor in each footwell, two bolts on each side.

FS4. The hydraulic brake line must be undone where it connects from the body to this subframe-mounted footbrake light switch unit (some Minis have a mechanically activated switch) and the relevant wiring must be disconnected by pulling of the spade terminals. The clutch slave cylinder should be taken off the engine assembly and left otherwise intact.

FS6.   The front of the subframe bolts to the front panel, right behind each bumper over-rider. This shot shows the position of the mounting bracket viewed from inside the engine bay with the subframe having been removed.

Also shown here is a modification to a later-type front apron panel (the only type now available) to allow an earlier type of front subframe to be fitted to it. This adaption can be carried out on a trial and error one-off basis or you can use a purpose made adaptor now manufactured by Austin-Rover.

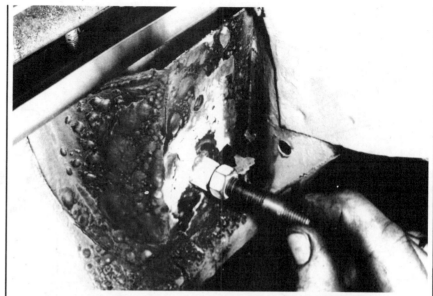

FS7.   Next the main mounting points at the top of the subframe towers are tackled. Earlier subframes are held in place by a pair of long bolts and here the ears of the tab-washers holding the bolts in place are being knocked back.

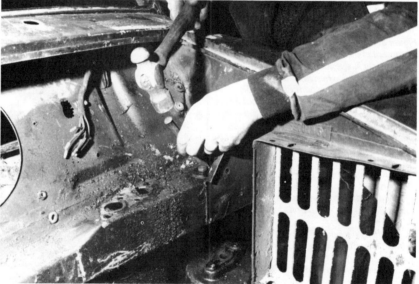

FS8.   Then, **with the subframe supported securely from beneath on both sides,** the bolts are undone with a socket and extension . . .

FS9.   . . . and the bolts and plate lifted out, after which the subframe (here less engine), can be lowered to the floor. It may be helpful to leave the wheels on in order to steady the subframe but, of course, they are not connected to the steering and so will turn with minds of their own, making it difficult to wheel around a subframe/engine unit!

N.B. Some early cars' subframe towers are connected by studs and nuts, rather than bolts, while all of the later cars have a large hexagon-head plug in place of the two bolts or nuts, and this must of course be removed instead of the sequence shown from FS7 to FS9.

Subframe removal with engine – résumé

First of all, make all of the disconnections necessary for normal engine (alone) removal – refer to the detailed account in the section 'Engine removal'. Also remove the complete exhaust system from the car.

1). Disconnect the gearlever or gear linkage.

2). Disconnect the knurled nut which holds the speedo cable to the left-hand side of the gearbox and take it out. This is frequently difficult to turn by hand so be prepared to use a pair of pliers or a self-grip wrench (but don't set the wrench in the auto-grip position, use it as if it were a pair of pliers, or the nut will be squashed.)

3). Take off the cap from the brake fluid reservoir, put a piece of polythene over the filler and screw the cap back on. This cuts down fluid loss when the hydraulics are disconnected.

4). *Single line braking system.* Remove the hydraulic pipe to the front wheels at the three-way connector on the bulkhead. *Dual-line system.* Undo and remove the hydraulic pipes to the front wheels at the pressure reducing valve or at the pressure differential warning actuator (according to model), which act as four-way connectors and can be found at the junction of the hydraulic pipes. Both are situated on the bulkhead.

5). Slacken the clip and pull off the brake servo pipe (if fitted) at the inlet manifold. NB. It is not necessary to remove the brake servo, as it would be if the engine was being lifted out of the car.

6). Disconnect the track rod ends from the steering arms.

7). *Hydrolastic suspension models only.* After having the system de-pressurised by a main agent, as described, undo and remove the displacer unit hoses at the transfer pipe unions.

8). Disconnect the subframe as shown in the photo-sequence.

9). Make a final check that all pipes and cables have been disconnected.

10). Lower the subframe and engine, or raise the body as described previously, making regular checks that everything really has been disconnected. There is, of course, no need to disconnect the driveshafts as though the engine was going to be removed without the subframe.

FS10.   With the front subframe off the car, it can be painted and rustproofed (although it's not particularly prone to rusting). Also the suspension can be worked on with great ease. All of these are useful plus points if a full scale restoration is being carried out. But don't forget to carry out the complete front end body rebuild before dropping the subframe away.

Rear subframe renewal

In the early days, Mini owners were resigned to renewing their car's rear subframes almost as frequently as they changed its tyres: a three-year lifespan was by no means unheard of. As the model's life has continued, the subframe has actually been made longer-lived (who says that things don't last as long as they used to?) but renewal

of a rear subframe is still something that needs to be carried out, especially when older cars are being restored. This section shows how to drop a subframe from the car but for information on stripping the subframe, see the sections dealing with rear suspension and rear brakes.

RS1.   In theory, removal of a rear subframe is really quite simple, but the problem is that by the time the subframe has rotted enough to require renewal, the fixing bolts are likely to be heavily corroded as well – and they're real piggies to get out once they are in that state!

RS2.   First step is to raise the whole of the rear end of the car, van or whatever (all Minis are pretty well the same in this area) and hold it there with a couple of axle stands and a length of timber situated just forwards of the rear subframe, reaching across the car.

RS3. Disconnect the hydraulic brake line from the brake compensator, (it stops the rear brakes locking up) and wrap the brake pipe union in masking tape to prevent it becoming damaged or the contents of the pipe becoming contaminated. Block the hole in the compensator too: an old bleed nipple is ideal.

Then take off the handbrake cable/s from the rear of the handbrake lever assembly (Figure 9 & 10). Also remove the access plate from the floor, and pull the cable through to beneath the car. Note that earlier models utilised twin cables which are removed by unscrewing both nuts at the ends of the cable adjusters.

Next, drain the petrol tank by removing the pipe that leads to the subframe-mounted S.U. electric fuel pump (where fitted) and remove the fuel pump itself or at least the pipework and wiring. Turn to 'Fuel tank removal' for information on removing the tank. Unfortunately, although it is possible to get away with pulling the tank to one side after disconnecting the mounting strap (so that you can get your left hand down the side of the tank when undoing the shock absorber mounting: (see next picture) the tank must come out if any of the subframe mounting bolts have seized and need the application of heat to free them. If the car is hydrolastic the system will have to have been depressurised by a main agent and the pipework subsequently disconnected.

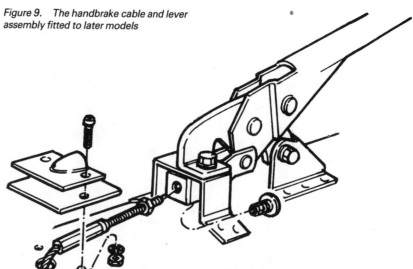

Figure 9. The handbrake cable and lever assembly fitted to later models

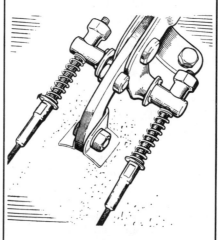

Figure 10. The handbrake cables and lever assembly fitted to early models

RS4. Both shockers must be disconnected from their mountings at the rear inner wings. The mounting nuts and washers should each sit beneath a black rubber cap. Don't be tempted to try to remove the bottom shocker mounting because although the nut can be removed, the shocker cannot.

RS5. Now support the subframe from beneath with a trolley jack and a stout piece of wood bridging the subframe. Undo the four bolts (two each side) found inside the boot on the floor. These bolts don't usually give problems; . . .

RS6. . . . these do! If you think ahead sufficiently, you can soak all the bolts found beneath the car with several doses of releasing fluid a couple of days before attempting the job.

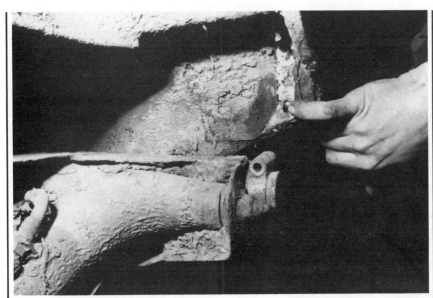

RS7.   Other 'solutions' entail cutting the heads off the fixing bolts (which is actually rather difficult without oxy-acetylene or a sharp chisel and a good arm – and a good aim!) Then, after the subframe is out, it's easier to get heat to where it counts when you come to remove the studs, as opposed to dissipating it in the subframe itself, and it also helps to get releasing fluid right in there. If the bolt still won't come out using a self-grip or stillson wrench, you may have to saw it off then drill out the bolt carefully aiming for the centre and retap the hole if necessary.

RS8.   The rear mountings are similar but the bolts go 'uphill'.

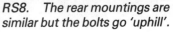

RS9.   The subframe can now be lowered to the ground but if the wheels are left on it makes the subframe easier to wheel away. The front mountings (A), rear mountings (B) and centre mountings reached through the boot floor (C) are shown arrowed.

RS10.   If the subframe is being renewed because it is rotten then no problem, except that the new one should be given extra coats of paint such as Hammerite or several coats of a rust proofer such as Waxoyl. However, if the subframe is taken out for any other reason, check it thoroughly for soundness, the crunch area being the vertical webs: If they are corroded the subframe must be renewed.

RS11.   When remounting the subframe, it makes sense to use either bright zinc plated or even the expensive stainless steel bolts (available through specialist suppliers who advertise in the motoring magazines on classic cars) to avoid the risk of any future problems with corroded mounting bolts.

RS12.   The section on rear suspension shows how to strip the suspension from the subframe but with a severely rusted subframe, the bolts holding some of the components can also rust solid like the example shown here.

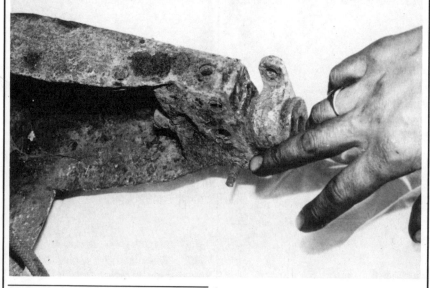

RSR1.   This is the subframe repair panel, ready made by a number of non-Austin-Rover Unipart firms. It's not a particularly fancy piece of work but it's very cheap and saves a lot of cutting out to shape and allows for various fittings on the base of the subframe.

Rear subframe temporary repair

Rear subframes most commonly rot out along their bases, and while it is certainly best to renew the whole subframe it is not always financially viable. This section shows how to carry out a simple temporary repair but it must be emphasised that if the subframe webs − the vertical bits above the flat, bottom section − have rotted out, the subframe has gone past the repair stage and, if you're particularly stretched for cash, a good second-hand subframe from the scrapyard would be the best proposition.

Tool Box

Linisher or angle grinder; several pairs of grips; drill; MIG, gas or possibly arc welder; basic tools for fuel pump and tank removal; axle stands or ramps.

Safety

DON'T work under the car without having it securely raised off the ground and front wheels chocked. Don't weld in the vicinity of the fuel tank − remove it first.

RSR2.   It is not wise to attempt to cut any metal away − even steel with some corrosion retains a bit of its strength − but it will be necessary to abrade the edges back to bright metal for welding purposes and it's sensible to take out some of the rot too.

RSR3. When a subframe-mounted fuel pump is fitted, disconnect the pipework and drain the fuel from the tank. Remove the tank for safety's sake, and unbolt the pump from the subframe.

RSR4. Over on the other side of the car, the repair patch is clamped up tight all the way along . . .

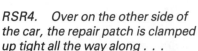

RSR5. . . . while this one has already been welded on with a series of MIG-'spot' welds using the SIP MIG with 'spot' nozzle attached. A series of holes were first drilled in the new panel where the welds were to go. It would be equally possible, though not as quick, to gas seam weld all the way down the edges or even to arc weld (unless the patch proved to be too thin).

RSR6. You are dead lucky if the pre-drilled holes line up with the pump mounting, and it may well be necessary to drill them out before bolting the pump back into place.

Rear apron renewal

Tool Box

Sharp bolster chisel, linisher, welding equipment, spanners for removing bumper — and plenty of releasing fluid!

Safety

Follow the normal bodywork safety procedures. See Appendix.

RA1. The rear apron fits against the flange which the bumper uses as a mounting, and on the closing plates at its two ends. Here the old apron has been cut from the flange with an air chisel but of course, an ordinary bolster chisel and hammer would do just as well.

RA2. After cutting away the apron flange, the flange which is left can be dressed to provide a good clean surface to which to attach the new apron. Use a linisher or grinding disc.

RA3. Sometimes the end closing plates have corroded away and need to be cut off and renewed. Use the old plate as a template for the new. This is from a MK I car.

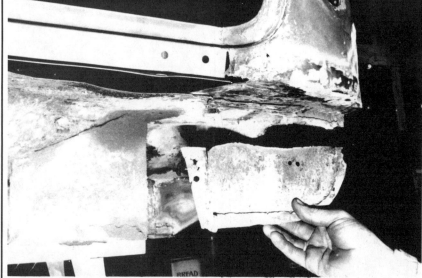

RA4. This closing plate is on a MK II Mini and its flange is being ground back to bright metal where the new apron flange will be fitted.

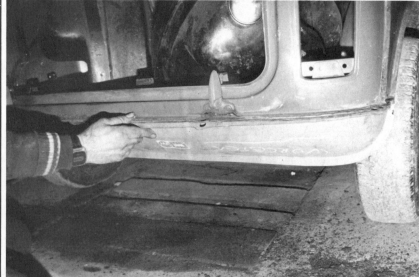

RA5. The new apron is being offered up here — make certain that the ends are pushed, pulled and tapped into a position giving a good fit, especially in the corners where they meet the car's rear panel and the closing plate.

RA6. Here the new panel is being spot-welded into place but it could just as easily be attached by MIG or gas welding, either MIG 'spot' welding through the seam as shown in other sections, or by running a series of stitch welds along all the edges.

If you're gas welding it would be prudent to remove the fuel tank first.

Door sliding glass channels renewal

Older Minis, Vans and Pick-ups with sliding window glasses suffer, in time, from a general deterioration of the sliding channels and after a time even fungus growth can set in. If you don't fancy window boxes on your Mini, here's how to go about slipping in some new sliding channels.

Tool Box

Cross-point and impact screwdriver, electric drill, new self-tapping c/s screws, sealing Mastic, scissors.

SG3. Put the bottom channel temporarily into place (see SG5) and cut off the frame channel so that it just meets the top of the horizontal channel.

SG4. The frame channel can now be finally pushed into place.

➡

SG1. This is a typical example of grot in the bottom window channels. Remove the window by taking off the window catches after undoing the screws that hold them in place. Then push both glass panels back, undoing the screw that goes downwards through the channel; push the glass panels forwards and take out the rear screw (arrowed). These screws are certain to be rusted in, so use plenty of releasing fluid and an impact screwdriver, or use brute force and ignorance and get some controlled heat onto the screws later. Now glass and channel slip out together from the bottom. The outer trim strip comes away along with the bottom channel.

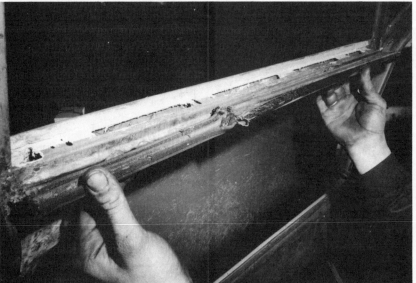

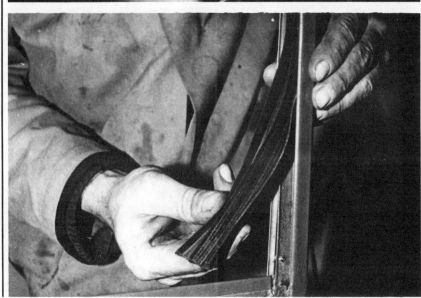

SG2. New channel for the door frame has to be fed in all the way around the frame, easing it in with a screwdriver if necessary.

SG5. The bottom channel could well still be too long, so fit one end snugly into place, mark the other, cut it off with a hacksaw and check it again for fit.

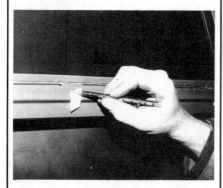

SG6. The channel is screwed onto the 'bridges' across the top of the door frame. Holes will need to be drilled in the new channel when it has been fitted but by then, of course, you won't be able to see where the bridges are! Mark their positions with a piece of masking tape with a pencil line drawn on to correspond roughly with the centre of the 'bridge'.

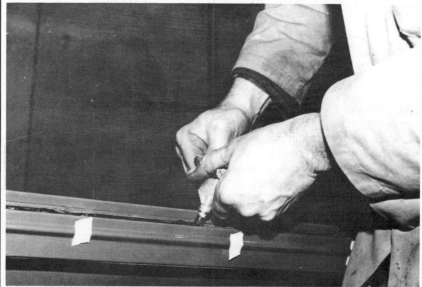

SG7. Now for one of the most vital stages! Use proper Mastic for this job and apply it generously because you are ensuring that no water can get down underneath the channel and into the door, other than through the proper drain outlets. First, run a line of Mastic along the inner edge of the door . . .

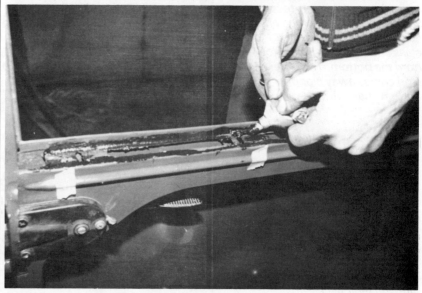

SG8. . . . followed by another along the outer edge, and more across the bridging pieces. Don't seal off the drain channels at each end and do check that both drain tubes are still open: see 'Door skin renewal' for further details.

SG9.   Just to be really thorough, run another line of Mastic along the inside of the finisher strip that fits along the inside of the window channel.

SG11.   Then, transfer your attention to the front of the channel and ease that into place . . .

SG12.   . . . followed by the rear of the channel. Of course, an extra pair of hands can be more than useful here!

SG10.   Now position both glass panels, the front one in the outer channel, in the middle of the channel and lift the whole lot, pushing both glass panels into their respective door frame channel slots as you go.

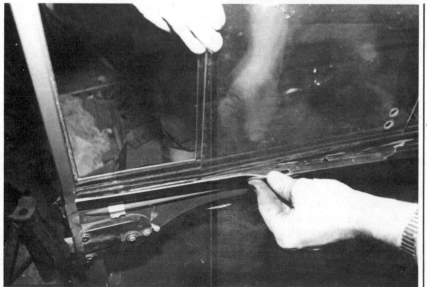

SG13.   Now the finisher strips can go back on, to hold the whole lot in place. Push it right under the channel as far as it will go. You may, in fact, wish to hold the finisher strip under the bottom channel all along, right from instruction SG10 onwards, it just depends how many pairs of hands you have available!

SG14.   Now you can see the relevance of the strips of masking tape, even though they won't all be used because the glass will be in the way. Use the correct tapping size of drill for whatever self-tapping screws you intend to use (they must have countersunk heads), keeping the drill as upright as possible within the restrictions of the window frame . . .

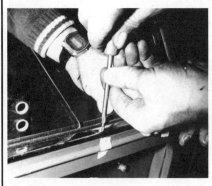

SG15.   . . . and screw the channel down to the door casing.

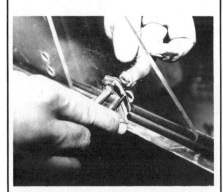

SG16.   Lastly, the catches that were taken off to allow full sliding of both windows, can be put back on, but don't forget to include the rubber sealing gaskets.

'Woodie' Traveller woodwork renewal and Estate side window removal and refitting.

The following instructions are a guide to removing and refitting whole sections (ie: complete side) which is the way in which the woodwork was originally fitted. No new woodwork is available from Austin-Rover but the Mini Spares Centre in London can offer woodwork for these cars in the original ash. This is likely to require some fitting and shaping and for that reason it would be wise to carry out repairs just to one side of the vehicle at a time, especially if the wood is disintegrating, to provide a frame — so to speak — of reference. If you are lucky enough to find good second-hand woodwork, fitting will be similar to that detailed here.

You can tell when ash has gone rotten by pressing it with something hard such as the handle of a screwdriver. If it is soft, the wood has rotted and should be renewed but if it remains firm, it is possible to get rid of any black staining or any other discoloration with 'Colorbac' wood colour restorer made by Sterling Roncraft or a similar proprietary product as obtainable from DIY stores and also from chandlers shops which can be found in any waterside resort, marina or other boating centre. From the same source can be found yacht varnish, which is vastly preferable to 'outdoor' polyurethane varnish, which does not adhere at all well to ash. When sanding ash, use an orbital sander (**never** a disc sander — it scores the wood) and never hand-sand across the grain of wood because, once again, the marks will be very difficult to eradicate. Paint, or preferably soak the wood in a colourless preservative and varnish very thoroughly when dry.

Before removing woodwork side sections, the sliding windows will have to be removed from that side.

Tool Box

AF spanners; both types of screwdriver; sealing Mastic; high quality exterior grade wood glue such as 'Cascamite'; possibly a set of woodworking tools; possibly paint/varnish stripper, paint brush, scraper; various grades of sandpaper; new fixing bolts; yacht varnish.

Estate sliding window removal and refitting.

1.   Take out the screws and remove the trim panels from above the sliding windows.
2.   Locate and remove the self-tapping screws holding both sliding channels to the body.
3.   Have an assistant push the tops of the glasses inwards from outside the vehicle while you support the bottoms of the glass panels. Remove the glass panels (complete with top channels) from the bottom channels.
4.   Refitting is a reversal of this procedure but be sure to seal the top channel with fresh Mastic, removing all the old hardened Mastic where necessary.

Side wooden frame removal and refitting.

With the glass removed, the complete side assembly can be taken off.

1.   Remove the interior trim liners from the body side and from the rear door pillar.
2.   On early cars, with the internal fuel tank, the tank must be removed before removing the left-hand frame assembly. (See relevant section.)
3.   Remove the rear door complete with hinges by taking off the hinges from the door pillar.

4. Disconnect the battery and remove the rear lamp assembly.

5. There are two wooden inserts: one against the front door pillar; the other between the cant rail and roof panel. Mark their positions, so that they can be refitted precisely, and then take them out.

6. Remove the nuts and plain washers from the studs which hold the frame in place, protruding through the side panel adjacent to the wheel arch. Access to two of the studs is within the spare wheel compartment.

7. Carefully ease the wood frame from the body, taking special care when easing it away from the rear bumper.

8. Refitting is the reverse of the removal procedure, but take note of the comments at the start of this section. Clean all the old sealing compound from the body panels and the woodwork and reseal with generous amounts of sealing compound. Any excess which squeezes out of the joint can be wiped away with stiff card and then with a paraffin soaked rag. Use new screws and insert them all before tightening any of them.

Rear door wooden frame

1. It is best to remove the rear door and take off the door lock assembly.

2. Take out the two screws from the middle of the inner door panel, taking care not to lose the two distance pieces.

3. Remove the door sealing rubber.

4. Unscrew all the self-tapping screws from the edge of the door and carefully ease the wooden frame from the door.

5. Refit exactly as described for the main side panel, remembering to locate all the screws before tightening any of them.

Roof rail repairs and scrapyard body parts in general

Whether you regard scrapyards as charnel houses to be avoided at all costs or transplant centres depends largely on how 'proud' you are of using someone else's left-overs, but it can also depend on how imaginative you are! Actually, in a world where resources cannot possibly last forever, there is something eminently sensible and wise about re-using durable car components, especially when you cannot purchase through normal channels some of the parts that the 'yard can offer.

Of course it would be stupid to spend hours cutting off a welded-on front wing when you can buy a new one for so little, especially when the second-hand one is likely to have a much shorter life. However, doors, screen glass, boot lids, bonnets, badges and trim, as well as much more, can be found at prices which are a small fraction of what you would have to pay new, even if the parts were available.

Of course, scrapyards do contain some dross (but then, so do some of the repair panel manufacturers' catalogues!) but it's up to you to separate parts that are worth having from those that are only fit for re-smelting.

Tool Box

Monodex cutter, hand drill, hacksaw, bolster chisel and hammer, range of spanners, screwdrivers and impact screwdriver.

Safety

Resist the temptation to 'rob' parts from cars that are stacked several high – deaths have been caused when piles of cars have toppled. Remember that fuel tanks are usually still in place. Scrapyards are usually littered with jagged metal and glass: it's part of the fun, but take care!

RR1.   This nest of Minis among and on top of a number of other cars was found at the author's local scrapyard, Stourport Car Spares. It is typical of the way in which many yards are 'organised' but it provides the enthusiast with more hope of finding the obscure bits and pieces he wants than the sort of dismantlers where all you see is a shop counter where you are brought whatever part you ask for, the cars having already been stripped out and the shells disposed of. Although you have to take the parts off yourself when buying this way, you do get a much better choice and can pick the best in the yard rather than having to rely on what you are brought.

RR2. The part needed here was the pillar top and the rail that runs beneath the roof drip strip. A good one was discovered on a Traveller body which, although slightly different around the rear top corner of the door, was adaptable for the job in hand.

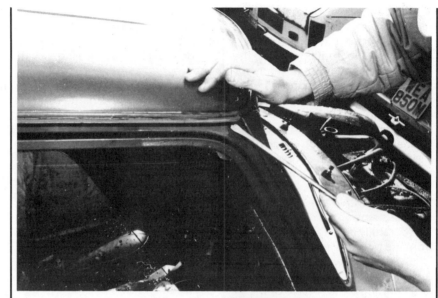

RR3. Obviously power tools are not much use in a scrapyard so you have to be prepared to do things the hard way. First, I drilled a hole in the roof.

RR5. Then a hacksaw was used to cut through both pillars.

RR6. Back in the workshop, the 'new' panel held against the very sad and sorry original. I had made certain that I cut off more than was going to be needed, just to be on the safe side.

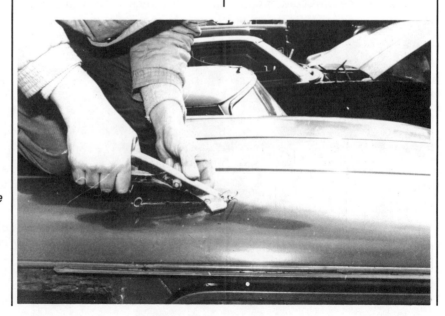

RR4. This enabled me to insert the blade of the Monodex cutter which was used to cut a slot along the length of the panel that I wanted to 'rescue'. The Monodex is famous for non-distortion of panels — and aching hands on the part of the user!

RR7.   This area contains a
complete box section with inner and
outer halves as well as the roof
section. The spot welds were all
drilled out and just the outer box
section was cut from the rest of the
panel.

RR10.   Again, the spot welds were
drilled through and then the panels
parted with the bolster chisel.
(Often, spot welds cling together
even after most of their diameter
has been drilled out.)

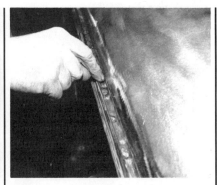

RR13.   . . . and the box sections
and guttering were welded through
the holes that had been drilled to
remove the spot welds.

RR8.   The repair panel was held in
place, and the old panel marked for
cutting.

RR11.   The old panel was taken
away with just a little more flange
distortion than would have been
ideal; this meant that the flanges
had to be dressed back to shape
with a hammer and dolly.

RR14.   Finally, front and rear
seams were leaded over, but this is
not an essential refinement of
course.

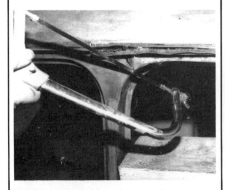

RR9.   When the old metal was cut
out from the front and rear pillars,
care was taken to leave more metal
in place than would be wanted and
then to grind the last of the metal
away a little at a time, offering the
repair panel up regularly to make
sure that it fitted closely.

RR12.   Front and rear pillars were
butt welded, which is why they had
to be a very accurate fit . . .

Leading body seams and
lead loading

It always seems sensible to me that
if you can seal off body seams so
that moisture can't get in, then no
corrosion can possibly take place.
You can use a seam sealer (and
indeed you should, if you want to
take every precaution), which is a
thick paste applied to the back of a
seam. But to seal off a seam
thoroughly, there can be nothing
better than to 'get some solder in
there'.

Tool Box

Solder paint (such as Fry's
'Fryolux') from motor factors —
check price first, as bad shock can
damage your health! Stick of 'body
solder'. Butane blow torch.
Stainless steel or hardwood spatula.

Safety

**Never risk breathing in lead
dust. Don't sand it with a power
sander of any sort. Wash hands
after soldering, especially before
eating.**

BS1.   This process is only worth
doing if the insides of the seams are
clean and fresh (ie if the panels have
been renewed). Paint solder paint
onto the surface of the clean metal.

BS2.   Play a blowtorch flame onto
the area to be filled (or a very soft
welding torch flame). Heat until the
solder in the solder paint flux forms
into little balls and flushes across
the surface. Then turn your
attention to the back of the seam
and heat from the other side. The
solder should be drawn towards the
heat and into the seam.

BS3.   When the solder has
flushed, be ready with a wet cloth to
wipe all the black flux away from the
surface of the panel. You may have
to rub vigorously.

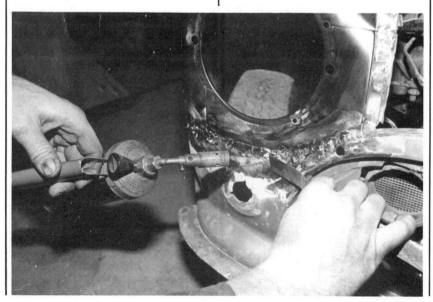

BS4.   Don't kid yourself — so far
this hasn't been the true art of 'lead
loading'! If you want to have a go,
feed a solder stick onto the panel,
playing the flame on it until it
crumbles, then oozes onto the
solder painted area. Continue
playing the torch on to the solder
until it goes as soft as butter but no
softer — it quickly gets too hot and
runs off, if you're not careful. Push
the solder where you want it with a
stainless steel or hardwood spatula.
File any excess off with a hand file,
NOT a power sander unless you
want to breathe very damaging lead
dust into your system!

Respraying

If you're new to respraying a car, or if you have tried before with poor results, you may be perplexed to see so little of this section dealing in detail with the business of actually putting the paint on the bodywork. This is because the pictures reflect what really happens when a high-class respray is carried out: preparation is easily nine-tenths of all the work, and that should mean several days of hard graft!

There is quite a lot to spraying and body preparation that could not possibly be covered in this book and this is dealt with in considerable depth in the *Haynes Car Bodywork Repair Manual* (published Winter 1984) also by Lindsay Porter, which, as the title suggests, aims to explain everything you need to know about car bodywork repair including detailed information on things such as arc, gas and MIG welding, use of fibreglass, lead loading and spraying and much more besides.

Although many of these are mentioned in this book, they are not covered in great detail for the obvious reason that there's only so much space and that is dedicated to the car of the moment!

There are no short cuts to adequate body preparation and if you try to take them, you will undoubtedly end up with an inferior finish at best, or at worst have to start all over again. So, here are the basic stages with a few hints and tips along the way.

Cleaning up

Before you even start to prepare for painting, you should strip the car down to its bare essentials and take an honest look at the trouble spots. I am assuming that any repairs have been carried out and that panels in need of renewal have been renewed or, if you're looking for a purely temporary repair, have been filled with fibreglass filler. If you see any sign of microblistering, which is tiny pimples in the paint, evenly spread, you must strip the paint back to

bare metal or the blisters will simply push their way through again. They are the result of water vapour in the finish coats or undercoats and unfortunately paint stripping is the only solution. If the microblistering is restricted to areas that have been repaired then, of course, only the blistered areas need stripping.

Loose and flaking paint, caused by spraying over paint that has not been properly 'keyed', also ought to be stripped and any car that has been sprayed with coat after coat of respray will need stripping or the fresh paint is likely to cause a reaction (wrinkling) in the paint.

There are ways of reducing the risk of reaction and they can be summed up here very briefly as: spray in oil-based paint (although that gives other disadvantages, too); spray in 2-pack, or spray a 2-pack primer (but with health hazards unless proper fresh-air breathing apparatus is used); or spray on a coat of isolator first, which must be sprayed fairly 'dry' and sprayed over within around 24 hours because it is hygroscopic (attracts moisture from the air). As I said, the topic needs more room to be covered properly!

Spraying equipment

The choice of spraying equipment is also rather important. Some recommend that a 'pro'-type compressor and spray gun are hired rather than a cheap spray set purchased. However, the typical hire shop set up can have three distinct disadvantages: the cost is usually high if the unit is to be used over a reasonable length of time; the user does not have the opportunity to get to know the whims and foibles of the particular set before it has to go back again; and worst of all, the equipment usually leads a hard life and is frequently half worn out or sub-standard in some other way.

The author's first respray was carried out on his front drive, using a cheap airless sprayer, which is little more than a powered garden sprayer. It was desperately slow and

there was a lot of arm-aching cutting back to do afterwards but the results were among the best the author has achieved! The point of this little homily is that the care and time taken in preparation and spraying are worth far more than the most expensive equipment.

A low cost spray system with a great deal to commend it is that manufactured by Apollo Sprayers of Birmingham, England. It does not use a compressor in the normal sense but instead a fan blower similar to that used in a vacuum cleaner. The pipe to the spray gun is large bore because the air supply is high volume, low pressure which has the advantage that there is less compressed air rushing around, whipping the dust off the walls and ceiling of the typical small domestic garage. On the minus side are the facts that the blower cannot be used to power other tools and also the short duty-cycle of the blower unit which means that it cannot be used continuously for long periods. Even so, the quality of spray achieved can be remarkably high with this unit.

RS-A. A big-hearted little system is that used by SIP in the Airmate Jet 30. This uses a very small compressor built along conventional quality lines and comes with a matching spray gun. This is the sort of unit that would make an ideal alternative to hiring a large compressor for a week or two, especially since the compressor unit can itself be used for other lightweight duties around the workshop. For spraying, of course, progress is very slow and the spray pattern is not as regular as that given by a compound with an air receiver.

RS-B. *Airmate compressors rise in size up to the type of unit that will do a worthwhile job of work for the most serious enthusiasts. Because they are fitted with an air receiver, a quantity of air can be stored which allows some leeway for the fluctuations in demand caused when heavier duty tools are used. These machines are perfect for those who want to equip themselves with a full 'pro'-style one man workshop at DIY cost.*

RS-C. *SIP also manufactures a quality spray gun suitable for the conscientious enthusiast. Known as the 'Jade', it can operate in a variety of modes and gives a high quality finish without having to go right up to the high cost and high air consumption of the full blown (if you'll excuse the pun) professional spray guns.*

Tool Box

A wide range of tools are called for and at almost every stage there are numerous alternatives — see text.

Safety

Paint fumes can be very dangerous, especially when the air is saturated with overspray. ALWAYS wear a top-quality face-mask, work in a well ventilated area and AVOID 2 pack Isocyanate paint unless you have a full, air-fed breathing kit such as the relatively inexpensive DeVilbiss kit and a compressor big enough to power your spray gun *and* provide you with a constant supply of fresh air.

RS1. *You can be certain that behind the Mini's trim strips, and quite probably behind the hinges and headlamps, there will be surface rust forming. Use a 36 grit disc on the angle grinder or drill and be sure to linish back to bare metal.*

RS2. *The insides of the guttering are also pretty certain to have rust scales and here a new abrasive disc which is still sharp along its outer edge should be used. Beneath the trim it didn't matter but here you will have to spot-prime and scrape on a thin layer of stopper to cover the scratches made by the linishing disc before going on to the next stage.*

RS3. *The only places where you can get away with brush painting are those that will be hidden by carpet or underseal, such as the insides of the wings. Brush marks will always show on exterior bodywork. We use a zinc-enriched cellulose-based paint so that any paint can go on top of it. DON'T use the much more common oil-based zinc or aluminium paint where you are going to spray over it, because cellulose paint will react very strongly to it.*

RS4.   Rotary sanders make circular marks which are extremely difficult to remove. This is a random orbit sander, powered by air and its advantage is that it does not leave scratch marks that remain visible through the paint, provided that you finish off with a fine grade, of course. Air random orbit sanders (or 'DAs'), as they are known, after the brand leader) consume a lot of air, so don't bother unless you own a large compressor. Black and Decker make an electric version (which should only be used with the dry, 'frecut'-type papers) which costs very little more than the air tool.

RS5.   The first job of all should be to flat the body all over with a medium grade of paper. One of the best tools for the job is this type of electric sander used with the 'frecut' type of dry paper cut into suitable sized strips to fit the sanding pad. Alternatively, use a hand held rubber sanding block with the same type of paper or, if you prefer to work in an old-fashioned mess, use wet-and-dry paper.

RS7.   Of course, the filler itself will only be ripple-free if it is flatted correctly. Flatting with a power tool or hand-flatting with a small rubber block just won't take the ripples out, and could create more! A specialist tool like this only costs a few pounds and is worth its weight in gold. You can buy self-adhesive strips to fit onto it. Alternatively, you could make your own tool with a piece of wood, wrapping a long strip of standard flatting paper around it.

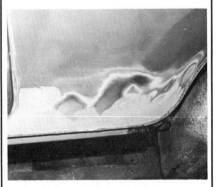

Preparation

After cleaning away unwanted paint and rust, the next stage is preparing the body. This is the most critical stage of all because the aim is to produce a bodywork surface that is flat and free of ripples, free of the sorts of minor blemishes that can easily ruin a good paint job and last but certainly not least, paintwork that has been flatted all over to provide a 'key' — a matt surface to which the new paint can stick without flaking off.

RS6.   The misuse of fibreglass filler has given it an undeserved bad name. It should never be used where structural strength is in any way needed but, used only to take the ripples out of a panel, or to true-up surfaces that have been welded together (this particular repair can be seen earlier in the book), it's a first-class material. If you use filler over paint (purists will say that you shouldn't but purists seem to have all the time and money in the world!), make sure that the paint is thoroughly flatted, as in the previous shot, to provide a key, otherwise the filler could break off.

RS8.   This area is a perfect example of where filler can be most useful. There was no corrosion here, but body distortion, since cured by repair work in other areas, had caused panel rippling. Two or three (or more if necessary) applications of filler are nearly always needed to level up depressions missed by the first layer(s) and to fill in any air bubbles that might have occurred.

RS9. Hand flatting has to be carried out in the dozens of tricky little areas where nothing else will reach: however, in such places there is rarely a problem with visible rippling which can only be seen on flat or flattish surfaces.

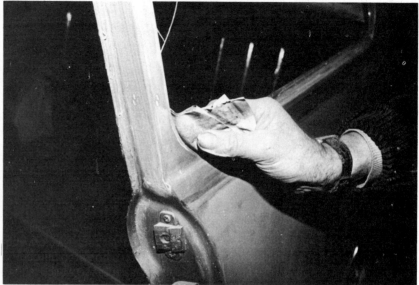

RS10. No filler was applied to the roof, there was no distortion and only the thickness of the original paint to contend with, so it was quite safe to machine flat here. You can see how easily you can break through the paint film on convex curves: in this case it didn't matter.

▷

RS11. There were several areas on the roof where localised breakdown of the paint film meant that sanding had to be carried right through to bare metal. Whenever you leave the edge of the existing paint under your respray, the edges should be 'feathered' gradually, as shown.

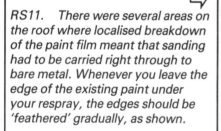

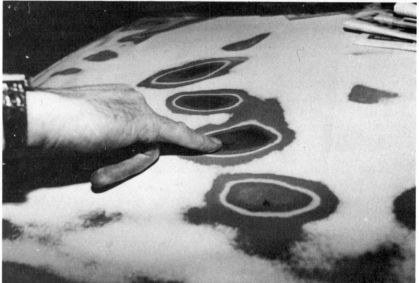

RS12. It is often easier to work on a door, bootlid or bonnet with the panel removed from the car. Doors with external hinges can then be sprayed under the hinges, and it is easier to spray the insides of doors and the areas partly covered by the hinge posts; also any stripping need not affect the surrounding panels.

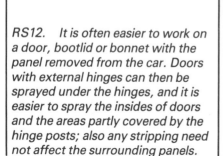

Masking off

RS13.   Many resprayers will not use newspaper for masking off because it is said to hold dust which can blow out into the paint. Most people don't actually find it a problem.

   If parts of the car floor are going to be sprayed, or if the doors or windscreen are out of the car, the interior should be very thoroughly masked off to prevent overspray from getting onto the steering wheel, dash or instruments. The headlining should also be masked off if the screens are taken out.

   The engine bay and wheels should be thoroughly covered over in any case. Spray finds its way onto the engine through the bonnet sides and through the grille opening too, while nothing looks more amateurish than over-spray on wheels and tyres.

RS14.   The best way of masking off (and this applies whether windows and other large components are left in place or taken off) is to start with a run of masking tape all around the part or orifice being masked, taking very great care to position it accurately.

RS15.   Then, take a sheet of paper, position another strip of tape half over the edge of the paper and press it down to the tape already fitted.

RS16.   A completely masked-off area should always look smooth and neat, if it is otherwise paint and dust from the first part of spraying can become trapped in crevices and blow out again onto the finished paint. Ideally, especially if you are going for a show finish, you should re-mask the whole car before spraying on the finish coat.

Spot-priming

RS17.   All of the filled areas should be spot-primed, as well as all those that have been sanded to bare metal or feather-edged. An ideal primer to use here is a high-build primer, spray putty or polyester spray filler, although you should wear breathing apparatus when spraying the latter. These special primers have the effect of priming the metal and of giving just a little depth for flatting out small blemishes.

RS18.   All the seam edges covered by trim should be thoroughly primed. (This particular tyre was bald and due for renewal but nevertheless wheels and tyres should be masked off when the finish coat is sprayed to cut down the risk of dirt being blown onto the paint).

RS19.   Where rust has been cleaned from door channels, etc, that cleaner area should be primed and then later, just before the finish coat is applied to the whole car, the finish coat should first be sprayed on to these and other awkward-to-get-at places.

RS20.   After it has been spot-primed, the body will have a patchwork appearance, but is now in an ideal state for the next stage of the respray.

Final preparation and spraying

The trouble with primer is that it flatters to deceive. Gloss paint shows every ripple, scratch and blemish on the surface of the bodywork but primer, being matt, has the opposite effect and makes things look a lot better than they really are . . .

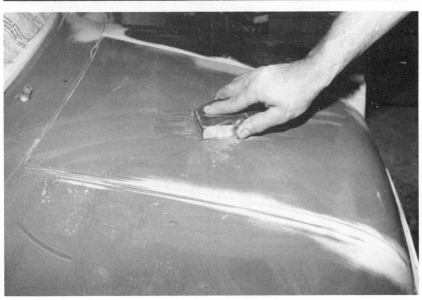

RS21.   Many professionals like to carry out their final flatting with 600 or even the finer 800 grade wet-and-dry which gives a finer finish than the 'frecut'-type dry use papers. If you're using oil-based laquer paints or two-pack (taking note of the health hazards) you may not need such fine flatting but cellulose tends to show up scratches more than any other of the common paint types.

RS22.   This, a different Mini with basically very sound paint, needed very little spot priming. If you're respraying a car with sound original paint, you will probably be able to get away with just carrying out this part of the work for 90% of the body; but it's a safe bet that at least 10% needs more work than just flatting when you look really closely!

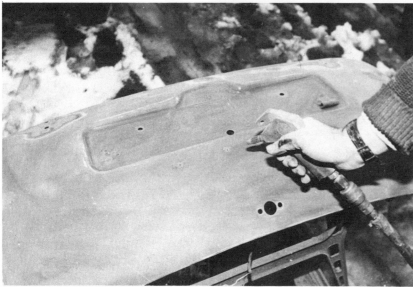

RS23.   After flatting, dry all the panels off with a clean cloth (not one that has been near polish; silcone contamination means that the entire finish will be ruined and you will have to start all over again with your preparation). Then, blow any remaining dust off the panel surfaces and out of the cracks and crevices and also blow the panel completely dry.

RS24.   The whole car should then be sprayed in primer or primer filler. Start at one 'corner' and work around the car one panel at a time in horizontal 'strips' each 'line' of spray half covering the one that went before. Then, the whole car will have to be flatted all over again. Before attempting to spray the finish coat on, you should consider adding two extra stages: 1) spray a thin coat of paint over the whole car. This will give enough gloss to show up any ripples, scratches or whatever. Be prepared to spend extra time putting problems right and note that polyester knifing putty can be very useful for getting rid of small blemishes fairly painlessly; 2) before spraying the finish coats, give all the 'fiddly' areas a coat of paint, such as door shuts and window openings and the edges of flanges. Trying to spray them at the same time as the final coat usually creates paint runs.

RS25. If you want your car sprayed in the harder wearing but slightly 'plastic' looking two-pack paint, you may consider sending it 'out' to be sprayed. You may wish to do this even if you want cellulose and don't feel too confident about spraying but want to do all the preparation yourself. Take a tip: always ask the sprayer to be responsible for the final flatting, even if it costs a little more (but get an idea of how much more before you leave the car). If you don't, no matter what goes wrong, you can be sure it will be 'your' fault. If he is responsible for making sure that everything is okay before spraying then it's up to him to make sure that things go as they should.

RS26. Many Mini owners cover their outer sills with one of the newer, rubberised hard wearing underseals to avoid stone chips. Here the sill has been masked off while the 'body schutz' is blasted on with an inexpensive air tool.

RS27. If you intend spraying a different roof colour, spray the roof first because then there's less to mask off when you spray the second colour. The interior had been stripped out of this Mini so masking at this stage was minimal. Note that no attempt has been made to mask off the pillars and top rails; they just had to be lightly flatted before the lower part of the car was sprayed. Allow the roof paint to fully harden (refer to paint manufacturer's process sheets, available from your paint supplier) before using masking tape on it.

Fitting up

Post-respray fitting-up has to be carried out with some care so that you don't scratch any of the beautiful new paintwork. Polish all the chromework before putting it back on the car, otherwise you will find it difficult to polish all the edges and corners. You will probably find that trim and fittings which seemed quite acceptable when on the car before it was painted, now look dull and full of blemishes. New bumpers and other available pieces of brightwork are remarkably inexpensive and certainly far cheaper than the re-chroming you might otherwise consider.

F3.   The grille and surround are held in place by the same screws.

F4.   The grille and surround are re-fitted as shown here during removal.

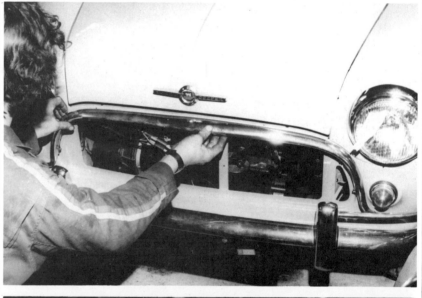

F1.   The 'cats whisker' type of grille surround is held in place by five or six self-tapping screws which pass through tags on the inner edge of the surround. Line it up very accurately before drilling or screwing holes in the front panel (if a new one has been fitted).

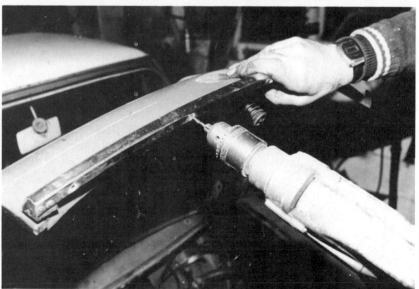

F2.   MK II car's top grille surrounds are fixed to the front of the bonnet with self-tapping screws or, as original, pop rivets. Here holes for the pop rivets are beng drilled in a new bonnet.

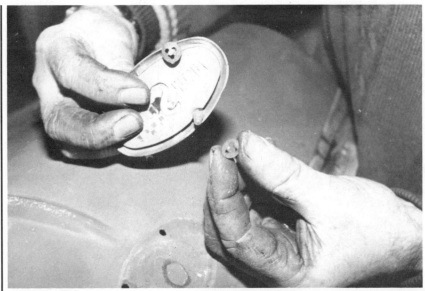

F5.   Some badges are held in place with steel grip washers. Legs stick out of the back of the badge which are pushed through holes drilled in the panel, and then the grip washers pushed on from behind. Some later badges use nylon inserts in the holes in the panel into which the badge legs are pushed. Most of the 'BL' era badges are glued on.

F6.   Chrome trim on Cooper doors is held by these small clips. They lever off with a screwdriver then push back on. Before refitting, dip each one in Waxoyl to preserve it: they are no longer obtainable as new items.

F7.   Door kick plates on early Minis are held by self-tapping screws; later cars had pop-rivets.

F8.   As already shown under 'Bonnet removal', the bonnet has quite a lot of adjustment within the hinges, however, room for boot adjustment is very limited. Even so, some movement can be obtained by slackening off the hinges then tightening fully when the bootlid is in position. In emergencies, more drastic steps can be taken — see 'Van and Traveller Rear Door Adjustment' and 'Boot Lid Adjustment'.

F9. Similarly, up-and-down adjustment of the doors is restricted although some is available. Remember to re-adjust the wedge and/or striker plate, too. The latter also gives in-and-out adjustment of the door and should be adjusted so that the door just compresses the rubber sealing strip and sits flush with the rear panel. If the sealing strip is too close to the door, you can gain a little leeway by pulling off the door sealing strip from those places where it is tight and either tapping the flange inwards or easing it over a section at a time with pliers or Mole grips.

F10. Later doors have these safety bosses beneath the handles. They are held in place with a single screw from inside the door and should always be fitted with the sealing gasket in place.

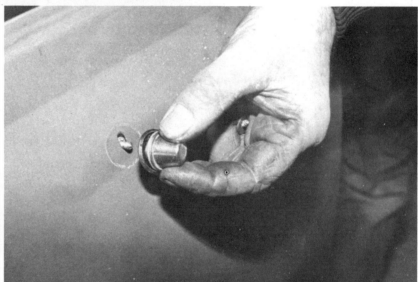

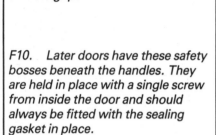

F11. Boot lid handles are refitted by attaching the lock first with two screws through the edge of the panel, after which the handle is fitted through the lock and the two remaining nuts fitted in place. Again, remember to fit the sealing gaskets behind all handle plinths.

F12. Little touches make all the difference! Here the radiator and shroud have been painted in their correct, original colours and the correct spiral thead, hexagonal head screw has been cleaned up and is being re-used. It is at this stage that you appreciate careful storage and, above all, careful labelling when stripping down.

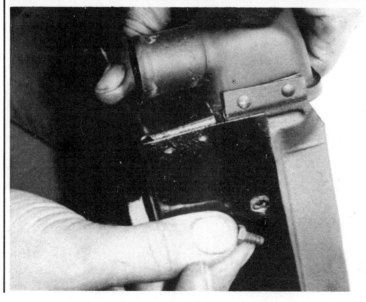

Rustproofing

After having put so much time,
effort and money into rebuilding the
car's body, it would be the height of
folly not to do something about
preventing, or at least delaying
further corrosion. Of course, all of
the seams and especially those
underneath the car should be sealed
with the special seam sealer made
for the job, before spraying on the
gloss coats of paint. However, most
long-term rust starts in box sections
and other enclosed areas and the
only way of holding back corrosion
in such structures is to inject a rust
retardant into all the enclosed
places where rust may form. The
cost of doing this is ridiculously low
compared to the cost of repairing
rusty bodywork and the stuff itself is
not too unpleasant to handle.

Having once injected rust
inhibitor, make a point of repeating
the operation every year, or two at
the most, in conjunction with a
thorough examination of the
underbody and touching-in of
damaged paintwork where
necessary.

*RP1.   Many people have
reservations about underseal and
prefer paint on the principle that you
can easily see when problems in
painted steel are starting, whereas
rust starting beneath underseal can
do its damage without being
spotted, while the underseal can
actually make matters worse by
trapping moisture against the metal.
Applied over a perfectly sound
surface, modern 'Body Schutz'-
type underseals are much improved
over the old-fashioned variety, but
they do need to be put on with an
inexpensive applicator and air line.
Regular steam cleaning will show up
any defects in older underseal and
remove it before it has a chance to
cause a problem. If you intend
inspecting the underside regularly,
underseal is probably not a good
choice; if you are the sort of person
to leave well alone, then underseal
is probably for you.*

*RP2.   Finnigans 'Waxoyl' is
probably the most well-known DIY
rust inhibitor. It is shown here with
the low-cost injector gun designed
to reach well into box sections.
Apply 'Waxoyl' (or any other
inhibitor) liberally. In winter, heat
the tin in hot water to thin the fluid
down, or thin it with white spirit.*

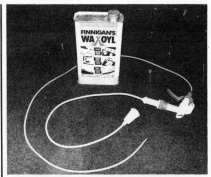

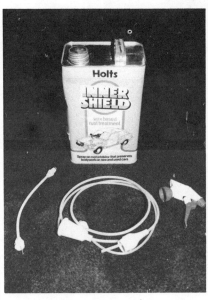

*RP3.   Holts make a similar product
called 'Inner Shield' and also market
a similar injector kit.*

*RP4.   Finnigans also sell a 'de luxe'
injector which takes the form of a
pressure can and spray operating on
the pump-up garden sprayer
principle. Once the initial can of
fluid has been purchased it can be
topped up from a standard can.*

RP5. The cheaper inhibitor injector kits leave something to be desired in that their coverage is relatively poor (make a long box from cardboard and try it for yourself). The DeVilbiss SGB-602 outfit is obviously more expensive than amateur kits, but it does give a very thorough and professional level of internal covering — as it should because this unit was designed to give a coverage which meets manufacturers' latest specifications.

RP6. Here the DeVilbiss unit is demonstrated as if being used to spray fluid into the bottom of the oddments pocket in the rear of the car, the internal trim would be taken out, of course.

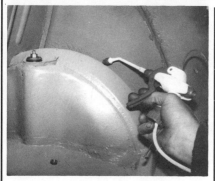

RP8. Here the cheaper Waxoyl applicator is used to protect the all-important seam between inner and outer reel wheel arch. Remember to treat the left-hand side on saloons before refitting the tank.

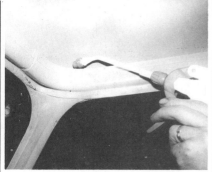

RP9. As you can see from the bodywork repair sections, the roof rail can, and does, eventually rot out. Again the simple hand-held 'garden sprayer' Waxoyling device is ideal for the job.

RP7. The SGB-602 uses a larger bore tube than the Waxoyl or Holts models, so it is necessary to use a much larger size of drill bit. This in turn means that you have to position the holes that bit more carefully to avoid their looking obtrusive. Make sure that you lay in a stock of blanking grommets before starting work.

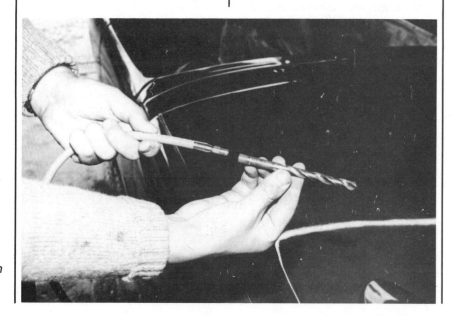

RP10.   The hand gun will just about do the job where the Mini's large crossmember is concerned, but the extension probe will allow the spray to reach right inside. Again, the DeVilbiss gun would be even better here, albeit at several times the purchase cost of the Waxoyl equipment.

RP11.   Small detail areas, especially those behind badges, are best rustproofed using one of the thinner, aerosol based inhibitors because they will 'creep' even more than standard 'Waxoyl'.

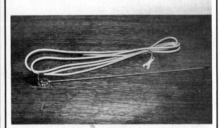

AF1.   This is the Unipart (BL's own accessory brand) roof aerial and is one of a range of good quality aerials marketed by the company. It always pays to spend just a little more to obtain an aerial that won't fall apart or rust solid within a very short time.

Roof aerial − fitting

Fitting an aerial to a car is quite a simple DIY task which should be well within anyone's capability. The aerial shown in this sequence is a Unipart roof aerial, many people considering the roof aerial to be the one that suits the looks of the Mini best of all. It certainly is a better bet from the practical point of view because wing mounted aerials are inclined to introduce corrosion into an already rot-prone wing and the corrosion then inhibits the performance of the aerial (most people have travelled in a car whose radio crackles when the car is on the move and this is usually due to rust preventing the aerial from earthing properly on the car's body, made intermittent by the movement of the car and whipping of the aerial). The other problem is that with a car as small as the Mini, there is nowhere on the front wings that is any distance from the electrical components of the engine and they can feed interference into the system. At the same time, there is virtually nowhere at the rear of a Mini where an aerial can be fitted — which only leaves the roof!

Tool Box

Electric drill, basic hand tools, Mastic.

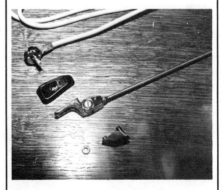

AF2.   The threaded connector on the end of the aerial wire pushes up from inside the car, the black plinth shown below it sits on the roof, the aerial platform sits on that and the washer, nut and finisher top off the assembly.

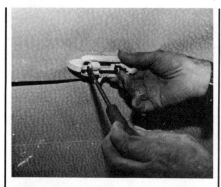

AF3. First step is to remove the interior light fitted to the centre of the roof, after first unclipping the plastic diffuser.

AF4. Then the whole front portion of the headlining can be slid backwards far enough to fit the aerial. It helps if you have one person at each side of the car, or, if working by yourself, you 'walk' the headlining back, first a little bit one side, then the other . . .

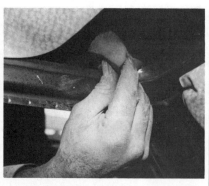

AF5. You will find a piece of foam rubber in the top of the door pillar. Reach inside and pull it out. (Incidentally, could this be why door pillar tops sometimes rot out?)

AF6. Place a tape square across the top of the roof and measure very accurately to determine the centre point. Mark it on masking tape.

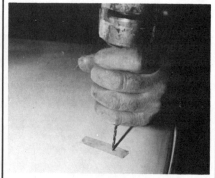

AF7. With the widthways centre line marked on the tape, you can mark the tape again to indicate the required distance from the front guttering.

AF8. The masking tape not only gives you a surface that you can write on, it also helps to stop the drill bit slipping. Go further by gripping the chuck of the drill WITHOUT PRESSING THE TRIGGER and turning the chuck and drill bit by hand in the normal direction of cut. Continue this process until the drill bit has just started to make itself a cut in the metal. Don't use a centre punch because it can easily dent the panel and don't ride your luck and hope that the drill bit won't skid across the roof — without taking these precautions, it almost certainly will!

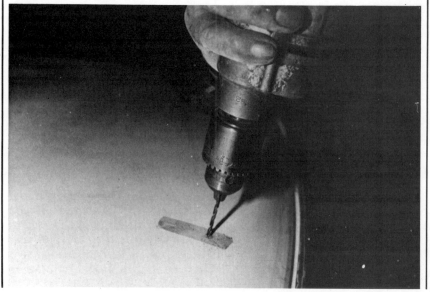

AF9. Then proceed as normal and drill through the panel using only light pressure on the drill. Note that a small drill size has been selected — around 0.125 inch (⅛ in.) here, to give a pilot hole.

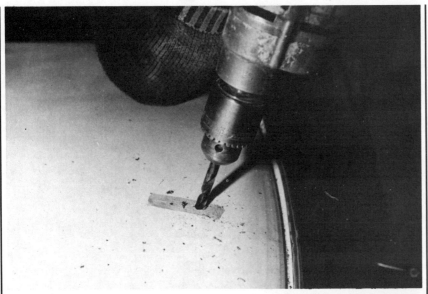

AF10.   Next, select a drill bit of the correct size to give a little clearance to the aerial thread and drill through.

AF11.   On the inside of the roof, clean the area around the hole with abrasive paper to ensure a good earth. You now need an assistant to hold the threaded part of the connector up from inside the car . . .

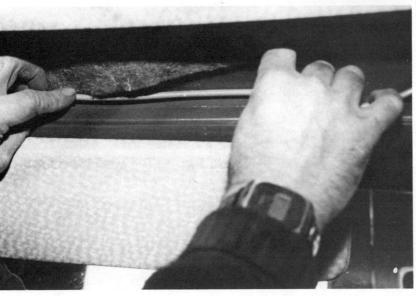

AF12.   . . . while the plinth, aerial platform, screw and nut are put in place from above. Incidentally, you should not paint the hole because the aerial needs to 'earth' against the car bodywork, however, you must put a trace of non-setting Mastic sealer under the plastic plinth to prevent water getting in.

AF13.   The aerial lead can be pushed into the hollow box frame around the inside of the roof . . .

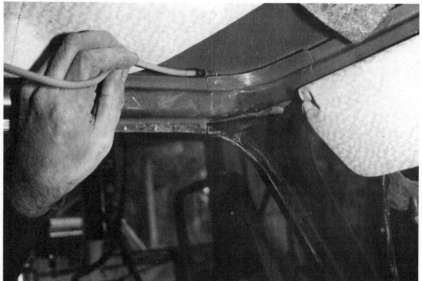

AF14. . . . and the end fed down the inside of the door frame.

AF15. The dashboard trim must be eased back, taking great care not to break or split it . . .

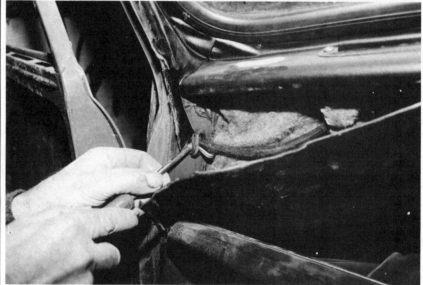

AF16. . . . and the wiring harness grommet at the base of the door pillar can be eased out with a screwdriver. Push the wire down from above and when the end appears, pull it through the same hole with a pair of long-nosed pliers. Alternatively, push a piece of stiff wire, formed into a loop at the end, into the hole and attempt to lasso the wire — it might work first time or you may need patience . . . push the aerial wire through the grommet and reinsert it. The route now taken by the cable depends entirely upon where your radio is sited.

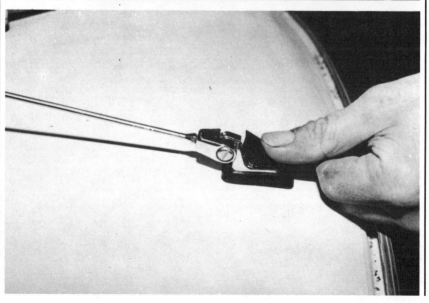

AF17. When the aerial has been correctly lined up, the nut can be tightened and the finishing cap pushed into place.

Fitting a wing-mounted aerial is very similar in principle although the actual method of fixing the aerial may differ. You may be able to feed the aerial wire through the inner wing and bulkhead using existing grommets or it may be necessary to drill holes and fit new ones.

4 Interior

Unfair though it may seem, any car is judged by most people first by the amount of shine on the bodywork (and never mind what is beneath the shine, or how long it is likely to last!) and secondly by the condition of the interior. You can rest assured that few people other than those who are in the know, will understand or care about the attention you have lavished on your car's structural soundness or the sweetness of the gearbox. However, the consolation of preparing an attractive interior is that it's one place where your hard work *will* be commented upon.

Trim removal & trim general

T1.   Front seats are easily removed with a pair of spanners on the two bolts (one each side) that hold the frame to the crossmember bracket. Note that this bracket gives two alternative seat settings (on top of the normal adjustment) although in its rearmost position the bracket can be a painful heel-cruncher, especially for those wearing sandals.

T2.   The alternative method of removing the seats, and the preferable one if the interior is to be sprayed, is by taking out the seat bracket retaining bolts that enter captive nuts in the front of the crossmember. (This is a special seat and supporting frame.)

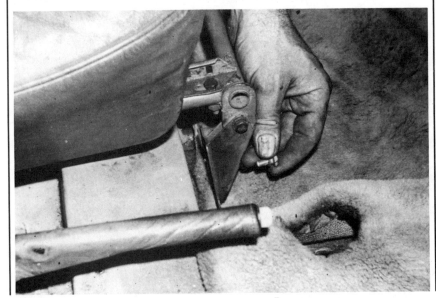

149

T3.   Nothing holds the rear of the seat in place in earlier cars, so the seat now lifts straight out. Later cars are fitted with catches.

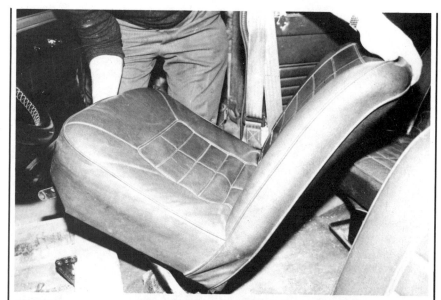

T4.   Damage to the rear of the seats is especially common to Van and Estate front seats, because awkward loads are often carried by these models. If you don't want to see a new panel stitched in by a trimmer — it probably won't be the exactly correct texture and/or colour — you may consider carefully removing the cover from the frame noting where the clips come from and how they are fitted, and repairing the splits with one of the many vinyl-weld type adhesives now on the market, or carefully gluing a patch onto the inside of the cover. ⇨

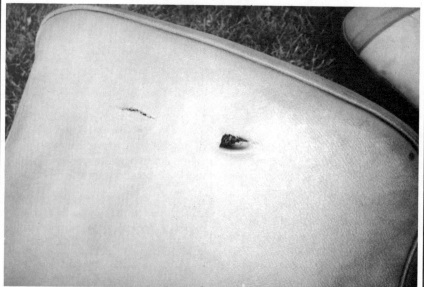

T5.   Removal of the dash side trim is straightforward. Take out Clubman air vents by unscrewing the plastic ring on the front of each vent anti-clockwise, after which the various pieces of the vent will come away. To take out the instrument panel, unscrew the four visible crosshead screws from the front of the panel, pull the black shroud forwards and disconnect (a) the panel light switch; (b) the temperature gauge wires; (c) the oil pressure gauge pipe and/or wires. The shroud now comes free and the instruments can be removed after unscrewing the knurled finger nuts that retain them. (Do remember to refit the interior light switch with a side-to-side movement. If it switches front-to-rear it can short circuit on the oil pressure pipe.) The speedo is taken out of the binnacle which fits behind the shroud. It is held by two screws, one each side: take care not to loose the shroud mounting brackets and spacers that are also fitted there. Pull the speedo forwards and detach the speedo cable, lamps and fuel gauge wiring. *DO NOT CARRY OUT ANY OF THESE OPERATIONS WITHOUT FIRST DISCONNECTING THE BATTERY.*

T6.   The trim ring is held in place by a series of bifurcated rivets, which are easily opened or closed with a screwdriver or pliers respectively.

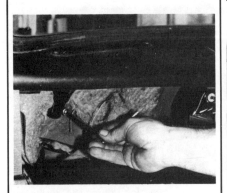

T7.   The dash top rail is also removed after the dash side trims have been taken out. A line of short bolts pass downwards through the dash top.

T8.   This is a Radford Mini Cooper, but customising of Mini dash panels has been a favourite occupation of Mini owners through the years. Before you rip out a non-standard dash, however, find out whether it is an interesting period accessory, or even an indication that more favourable things have been done to your car.

T9.   'Special' dash boards often require special framework to hold them in place. If you want to retain yours, make a written note or drawing of where it all came from – you probably won't be able to find out from any other source if you forget.

T10.   The steering column is fixed to the dash by a bracket (arrow) and to the rack by a clamp bolt which must be removed completely before the column can be pulled off. Disconnect all the wiring, too.

Later models are fitted with a steering lock (see figure 11) which can fail and refuse to unlock whilst you are parked in some expensive, or embarrassing place. The heads of the shear bolts are designed to break off as they are torqued up leaving, in theory, no way of getting them out. In the comfort of your own garage, you can drill the heads of the shear bolts off, or drill a smaller hole and insert a stud extractor.

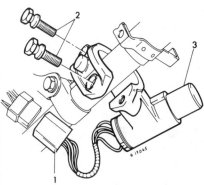

Figure 11.   Steering lock/ignition switch assembly.
1   Multi-plug connector
2   Shear bolts
3   Steering lock/ignition switch

The author once found himself in an expensive car park with a seized lock, but got out of trouble by dashing round to the nearest hardware store and buying a centre punch and hammer, then using the punch as a drift to turn the shear bolts. A fourth way out is to saw a slot into the head of the bolt and partly into the metal body of the lock if necessary, and then to use an impact screwdriver to free the bolt.

You can easily activate the ignition by removing the wiring switch from the bottom of the main switch body and operating it by hand. What's that flashing blue light . . . ?

151

T11. To remove the rear seats, you first undo the two nuts that hold the top of the backrest to the rear parcel shelf, from inside the boot.

T12. The seat then lifts up at the back, the two bolts coming out of their holes . . .

T14. . . . and the whole seat backrest to lift away.

T16. . . . which leaves the cover free to be taken out.

T13. . . . which allows the locating rods in the floor to lift up and out . . .

T15. The rear parcel shelf cover may be held with self-tapping screws or pop rivets. If the latter, carefully drill their heads off . . .

T17. Finding correct replacement trim parts can be extremely difficult and to find a set of early Cooper seats like these can take a great deal of searching.

T18.   Untidy wiring is a real eye-sore as well as a potential safety hazard. Take trouble to tape any ancillary wiring into a loom (see 'electrical' section) and buy wiring clips to hold the wiring either behind the trim or, if necessary, beneath the dash.

T18A.   This demoralising sight is where all absolutely first-class interiors start from. The first step to a beautiful interior is the use of seam sealer along all the body joints, to ensure that no water can force its way into the car, especially where you have fitted new panels. For the same reason, the windscreen must have a sound frame, sound rubbers and be correctly fitted.

Carpets

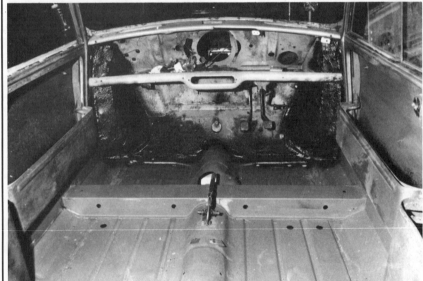

T19.   Before fitting new carpets, take the opportunity to clean the floor area thoroughly. Here foam rubber 'sound proofing' has been glued down to the floor and is being carefully scraped off.

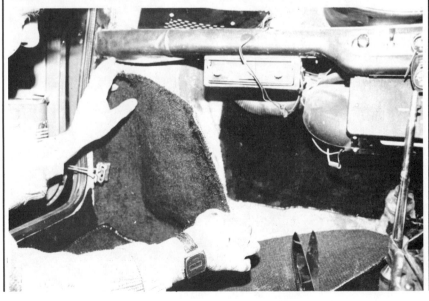

T20.   It is extremely difficult, if not impossible, to get hold of factory-original carpet material. Some of the carpets offered by the cheap-car-carpet companies are of dreadfully poor quality. These carpets, which were better than average but not wonderful, were bought from the Mini Spares Centre. The inner wheel arch pieces were ready formed and were glued in place.

T21.   Where the carpet fitted the dipswitch at the toe-board, it was trimmed to shape. An alternative would have been to remove the dipswitch, make a hole in the carpet for the wiring and screw the dipswitch down through the carpet.

T22.   There was no getting away from having to trim the carpet around the handbrake and gearchange mechanism, although at least the gearchange grommet and bezel covered the edge of the carpet.

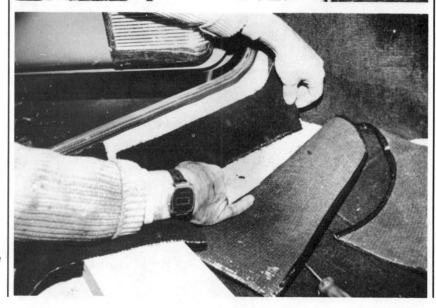

T23.   Sill pieces were ready formed but were a poor fit, so some extra trimming was necessary.

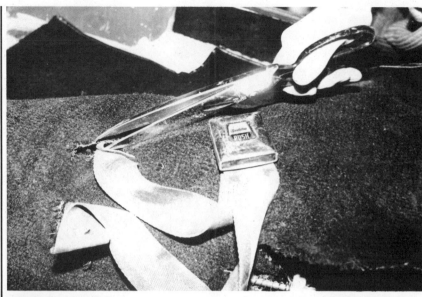

T24.   Slots had to be cut into the carpet for the seat belt floor straps.

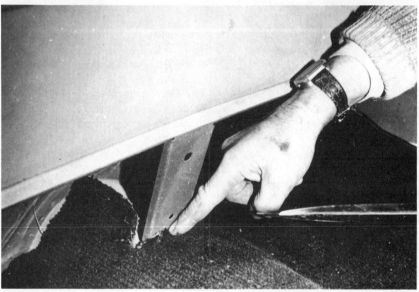

T25.   And then the rear carpet was cut in a T-shape to fit around the rear seat support bracket.

Unless carpets are clipped down to the studs provided, they will slip about, look untidy and make a thorough nuisance of themselves. If new panels have been fitted screw new studs down with self-tapping screws. If extra sound-deadening felt has been laid, the studs will need to be raised to compensate with packing pieces — marine grade plywood is fine.

T26.   When you receive your new carpets, start by placing them in the car, feeling for the position of the stud and marking it with chalk. Press the clawed ring down onto the top of the carpet . . .

T27. . . . so that the claws protrude through the carpet.

T28. Place the clip over the claws and fold the claws inwards with a screwdriver. Simple!

Headlining removal and refitting

Early saloons

1.   Mark the position of the rear edge of the front liner to act as a reference when refitting.
2.   Remove by gripping the outer edge of the liner, exerting a gentle inwards pressure and pulling rearwards.
3.   Mark the position of the rear liner at its front edge and remove in the same way, but of course, by pulling it forwards. When a roof lamp is fitted, it must be removed first, of course.
4.   Refitting is the reverse of the above, the rear liner going in first. Make sure that the rear liner is pushed fully home. When refitting make sure that the wires are pushed through the front liner before it is pushed fully home.
5.   When refitting the front liner, check that the three retaining hooks on the forward edge of the rear liner engage in the three sockets in the rear edge of the front liner.

Later saloons

This is one-piece headlining of more conventional type.

1.   Undo the two screws either in the sides or in the support rail, in the middle.
2.   Take out both front and rear screens (See relevant section of this book) and take out both screen rubbers.
3.   Pull the door seals down from their top edge.
4.   Peel the edges of the headlining from around the door aperture and front and rear screen apertures.
5.   Spring the headlining support bars over the top of the side rails and remove complete.
6.   When refitting, start at the back, glue to the rear window aperture and then fit the rear screen. Then pull forwards and fit from the back.

Countryman and Traveller

The procedure is very similar to that for the early saloon, with the following differences:

1.   Mark the positions of both front and rear liners on the cant rail so that they can be refitted in the same position.
2.   Remove the trim liner from over the rear door.
3.   When refitting, make certain that the clip on the front liner enters the bracket on the front edge of the rear liner.

5 Mechanical Components

Suspension & brakes (general) & depressurising Hydrolastic systems

When the Mini was introduced, it was fitted with a revolutionary rubber suspension system: rubber cone-springs were mounted vertically in the front subframe and horizontally in the rear. In August 1962 the highly successful Austin/Morris 1100 models were announced and they had 'Hydrolastic' suspension which used a mixture of water and alcohol, inside special chambers, as the springing medium. Minis went over to Hydrolastic in 1964, but the system was phased out between 1969 and 1972 (depending upon model) and the good old rubber suspension reintroduced. Incidentally, the Vans, Pick-ups and Estates stayed with rubber suspension all the way through.

Tool box

A range of standard workshop tools will be required for work on suspension and brakes and some special tools might be required (they may be available for hire, or on loan): front suspension compressor; Hydrolastic suspension depressurising tool; brake pipe flare forming tool; brake bleeding equipment.

Safety

NEVER attempt to let down a Hydrolastic suspension system without the proper, approved tool – it may be best to leave the work to your main agent who will make a very modest charge indeed for the work. The suspension is pumped up to a pressure OVER 10 TIMES HIGHER THAN TYRE PRESSURES, so uncontrolled release could be very dangerous indeed. NEVER work on a car supported by a jack; always support the car on axle stands with wheels chocked when working on suspension or brakes.

Brake dust can be lethal! NEVER blow it away: it is probably best to work out of doors and to dampen the area with a garden-type hand sprayer. Collect dust with a damp rag then dispose of it in a sealed plastic bag.

Depressurising the Hydrolastic system

S1.   *You should not try to depressurise Hydrolastic suspension yourself for safety reasons, and it's a very inexpensive job to have carried out for you by a BL dealer. It is quite O.K. to drive a Mini with deflated suspension at speeds up to 30mph, but remember that it is travelling along on its body-mounted rubber bump stops so take extra care on very bumpy stretches (the crashing around inside your cranium should slow you down!). In an emergency, you can pump up the suspension with air from a foot pump or air line (50 to 70 psi should do the trick) but the suspension will be very soft. This picture shows the positions of the pressure valves, mounted on the rear subframe.*

Checking Hydrolastic system for leaks

Hydrolastic suspension systems are notorious for 'going down' and although some cars are never affected, others can become annoyingly afflicted by the leaky fluid gremlins. To check whether your Hydrolastic Mini is riding low, check the following table and measure the wing height front and rear and on both sides ('Wing height' is the vertical distance from the middle of the wheel to the edge of the wheelarch).

Early cars: front wheels 12¾ – 13¼ inch (324-336mm), rear wheels 13¼ -13¾ inch (337-340mm). Later cars: front wheels 12⅜ -12⅞ inch (315-350mm), rear wheels 12⅞ -13⅜ inch (325-340mm).

Early cars should, in theory, be pressurised to 263 psi while later cars should be at 282 psi, but your main dealer will undoubtedly go by actual wheel arch heights rather than pressure readings when your Mini's suspension is 'pumped up'. 'Later cars' in this instance, by the way, start at the following car numbers:

Saloon (Austin): RHD 830899, LHD 832055.
Saloon (Morris): RHD 370004, LHD 370197.
Cooper (Austin): RHD 830061, LHD 829417.
Cooper (Morris): RHD 830127, LHD 829490.
Cooper 'S' (Austin): RHD 820487, LHD 820514.
Cooper 'S' (Morris): RHD 820705, LHD 820706.

These numbers seem to imply that the recommended change over took place very late in 1965. In fact I strongly suspect that the height changes are no more than recommendations from the manufacturers and that, unless you want to impress the most fanatical of all concours judges, you have the suspension pumped up to whatever

height suits you, within reason (although deviating too far from the recommended settings could lead to odd suspension behaviour and rapid front tyre wear).

Common leak areas include the displacer hose connections at the front, just ahead of the master cylinders (see figure 12).

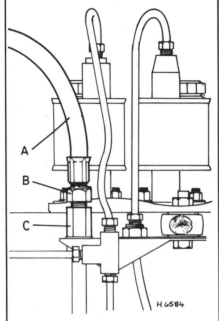

Figure 12.   Hydrolastic displacer hose connections.
A   Hose   C Connector
B   Hose union

S2.   On the other side of the car, the connector (arrowed) is just inboard from the radiator. Check connectors for any signs of fluid leakage or 'droplets' of rust formed by drops of hydraulic fluid escaping. Tighten the connectors up if any traces are discovered, although this one can be very difficult to get at.

S3.   Pull up the boot (arrowed) at the bottom of the front displacer unit to see if the displacer is leaking.

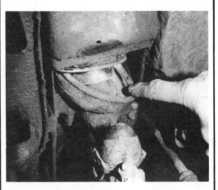

S4.   Do the same at the top of the boot.

S5.   The rear displacer unit sits inside the rear subframe and, once again, the boot should be pulled off and the displacer unit checked for leakage.

Brakes pull to one side

It must be said that Minis with dual circuit brakes (up to August 1984, when disc brakes and 12 inch wheels were fitted as standard) often suffer from erratic pulling to one side under braking. If this should happen, make absolutely certain that all of the hydraulic lines have been properly bled, that all hydraulic components function correctly, that there is no contamination of the brake drums and shoes. If the problem still persists, try swapping *one* brake shoe from left to right of the front brakes. Unfortunately the problem has been known to persist on some 'dual-circuit' Minis in spite of all these measures having been taken: then the only answer is to renew all components, one at a time, until the culprit is found.

Rear brake limiter

The Mini has so little rear end weight that it was necessary on earlier cars to restrict the amount of hydraulic pressure available to the rear brakes to prevent them locking up before the front brakes. Two types of limiter were fitted but neither type can be stripped and rebuilt. If your Mini locks its rear brakes (and the front brakes are not faulty in any way), consider renewing the limiter valve or repairing the later type.

The earlier, single circuit system, pressure reducing valve is mounted on the rear subframe while the later type with four pipe connections, is mounted on the bulkhead crossmember. Before removing either, remove the master cylinder filler cap, place a piece of plastic sheet over the filler and screw the cap down tightly. This helps to reduce fluid loss as components are removed and makes brake bleeding simpler. (Note: not all dual-circuit braked Minis are fitted with a limiter at all.)

Brakes & suspension (rear) – dismantling

All Minis are fitted with drum rear brakes with a single wheel cylinder and brake adjuster. Sizes of wheel cylinder varied from model-to-model so always take the old one as a pattern when buying new wheel cylinders.

See 'Suspension & brakes (general)' section for tools and safety.

BSR1.   The brake adjuster (arrowed) is near the top at the rear of the backplate. The recess around it should be covered over with a plate but they frequently rust and drop off, as this one has. This allows the adjuster threads to rust solid even more quickly than normal. The adjuster head also rusts and rounds off, especially if a special adjuster spanner is not used. Problems of this sort can be overcome by changing the wheel cylinder. Keep the area around the adjuster threads packed with high melting point grease to avoid future adjuster problems. Also it is a good idea to cut a short length of plastic petrol piping and slip it over the adjuster for additional protection, but ensure that there is plenty of grease on the threads too, because the piping will only keep rust off the exposed part of the thread and, of course, adjusters seize where the thread is inside the adjuster body.

BSR2.   Before attempting to remove the brake drum, slacken the adjuster off so that the shoes do not bind on the unworn/rusty parts of the drum and stop it from coming off.

BSR3.   The drum itself is held by two crosshead screws. If they won't come out, use an impact screwdriver, or tap the end of a standard screwdriver with a hammer. Sometimes the screw heads are burred into uselessness, giving the screwdriver nothing to grip on: drift them round (anti-clockwise) with a centre punch and renew them or, as a last resort, use a screw extractor (Eaziout).

BSR4.   The drum should pull straight off, but may need tapping all the way round with a soft-faced hammer or even a piece of wood used as a drift with an ordinary hammer. DON'T use a hammer directly on the drum; it can easily crack. ⇨

BSR5.   Shoes take quite a lot of levering off. Try easing the ends of each shoe, in turn, out of their retaining slots before removing the shoes complete with springs. Note how they are assembled (springs behind shoes) so that you refit them correctly.

BSR6.   A new wheel cylinder just bolts onto the backplate in place of the old one after undoing the brake pipe and the single retaining nut.

BSR7.   With the brake shoes out of the way, take the opportunity to take out and clean the brake adjuster wedges, renewing them if worn too badly. Grease thoroughly using only special BRAKE GREASE during reassembly.

The rear suspension radius arm has to be removed when the radius arm bearings wear (you can't change them yourself without special tools, but you can save money by removing and delivering the radius arm unit to the agents yourself); when Hydrolastic rear displacer or rubber cone has to be renewed; when the subframe is changed and when the suspension height is to be altered on rubber suspension cars (see 'Tuning ' chapter).

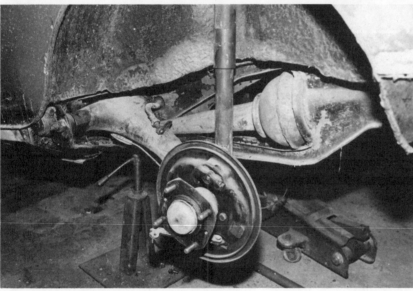

BSR8.   It is not necessary to strip off the brake components, of course, but it is important that the car is supported by substantial axle stands and not just by a jack.

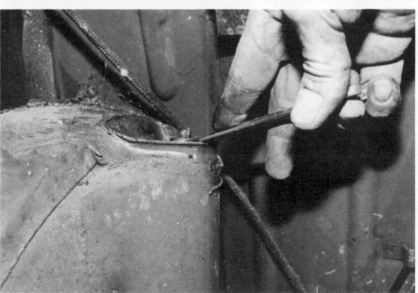

BSR9.   Start by taking off the shock absorber top mounting nut from the side being worked on. The saloon left-hand shocker mounting point is behind the fuel tank — see 'Fuel tank removal' — but only release the fuel tank, leaving the fuel pipe in place. Tip the fuel tank inwards at the top far enough to get your hand behind it. On very early cars, the tank has to be drained and the drain tap removed.

BSR10.   *Disconnect the metal brake pipe from the flexible brake pipe then take the flexible pipe off its bracket on the radius arm. Clamp the pipe with a brake pipe clamp if you don't want to lose too much fluid.*

BSR11.   *Take out the four bolts and spring washers that attach the radius arm to the subframe.*

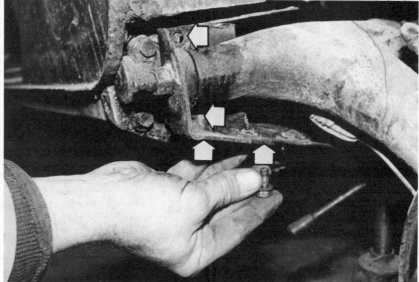

BSR12.   *Then take off the large nut that holds the other end of the radius arm bearing into the subframe. (This shot was taken with the radius arm removed, of course.)*

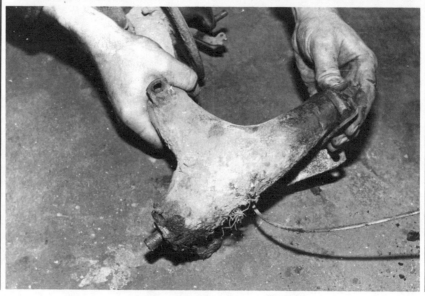

BSR13.   *Another 'fast-forwards' shot, this one shows the handbrake cable still attached. It's easier to detach it at the handbrake if the radius arm is not going to be moved far from the car such as when raising or lowering the (rubber) suspension, but it is best to remove the split pin and clevis pin at the backplate if the radius arm is to be taken right away.*

BSR14. With all disconnections made, pull the radius arm down to free the shock absorber . . .

BSR15. . . . then out and away from the mounting brackets.

BSR16. The suspension 'trumpet' seats in this nylon cup: it breaks up if not lubricated regularly.

BSR17. The trumpet and rubber cone can now be removed from the subframe.

When dismantling the suspension of cars with the Hydrolastic system, the system should already have been depressurised as described earlier in this section. After removing the 'trumpet' (or strut) and disconnecting the Hydrolastic pipe from the displacer, the displacer unit itself is unclipped by turning it anti-clockwise before removal (see Figure 13).

Figure 13. Rear Hydrolastic displacer unit separated from locating plate.
A   Displacer unit   C   Locating plate
B   Locating lugs   D   Subframe

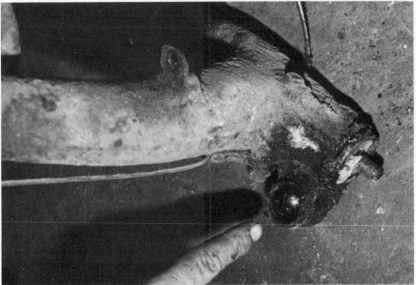

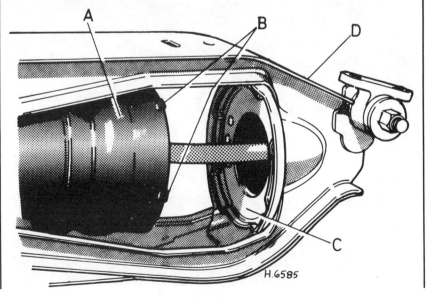

H.6585

BSR18. Sometimes the ball jams in the end of the trumpet, in which case it will have to be driven out with a soft metal drift. Look closely at the ball and, if it's all pitted, renew it.

BSR19. This is the grease nipple that can prevent much trouble with radius arm wear. It is often neglected, which allows the bearings to wear out rapidly.

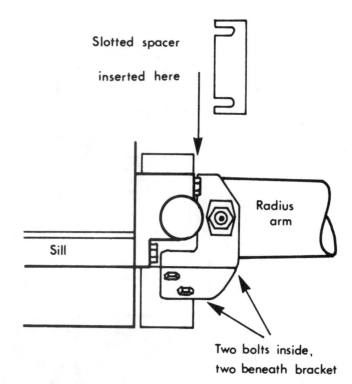

Figure 14. Adjusting toe-in of rear wheels at radius arm mounting.

When refitting the radius arm after renewing the subframe, be sure to have the toe-in of the rear wheels checked. Toe-in should be about 0.062 in. If it is more, insert shims between the radius arm to subframe horizontal mounting bolts (see Figure 14). When refitting, always pack the nylon cup with new grease and make absolutely certain that the trumpets' balls seat properly in their cups before weight is put on the wheels.

Brakes & suspension (front) – dismantling

See 'Suspension & brakes (general)' section for tools and safety.

BSF1. On paper, the Mini front suspension, steering and driveshaft set-up seems horribly complicated, but in practice BMC's development engineers did a brilliant job of making it a relatively straight-forward system to work on. The top suspension arm (A) pivots on the subframe and joins to the hub assembly via a ball joint at its outer end. The bottom suspension arm or wishbone (B) is attached in a similar fashion. Also at the bottom is a tie-rod (C) which stops the assembly from moving back and forth. In the centre, the driveshaft (D) drives the front wheels. The top suspension arm compresses a rubber cone or Hydrolastic displacer unit to provide suspension.

Hub/Brake assembly — dismantling

BSF2. The brake calipers can be taken off (disc brakes only) without disturbing the hydraulic system. Knock back the retaining tab washers, remove the bolts and support the caliper so that there is not too much strain on the hydraulic pipe.

Drum braked cars:

Put a piece of plastic beneath the master cylinder reservoir cap to prevent too much fluid loss, take the wheel flexible hydraulic pipe from the connection to the metal pipe which leaves the hub free to be removed.

BSF3. Pull the split pin out of the large nut which holds the hub in place.

BSF4. Lock the hub with a tyre lever, or something similar, held between the wheel studs and undo the hub nut. It may require quite a lot of force to remove!

BSF5. Save the nut and the thick washer beneath it, but discard the split pin: use a new one next time!

BSF6. Undo the nut on the ball joint holding the steering arm to the steering rack.

BSF7. The steering arm is taper-fitted to the ball joint and such tapers contain their own, natural 'stiction'. Give the end of the arm a couple of sharp blows with a hammer (you'll split the rubber boot if you hit it!) to shock it free. If that doesn't work, try holding another hammer up against the opposite side of the joint. If that doesn't work GO TO BSF8 and/or keep trying.

BSF8. A ball joint splitter (there are several fairly inexpensive types in the accessory shops) is being used on the top suspension joint here and the ball is being struck. You sometimes have to try the lot!

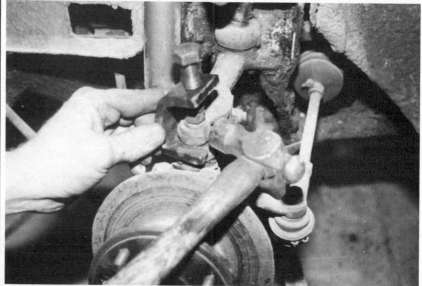

BSF9. In the end, though, they do come off as this shot of the steering arm on the other side of the car shows!

BSF10. Then, you have to go through the whole thing again with the bottom suspension ball joint.

BSF11. Lever the top suspension arm upwards against the springing to remove it from the top ball joint . . .

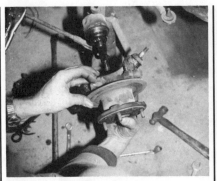

BSF12. . . . at which point the whole hub assembly pulls cleanly off the end of the driveshaft.

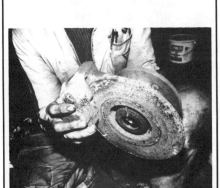

BSF13. What a mess! It is possible to have discs skimmed, but when they get into this disgusting state they are really ready for renewal. In any case, Cooper discs are a bit on the thin side to start with, so you can only shave a whisker with any confidence!

Mini drums, on the other hand, are notorious for going out of true and giving snatchy braking. They often benefit from being checked and skimmed internally by a good engineering shop, if they are in sound condition.

To remove the front drums, see previous section on rear drum removal but note that after 1964 there were two front wheel cylinders/adjusters, instead of one.)

BSF14. The brake assembly (of whichever type) pulls away from the hub assembly.

Figure 15 shows the actual layout of the front hub components of both brake types with the brake disc/brake drum and backplate assembly removed.

Figure 15. Exploded view of the front hub components

A	Drum brake models	7	Taper roller
B	Disc brake models		bearing and
			spacer set
		8	Outer oil seal
		9	Distance ring
1	Swivel hub	10	Driving flange
2	Driveshaft	11	Thrust washer
3	Water shield	12	Castellated hub
4	Inner oil seal		nut
5	Oil seal spacer	13	Wheel stud
6	Ball bearing and	14	Wheel nut
	spacer set	15	Thrust washer

BSF15. The disc itself is removed by taking out the four setscrews holding it in place . . .

BSF16. . . . and tapping it free of the driveshaft mounting.

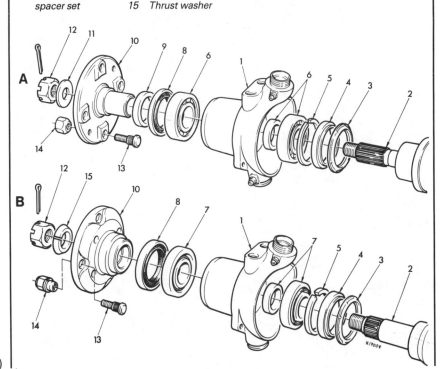

BSF17.   This shot illustrates the differences in thickness, smoothness and thus brake quality between old and new brake discs.

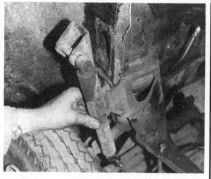

BSF18.   The front shock absorber is fitted on simple bushes top and bottom, while the mounting bracket complete can be removed if required.

BSF19.   Previous shots have shown how the steering rack is disconnected from the steering arms. The rack itself is held to the floor by two U-bolts, and the steering column to the rack by a pinch bolt which must be completely removed before the column and rack can be parted.

BSF20.   Steering ball joints (track rod ends) screw into the ends of the rack: they have an internal thread and flats for 'spannering' them on or off. There is also a locknut against the back of the track rod end which must be freed before the track rod end can be removed. If it has to be renewed, use the position of the locknut as an approximate guide for fitting its replacement, then have the track re-adjusted at a reliable garage as soon as possible: *bad tracking is notorious for ruining Mini tyres.*

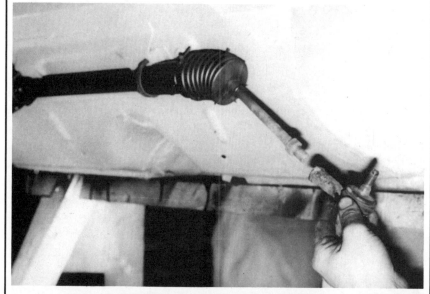

BSF21.   At the base of the front suspension trumpet, covered here by the rubber boot, is a ball and cup, very similar to that of the rear suspension. (The cup shown was damaged during removal.)

BSF22.   The cup often wears through, and the suspension then gives out a horrible, irritating squeak! Use of this much neglected grease nipple is the answer, after first changing the cup of course.

BSF23.   To get at the front suspension trumpet, you really have to compress the front suspension rubber with a special tool, similar to the one used here on the Practical Classics *magazine project Mini.*

BSF24.   This has the effect of taking the pushing force out of the rubber spring so that the whole trumpet and ball can be removed. If you really had to, you can renew the cup without a compressor by levering the trumpet away from the rubber — but it's extremely tough going!

Figure 16 shows how the trumpet (or strut) looks as it is taken out. Its equivalent on hydrolastic suspension models does not need the suspension to be compressed. Instead, the system must be depressurised after which the trumpet can be prised out.

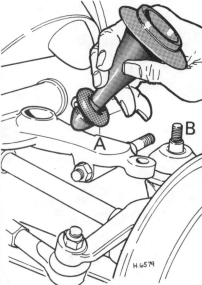

Figure 16. Suspension strut removal — rubber cone spring suspension.

A   Upper suspension arm
B   Upper swivel hub balljoint

BSF25.   If the driveshafts are removed, check that the rubbers are in good condition. Now is the time to do it because removing so many components just to renew split rubbers can be an annoying business!

BSF26.   Fitting the hub assembly back into place is basically a reversal of dismantling, except that the brakes must be bled thoroughly afterwards if hydraulic hoses were disconnected.

BSF27.   In order to properly complete the job, the steel shroud which fits around the brake disc must be replaced. If it has been dismantled for cleaning, the two halves should first be bolted together off the car and then the supporting strap fitted when the shroud is in place on the top of the steering arm joint, as shown.

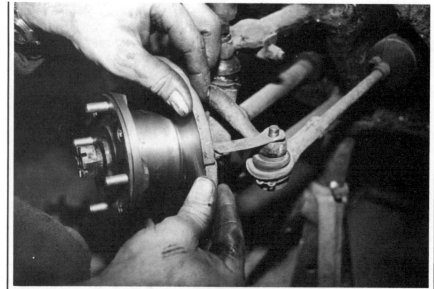

BSF28.   If at any stage you wish to overhaul a caliper, remove it as shown earlier in this section and disconnect the flexible pipe from the back of the caliper, after slackening with a spanner, then unscrewing the caliper from the hose.

BSF29.   Before removing the hose it should be carefully clamped with a self-grip wrench, or preferably a proper hose clamp to prevent the escape of fluid.

BSF30.   You should strip calipers and the master cylinder (it's amazing how often it fails if the calipers or wheel cylinders are overhauled, but the master cylinder ignored). See Haynes Mini Owners' Workshop Manual *for details.*

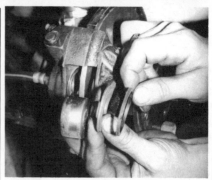

BSF31.   Provided that pistons are not scored or pitted, new seals will do the trick, otherwise exchange calipers will be needed. Don't compromise with braking system components — if in doubt, renew!

Master cylinder renewal and fitting new seals

It cannot be over-emphasised that when working with brake hydraulics, scrupulous cleanliness should be observed. Even minute particles of dirt and oil/grease are the enemies of brake hydraulics. It is dangerous to use old brake fluid, even if clean. If you are giving the braking system a major overhaul, consider the use of silicon-based hydraulic fluid. It is far more expensive than conventional fluid, but unlike standard fluid is not hygroscopic and therefore does not create internal corrosion. It also has a longer service life and better heat tolerance than conventional fluid.

Single circuit systems

MCR1. Start off by detaching the brake pedal from the master cylinder pushrod: pull out the split pin and take out the round clevis pin. Connections are found behind and beneath the heater ducting which runs beneath the dash. It may be helpful to disconnect and remove the ducting. This illustration shows a master cylinder that has already been removed.

MCR2. From inside the engine bay, unscrew the brake pipe union from the top of the master cylinder and carefully bend the brake pipe away to clear the master cylinder.

MCR3. Take off the two nuts and spring washers holding the master cylinder and lift it away from the bulkhead.

All of the references in the following overhaul sequence are to figure 16A.

A. Prepare a clean surface on the workbench covered with newspaper.
B. Tip the remaining fluid from the master cylinder through the filler opening.
C. Take the dust cover right off (item 3).
D. Take out the circlip (item 4) using a pair of circlip pliers, and lift off the pushrod and dished stopwasher (item 5).
E. Tape the bottom of the master cylinder on a wooden block until the piston (item 7) comes out of the cylinder bore.
F. Pull out the piston, followed by all remaining parts (items 2 and 8).
G. Remove the secondary cup seal by stretching it over and off the end of the piston.
H. Lay the parts out in the order of removal and carefully wash each one in clean hydraulic fluid and then dry them with a clean, lint-free rag so that all metal surfaces can be inspected.
I. Examine the cylinder bore and piston carefully for signs of scoring or ridges in the bore. If there is any sign of scoring or ridges, renew the whole master cylinder: brakes are too important to take chances with!
J. If the bore and piston are perfect fit **NEW** seals (*never* re-use old ones − they are inexpensive in any case). Begin by thoroughly lubricating the internal components in fresh, clean hydraulic fluid.

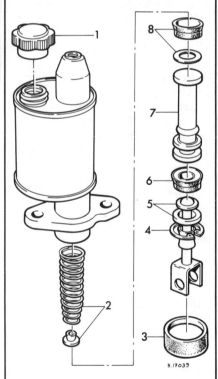

Figure 16A Single circuit master cylinder.

1	Filler cap	6	Secondary cup seal
2	Spring and spring retainer	7	Piston
3	Dust cover	8	Piston washer and main cup seal
4	Circlip		
5	Pushrod and stop washer		

K. Using fingers only, place the secondary cup seat in position on the piston with the lip of the cup facing the opposite (drilled) end of the piston.

L. Position the non-return valve over the large diameter of the spring and the spring retainer over the smaller diameter, and place this assembly into the cylinder bore, larger diameter first.

M. Now insert the main cup seal into the cylinder bore, lip end first followed by the washer.

N. Insert the piston assembly into the cylinder bore followed by the pushrod, dished washer and circlip. Ensure that the circlip fully enters its groove.

O. Lubricate the new dust cover with rubber grease (not the normal type, which rots rubber), and stretch it over the pushrod and into position on the end of the cylinder.

Refitting the master cylinder is a straightforward reversal of the removal sequence. If there is a great deal of play in the brake pedal to master cylinder pushrod joint, which frequently happens after prolonged use, fit a new clevis pin. This after welding up the ovality in the brake pedal rod and redrilling it to clearance size, so that the clevis pin moves freely. If the master cylinder pushrod holes are worn, replace the pushrod with a new one if possible, or it may be necessary to purchase a new master cylinder complete. It will, of course, be necessary to bleed the complete brake system — see the relevant section.

Dual circuit master cylinder (early type)

Removal and refitting are very similar to that of the single circuit type except, of course, that these are two pipe connections. When reconnecting, fit the two pipes to the master cylinder before bolting it back down, otherwise the pipework may be difficult to align with the cylinder body. (Pipework and mounting details in figure 16B.)

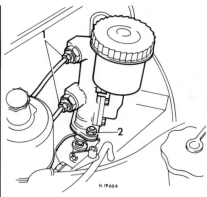

Figure 16B   Removal of the early type dual circuit master cylinder.

1 Hydraulic pipe unions   2 Retaining nuts

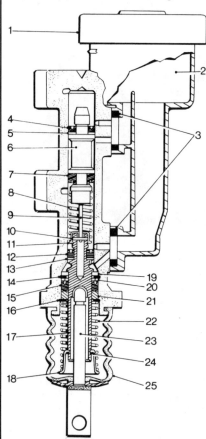

Figure 16C   Early type dual circuit master cylinder.

1	Filler cap	14	Circlip
2	Plastic reservoir	15	Cup
3	Reservoir seals	16	Circlip
4	Main cup	17	Piston
5	Piston washer	18	Spring retainer
6	Piston	19	Stop washer
7	Main cup	20	Washer
8	Spring	21	Bearing
9	Piston link	22	Spring
10	Pin	23	Pushrod
11	Pin retainer	24	Spirolex ring
12	Main cup	25	Rubber boot
13	Piston washer		

Figure 16C is relevant to the following instructions.

A. Prepare a clean surface on the workbench, covered with newspaper.

B. Tip the remaining fluid from the master cylinder through the filler opening.

C. Mount the master cylinder in a vice with protected jaws so that the mouth of the cylinder bore is uppermost.

D. Slide off the rubber boot, compress the return spring and using a small screwdriver, remove the Spirolex ring from its groove in the primary piston. Take care not to distort the coils of the ring or score the bore of the cylinder.

E. Using a pair of circlip pliers, remove the piston retaining circlip.

F. Carefully move the piston up and down in the bore so as to free the nylon guide bearing and cap seal. Lift away the guide bearing seal.

G. Lift away the plain washer.

H. Using a pair of circlip pliers, remove the inner circlip.

I. The primary and secondary piston assembly, complete with the stop washer, may now be withdrawn from the cylinder bore.

J. Lift away the stop washer.

K. Compress the spring that separates the two pistons then using a small diameter parallel pin punch or a suitable round nail with the point sawn off drive out the roll pin that retains the piston link.

L. Inspect and note the positions of the rubber cups (look for the moulded indentations) and then remove the cups and washers from the pistons.

M. Undo and remove the four bolts that hold the plastic reservoir to the body and lift away the reservoir.

N. Recover the two reservoir sealing rings.

O. Unscrew and remove the hydraulic pipe connection adaptors, discard the copper gaskets and then recover the spring and trap valves.

P. Wash all parts in clean hydraulic fluid or methylated spirits and wipe dry.

Q. Examine the cylinder bore and

piston carefully for any signs of scoring or ridges in the bore. If there is any sign of scoring or ridges, renew the whole master cylinder. If the bore and piston are perfect fit **NEW** seals (*never* re-use old ones).

R. Reassembly of the master cylinder is the reverse sequence to dismantling but the following additional points should be noted.

(i) All components should be assembled wet by dipping in clean brake fluid.

(ii) Locate the piston washer over the head of the secondary piston, convex surface first and then carefully ease the secondary cup over the piston and seat it with its flat surface against the washer.

(iii) Fit new copper gaskets to the connection adaptors.

Dual circuit master cylinder – later type

Removal and replacement is very similar to that of the earlier types of master cylinder, as described in the previous sub-sections, except that this type has an electrical brake warning connector which must also be removed. The entire system

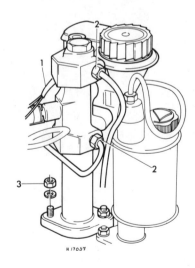

Figure 16D   Removal of the later type dual circuit master cylinder.

1   Electrical wiring to failure switch
2   Hydraulic pipe unions
3   Retaining nuts

must of course be bled on reassembly: see the relevant section. (Pipework and mounting details in figure 16D.)

Figure 16E is relevant to the following overhaul sequence.

A. Prepare a clean surface on the workbench, covered with newspaper.

B. Tip the remaining fluid out of the master cylinder through the filler opening.

C. Mount the cylinder in a vice with protected jaws, so that the reservoir is uppermost.

D. Unscrew the two reservoir retaining screws and lift the reservoir off the master cylinder body. Carefully withdraw the two reservoir sealing washers from the outlets.

E. Push in the pushrod as far as possible, and using pliers extract the secondary piston stop pin from its recess.

F. Release the pushrod rubber boot from the end of the cylinder, push the pushrod in and extract the retaining circlip. Now lift away the pushrod assembly.

G. Remove the master cylinder from the vice, tap it on a block of

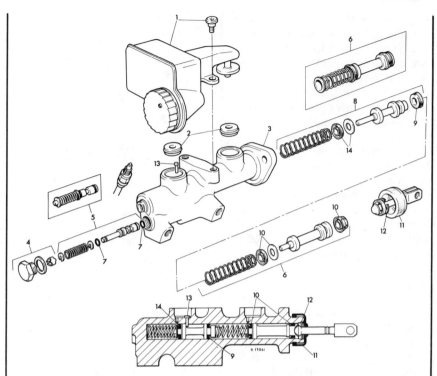

Figure 16E   Later type dual circuit master cylinder.

1   Reservoir and retaining screw
2   Reservoir sealing washers
3   Master cylinder body
4   End plug assembly
5   Pressure differential piston (insert shows alternative assembly)
6   Primary piston and spring (insert shows alternative assembly)
7   Piston rubber seals
8   Secondary piston and spring
9   Secondary piston seals
10   Primary piston seals
11   Dust cover
12   Circlip
13   Stop pin
14   Secondary piston seals

wood and withdraw the primary and secondary piston assemblies from the cylinder bore.

H. Unscrew the brake failure switch from the cylinder body.

I. Unscrew the end plug and washer, then remove the distance piece and pressure differential piston assembly.

J. Note the position and direction of fitting of the rubber seals on the piston assemblies, and then carefully remove them.

K. Wash all the parts in clean hydraulic fluid and dry with a lint-free cloth.

L.   Examine the bore of the master cylinder carefully for any signs of scores or ridges. If found to be smooth all over, **NEW** seals can be fitted. If, however, there is any doubt about the condition of the bore, then a new cylinder must be obtained and fitted. Never re-use old seals, as they will have deteriorated with age even though this may not be evident during visual inspection.

M.   Reassembly of the master cylinder is the reverse sequence to dismantling, but the following additional points should be noted:

(i)   Thoroughly lubricate all components in clean hydraulic fluid and assemble them wet.

(ii)   Refit the seals onto the pistons using fingers only, and ensure that they are fitted the correct way round.

(iii)   When refitting the secondary piston assembly, push the piston down the bore using a soft metal rod or wooden dowel and insert the stop pin. The primary piston and remaining components can then be fitted.

Brake pressure failure warning light actuator – overhaul

This unit, fitted only with the earlier type of dual circuit braking system, operates the warning light which informs the driver of failure of one of the hydraulic systems. The lamp sometimes comes on after simple brake bleeding. It should go off after a hard application of the brakes but if not, re-bleed the brakes. If at any time, the light comes on and stays on; there is a fault in one of the hydraulic systems, or a fault in the actuator or switch. If the brake warning light does *not* come on when the brake pedal is pushed but *does* come on when the test-push on the switch is operated, then everything is okay.

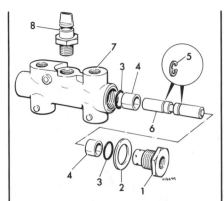

Figure 16F   Pressure differential warning actuator.

1	End adaptor	5	Circlip
2	Copper washer	6	Piston
3	O-ring	7	Body
4	Sleeve	8	Switch

Overhaul

Follow the same sort of procedures regarding care and cleanliness as you would follow when dismantling any hydraulic parts. (All references are to figure 16F.)

A.   Clean off the unit very thoroughly so that no dirt or grit gets inside, as it is removed.

B.   Disconnect the hydraulic pipes, disconnect the electrical connections and take off the unit.

C.   Take out the end plug (item 1) and discard the copper washer.

D.   Unscrew the warning light switch (item 8).

E.   Tap the body on a block of wood to 'encourage' the shuttle valve piston assembly to poke its head out (item 6), then remove.

F.   Strip the assembly and examine the bores as for a brake master cylinder. If there is *any* scoring renew the whole unit. Otherwise renew the seals. **NEVER** refit old seals (item 3). Replace the copper washer (item 2) with a new one.

After refitting the unit and bleeding the system, check carefully that the warning light functions correctly, re-bleeding as necessary. Insert the hydraulic pipes into the actuator body before refitting it to the car: alignment of the pipes thus becomes easier.

Brake lines

Tool Box

Open ended spanners; Brake pipe forming tools if making your own pipework.

Safety

If you make your own brake pipes, make absolutely certain that all flares are properly formed so that a good seal is achieved inside the brake pipe union. Always renew brake pipe nuts with those of the correct type. Make certain that you, or whoever makes the replacement pipe, make a 'single' or 'double' flare, to match the one of the pipe being replaced. Use Kunifer rather than steel tubing because it will not corrode. Copper stands a theoretical risk of snapping after work-hardening from the vibration found in certain locations.

BL1.   Always use the old brake pipe as a pattern for making the new one. Even if it breaks as you remove it, it will still be invaluable for this purpose. Don't bother straightening it to measure the new length of pipe; instead lay the old pipe against the new one a section at a time, rolling the new pipe against the old at the bends.

BL2. If you have access to a proper pipe cutting tool, use it, because the quality of cut will be much higher. You tighten the cutter until it touches the pipe, turn the cutter a couple of times round the pipe, tighten half a turn, rotate the cutter round the pipe again, and so on until the pipe is cut through.

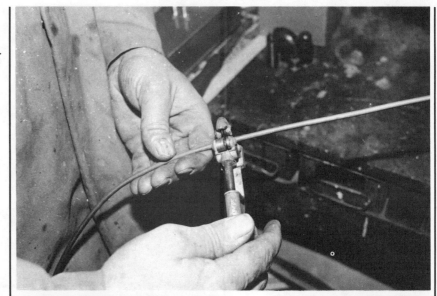

BL3. If you hacksaw through the pipe (a 'junior' saw is best) you must then file the end dead square.

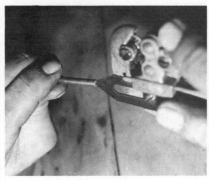

BL4. Whether you use a cutter or a saw, use a de-burring tool to clear any burr from the inside of the pipe. Then blow through thoroughly to get rid of any swarf or filings.

BL5. Place the wing nut (A) of the flaring tool over the pipe, push the end of the pipe into the throat of the tool and fit the collets (B) each side of the pipe with the pipe sticking out of the collets by a small fraction.

BL6. Next, use the dolly (C) to push the collets back into the throat of the tool and the pipe end dead level with the front of the collets.

BL7.   The dolly is pushed into the receiver on the end of the screw thread which acts like a press, pushing against the collets and pipe. The collets are held tight into the throat of the tool by the wing nut (left) which screws onto a thread on the back of the collets and draws them back into the taper of the throat.

BL8.   With pipe tightly gripped, the dolly is changed for a flaring tool which is forced into the end of the pipe by the screw thread and handle in the foreground.

BL9.   When a double flare is required, a single flare is first formed and then the 'Number One' flaring tool changed for a 'Number Two' which is again forced into the end of the pipe making a double flare.

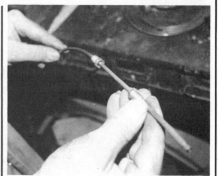

BL10.   Before the other end of the pipe is flared, both nuts must be slipped onto the pipe (facing the correct ways of course).

BL11.   To illustrate the point — both of them, in fact — from left to right is a double flaring tool; a double flared pipe with 'female' nut (for fitting to the 'male' ends of the flexible brake pipe); a single flared pipe with 'male' nut for fitting to wheel cylinders, brake light switches and other fittings with an internal thread.

BL12. After making the pipe as a long straight piece, use the old pipe as a guide to bending the new piece of pipe to fit the car. Don't bend the pipe too acutely.

BL13. You will probably have to make final adjustments when fitting up. Make absolutely certain that new pipes cannot chaffe on wheels when they are on full lock, or on the full limits of suspension travel, and that they cannot rub on any other moving parts or cause an electrical short-circuit, and that any long runs, such as under the car's body or along the rear subframe, are properly supported. Pipes have to meet their unions squarely or you will have difficulty getting the nuts to screw in or on. If you have great difficulty, take the union off or loosen it, fit the pipe nuts up and then refit or retighten the union.

If you intend renewing a complete set of brake lines, you may well be better off going to a firm like 'Handy' who make, for specific cars, complete brake pipe sets all of the correct length and with flares and nuts already fitted.

Flexible brake hoses

FBP1. In time, flexible brake hoses can perish and become weakened. Check them by bending them back: if any cracks or any other form of deterioration then shows, renew the hose before it gets to the stage where it can burst when the brakes are applied hard, which is always the time when you need them most, of course!

You may wish to go over to a rather more expensive but tougher type of flexible hose such as the 'Aeroquip' hose covered in braided metal. Removal and refitting of all types is as follows:

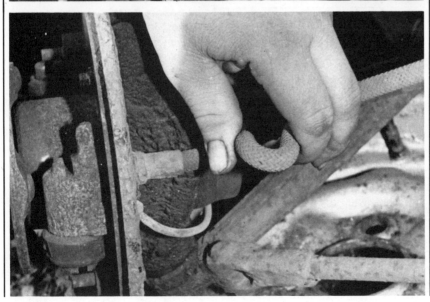

FBP2.   First, unscrew the brake
master cylinder cap and screw it
back down tight with a piece of
plastic sheet beneath it. This seals it
and greatly reduces the amount of
fluid lost, and thus the amount of
brake bleeding required.

FBP3.   Now release the union
joining the rigid brake pipe to the
end of the flexible hose. In this case,
it lay beneath where the radiator
would have been, had it been fitted,
so this view is from inside the
engine bay.

FBP4.   With a spanner to lock the
flexible hose as shown here from
inside the wheel arch . . .

FBP5.   . . . the retaining nut and
spring washer can be removed and
the flexible pipe pulled away from its
bracket or, as in this case, from the
mounting point in the front
subframe.

FBP6.   It is now a simple matter to
unscrew the brake wheel cylinder
end of the flexible pipe in the usual
anti-clockwise direction.

Bleeding the brake hydraulic system

After the fitting of any brake lines or
brake components, it is essential to
bleed all air out of the brake
hydraulic systems otherwise air
bubbles trapped in the pipe will
compress instead of pressure being
available to work the brakes. The
main symptom is pedal 'sponginess'
(softness when the brake pedal is
pushed), compared with the firm
'pedal' which is obtained from air-
free brake lines.

When bleeding the brakes,
remember to top up the reservoir
with fresh fluid every 6-8 strokes of

the pedal. Do not re-use even fresh
fluid as it comes out of the braking
system, because it will almost
certainly be aerated by tiny bubbles,
which is exactly what you are trying
to get rid of, and do not use old
brake fluid that has been standing
uncovered to the air because brake
fluid is hygroscopic, which means
that it absorbs water vapour from
the atmosphere. Once water is
absorbed, the high
pressures/temperatures inside
brake pipes, make it form a vapour
lock which has the same effect as
air in the brake lines or even render
the brakes totally ineffective in
severe cases.

Brake bleeding involves
slackening off a bleed screw on
each of the wheel cylinders in turn
and pumping fluid through the
system until all the air is expelled.
Bleeding single-circuit brakes is
straightforward but the procedure
for dual-circuit brakes is a little more
complex. Details follow.

When bleeding brakes, it is
strongly recommended that you use
one of the many so-called 'one-
man' brake bleeding kits. These
incorporate a one-way valve so that,
as the foot is removed from the
brake pedal in the following
process, air is not drawn back into
the system. However, the system is
not infallible because it is often
possible for air to be drawn through
the bleed tube where it push-fits
onto the bleed screw, but such
systems are invariably superior to
the more long-winded system
involving a clean jam-jar, a length of
clear plastic tubing that is a tight fit
over the bleed screw and a ring
spanner.

Brake bleeding without a 'one-man' kit

Clean the area around the bleed
screw. Push the clear plastic tube
over the bleed screw after first
locating the ring spanner on the
screw with enough clearance to first
untighten and then retighten it.
Pour an inch or so of brake fluid into

a jam jar and hold the free end of the plastic tube beneath the level of the fluid in the jar. (Check that the master cylinder is topped up.) Have an assistant inside the car with a foot on the brake pedal. You position yourself near to the wheel cylinder and release the bleed screw by half a turn or slightly more. Say the word 'Down' to your assistant, who should push the pedal right down to the floor steadily, but not too slowly, taking perhaps a couple of seconds. He/she should then reiterate the word 'Down' to indicate that the stroke is complete. You then retighten the bleed screw to prevent air re-entering the system, and tell your assistant to let the pedal 'Up'. He/she says 'Up' to tell you that it is now up! As the pedal is pushed down, you may see nothing at first as air is pushed out of the system or you may see bubbles rising through the fluid in the jar. Continue bleeding at each bleed screw until no more air is pushed out, which can take anything from half-a-dozen to dozens of pumps, depending on the length of the brake line, whether a servo is fitted and whether any bubbles of air are trapped in the pipe. Try asking your assistant to give four steady pushes to every two hard, rapid pushes. If your assistant notices any pressure at the pedal, you may not have slackened the bleed screw sufficiently. The master cylinder level must be kept up through this whole process.

Brake bleeding with a 'one-man' kit

It becomes possible with such kits to bleed brakes without an assistant (although the author would always go back later and re-bleed for a couple of strokes with the aid of an assistant, to make certain that no air was creeping back in). Even with an assistant, bleeding becomes much quicker because the bleed screw does not have to be tightened/untightened between each stroke.

Brake bleeding general notes and sequence

During bleeding top up the master cylinder every 6-8 strokes. THIS IS VITAL because if you do not and the fluid level falls too low, you will draw air into the system and have to begin bleeding the whole system again from scratch. DON'T SPILL FLUID ON THE PAINTWORK OF YOUR CAR because it can act like paint stripper and remove or at least damage your paintwork. Wrap a rag around the neck of the master cylinder to catch any fluid spillage (it makes a mess of the engine bay too) and use a flash lamp to check the fluid level. If you have renewed something at one of the extremities of the brake system, such as a wheel cylinder or flexible pipe, you should easily get away with bleeding only the section of brakes which you have worked on. If you exchange the master cylinder or a major section of pipework you will have to bleed the whole system as follows:
1.   Bleed the l.h. front brake.
2.   Bleed the r.h. front brake.
3.   Bleed the l.h. back brake.
4.   Bleed the r.h. back brake.
5.   Go all the way round the whole system once more to remove any air bubbles that may have been pushed from one part of the system to another. If the pedal still feels spongy, repeat the process until a) no more air bubbles can be seen to come out and b) the pedal ceases to feel spongy.

Early type dual circuit brakes (with separate warning actuator)

The process is exactly the same as for single-circuit brakes but with the following important differences:
1.   If only half the system has been disconnected, it should only be necessary to bleed that half of the system, provided that no air has entered the other half.
2.   If the entire system has to be bled, refer to figure 16G and bleed

the brakes in the sequence A, B, C, D for right-hand drive car and B, A, D, C for left-hand drive vehicles.
3.   The brake pedal should be depressed rapidly then held down for THREE SECONDS before releasing. Wait FIFTEEN SECONDS between each individual pump of the pedal.
4.   After bleeding is complete, check that the pressure warning actuator operates correctly. If the light is 'on', press the pedal hard, when it should go off. If it fails to do so, there is a fault in the warning actuator, OR the pressure is unbalanced and the braking system is faulty or needs re-bleeding. If this fails to cure the trouble, investigate the actuator and switch.
The system works correctly when the warning light does *not* come on as the pedal is pressed but *does* come on when the test-push switch is operated.

Later type dual circuit brakes (with warning switch incorporated into master cylinder body)

1.   First, before bleeding the brakes, remove the brake failure pressure switch from the side of the master cylinder body. *NB: if the master cylinder has been renewed, and there is a plastic spacer between the pressure switch and master cylinder body, leave it in place until bleeding has been completed and then discard it.*
2.   Again, if only components in one half of the system have been disturbed, only that half will need to be bled. If the entire system has to be bled, however, you must check in your handbook to see whether your Mini's system is diagonally-split or front-to-rear split, which is the system used on latest Minis.
3.   For diagonally-split systems, refer to figure 16G and bleed in the order A, B, C, D for right-hand drive cars and C, D, A, B for left-hand drive cars.
4.   If the system is split front-to-rear, bleed the brakes in the order

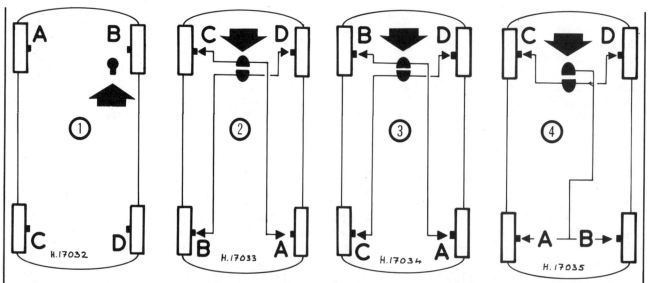

Figure 16G   Brake hydraulic system bleeding sequences.

1   Bleeding sequence for single circuit braking systems – see text.
2   Bleeding sequence for early dual circuit braking systems with separate pressure differential warning actuator – see text.
3   Bleeding sequence for diagonal split dual circuit braking systems with inbuilt pressure differential warning actuator – see text.
4   Bleeding sequence for front-to-rear split dual circuit braking systems with inbuilt pressure differential warning actuator – see text.

A, B, C, D (figure 16G) irrespective of driving position.
5.   As with the earlier dual-circuit system, the pedal must be held down for THREE SECONDS at the bottom of each pump of the pedal and FIFTEEN SECONDS left after the pedal is released before pumping it again.
6.   Refit the brake failure pressure switch after completing the bleeding operation.

Engine gearbox removal

As I have shown in other parts of this book, particularly in connection with front subframe removal, the engine can be removed downwards complete with the subframe (see

'Front subframe removal' section) or uphill, through the bonnet opening, leaving subframe and front suspension behind. Of the two, engine removal through the bonnet opening is the easier, especially with Hydrolastic suspension Minis.

Tool Box

Full range of socket, ring and socket spanners, pliers, range of screwdrivers, large lever, engine hoist.

Safety

Never work, or stand, beneath an engine held up on a winch; the sturdiest of models can give way and ropes can break. If

possible, make a mechanical fixing to the engine rather than using ropes. THE ROCKER BOX COVER STUDS ARE ONLY MARGINALLY STRONG ENOUGH. THE FIXING METHOD SHOWN UNDER "ENGINE REFITTING" IS PREFERABLE.

ER1.   This is a Cooper engine but in fact the basic principles of removing any Mini engine are the same. There are minor differences between models such as Coopers with LCB manifold, for example, when the manifold is disconnected from the exhaust pipe and then left on the engine while the engine is removed. **BEFORE STARTING WORK, DISCONNECT THE BATTERY.**

ER2. First step is to remove the bonnet by undoing the nuts from the fixed studs in the hinges. Prop the bonnet open with the bonnet stay. Mark the relative positions of the bonnet bracket/hinge with a soft pencil to aid accurate refitting.

ER3. Then lift the bonnet away and store it somewhere safe. Also, if the car's paintwork is not to be damaged, drape a couple of large old blankets or something similar over the wing tops.

ER4. The author purchased an engine hoist from Intec Project Engineering who make two models of heavy duty but relatively inexpensive engine hoists. This is their larger model and has a boom that extends outwards giving three different reaches. The hire of one of these hoists would be well worth considering from local tool hire firms (addresses will be found in the phone directory) and there are screwed types of hoist available, but these hydraulically operated tools are far superior.

ER5. The other advantage of the Intec hoist is that it will fit into the boot of a medium sized car, even a sports GT like this MGB.

ER6. Meanwhile, back in the engine bay . . . the heater cable was disconnected by undoing the clamp that holds the outer casing and the pin through which the inner cable passes.

ER7. An early job must be to take out the fresh air/heater trunking. If the earlier, paper covered type is fitted, take care not to collapse it. You can, if you wish, simply wire the trunking back out of the way.

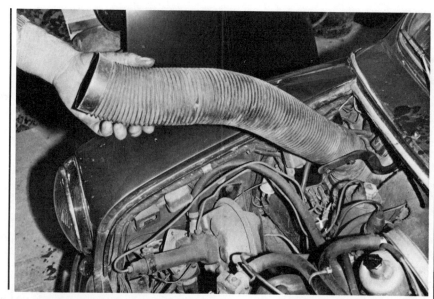

ER8. Before removing plug leads and distributor cover, mark each lead with blobs of paint or bands of tape or by any other means that takes your fancy so that you know instantly where each lead goes when you reassemble. Take care not to drop and lose the small brass washer that goes beneath the knurled nut that holds the H.T. lead to the coil on earlier models.

ER11. . . . making it extremely sensible to tag, at the very least, the two coil leads so that you will know which way round to reconnect them. (The trouble with connecting these two up wrongly is that the car will run, but with a small loss in efficiency.)

ER9. Getting down into the second level now . . . take off the starter solenoid and, if necessary, tag the leads that come from it.

ER10. The same applies to the dynamo or alternator and the coil, where the number of leads is greater . . .

ER12. Now the alternator or dynamo can be slackened off on the adjuster, the fan belt slipped off the pulley, and with adjuster and two pivot bolts taken out, it can be lifted away.

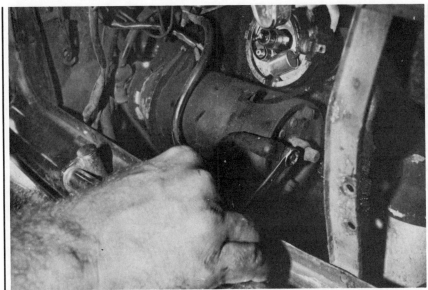

ER13.   It's a good idea to remove the grille at this stage: some are held in with a few self-tapping screws, others have 'accessory' finger-and-thumb screws, a few are fixed by pop-rivets. In the latter case drill the heads off and replace the grille later with more pop rivets or with self-tappers.

ER14.   After undoing the starter motor cable, the starter motor itself can be unbolted and removed through the same opening. Don't forget the earth strap which on early models is fixed to the flywheel housing bolts.

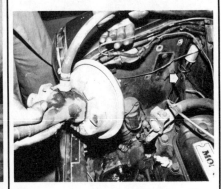

ER15.   The servo hydraulic pipework can be unscrewed (when a servo is fitted) and it saves a lot of fluid spillage if the two unions are connected temporarily to one another by a length of plastic or rubber pipe. The vacuum pipe can be left on the servo but released from the manifold while the unit itself is usually bolted through the bracket arrowed.

ER16.   The carburettor(s) are removed by disconnecting throttle and choke cables from the carb(s), fuel feed pipe and the emission control pipework (if fitted). Some prefer removing the carbs separately from the manifold.

ER17.   The inlet manifold shares the same studs as the exhaust manifold. ''But how do you get at them?'' you ask. It is difficult, but just think of it as a kind of Yoga for fingers!

ER18.   Unbolt the clutch slave cylinder from the flywheel housing but don't disconnect the hydraulic pipe from it. Wire the slave cylinder somewhere convenient but well out of the way of the engine as it comes out.

ER19.   Take out the bolt that holds the top engine steady in place and swing the steady leftwards and well out of the way.

ER20.   Now take the opportunity, if you wish, of draining the block and radiator. Push a plastic tube over the end of the drain tap (if fitted), or even leave draining the engine until later, so that you can enjoy the luxury of grovelling around on the floor in the dry in the next stages.

ER21.   There have been three different types of gearchange fitted to Minis. The remote-type change bolts up to the gearbox casing via four bolts on the front end of the remote change casing (arrowed). On models with a direct change (the pudding-stirrer type), disconnect the rubber boot fitted to the base of the gearstick, inside the car and slide it up the stick a little, from under the car, take out the two bolts holding the stick into the gearbox and remove the gearstick along with the anti-rattle spring and plunger from inside the housing.

The third type is the later rod-change type of remote control (see Figure 17). Start by drifting out the roll pin which holds the collar of the remote control extension rod to the selector shaft (arrow 1). Undo the bolt holding the steady rod to the differential housing (arrow 2) and remove it. Both are now released from the gearbox.

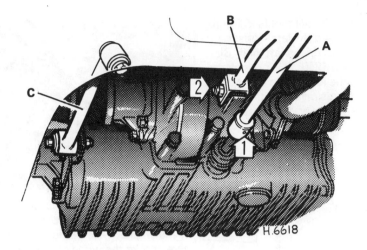

Figure 17. Gearchange and lower tie-bar attachments on the rod — change-type gearbox
A Extension Rod
B Steady rod
C Lower tie-bar
(1 & 2 — see text)

ER22. On the rear of the gearchange housing is a large 'cotton reel' rubber mounting which attaches the housing to a large bracket underneath the floor; it is held in place by a nut and flat washers.

ER23. Shown with the engine out of the car, this is the rubber coupling at the inner end of each driveshaft. Undo and remove the two U-bolts holding the driveshaft to the coupling and move the driveshaft out of the way.

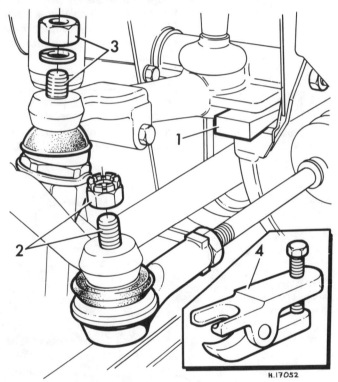

Note. When refitting the early type of coupling and when removing or refitting the later type, it is necessary to release the upper suspension swivel arm (Figure 18, item 3) using a ball joint splitter like the one shown in Figure 18 as item 4 or as described in the section on 'Front Suspension'. This is so that the top of the swivel hub can move outwards, and therefore give sufficient clearance. Workshop manuals usually suggest releasing the steering tie-rod ball joint too (Figure 18, item 2) but it will probably be OK to turn the steering to right lock when working on the

Figure 18. Separation of the suspension and steering balljoint assemblies
1 Packing wedge
2 Steering tie-rod balljoint assembly
3 Swivel hub balljoint assembly
4 Unversal balljoint separator

right-hand side and left lock on the left, thus extending the steering arm sufficiently far out of the rack to give clearance. Remember to use a wedge (Figure 18, item 1) to hold the suspension compressed. This is in place of the rebound rubber which must be removed before jacking the car up and taking the front wheels off.

There is a special tool (see Figure 19) for releasing the later, offset sphere type of driveshaft joint, BL number '18G 1240'. It is possible to withdraw the joint using a tyre lever or something similar pivoting the lever against the end cover retaining bolt directly below the joint.

ER24. *This is the oil pressure gauge take-off pipe fitted to the rear of the engine. Disconnect the pipe here or take the wires off the sender unit if an electrically operated gauge is fitted. Also disconnect the wires from the water temperature gauge sender unit.*

Before attempting to lift the engine, make sure that the parts shown in Figure 20 (not necessarily mentioned/shown in the photo-sequence) are removed. Unbolt the oil cooler (where fitted) and remove it, taking care not to damage it, as the engine is removed. Remove the ignition shield from the front of the engine (where fitted). Disconnect the fuel inlet hose from the mechanical fuel pump on those Minis with such a pump. Take out the heater/demister blower unit from the engine bay and, if necessary, take off the horn.

ER25. *Undo the bolts holding the engine mountings to the front subframe (two bolts at each end), leaving the engine free to be lifted out.*

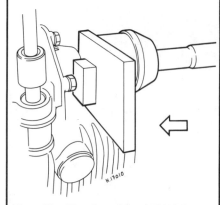

Figure 19. Use of special tool 18G1240 to release offset sphere driveshaft joint

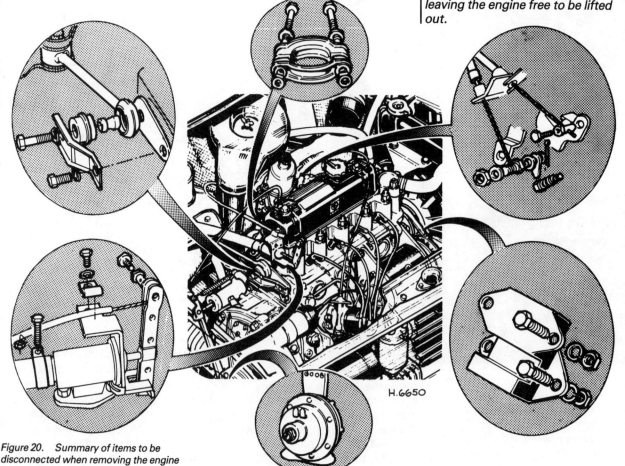

H.6650

Figure 20. Summary of items to be disconnected when removing the engine and manual transmission.

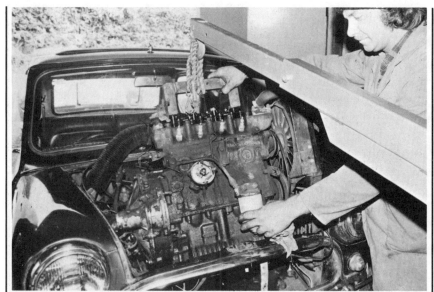

ER26.   Lift the engine a little, then, making absolutely certain that it is safe to do so . . .

ER27.   . . . undo the bolt that holds the normally virtually inaccessible speedo to the gearbox . . .

ER28.   . . . and pull out the speedo cable and drive gear complete. REMEMBER TO PUT IT BACK AT THIS STAGE WHEN REFITTING THE ENGINE!

ER29.   With the engine out of the way, take the chance to clean the engine bay with a grease solvent, and perhaps even to rub it down and repaint it.

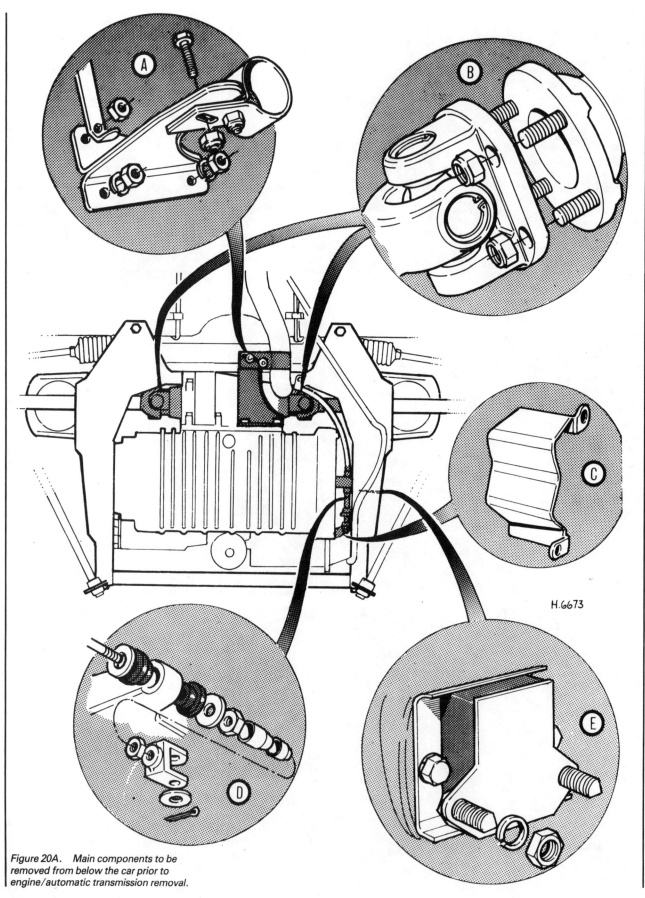

H.6673

Figure 20A.   Main components to be
removed from below the car prior to
engine/automatic transmission removal.

Engine removal – automatic transmission models

The procedure is much the same as for manual transmission models but with the following differences in approach. (All references in the following text to figure 20A.)

1.   Beneath the car, disconnect the exhaust pipe strap from the support bracket on the differential housing. Then take off the support bracket (item A).

2.   If the driveshafts are fitted with Hardy Spicer (Hooke's type) UJs at their inner ends, undo and remove the nuts holding the two UJs to the differential flanges. However, if the driveshafts are fitted with offset sphere joints at their inner ends, remove them as follows: release the steering arm balljoints using a balljoint splitter. Undo the front suspension swivel hub balljoint as shown in the section on front suspension and allow the tops of the swivel hubs to hang outwards, taking care not to strain the brake flexible hoses. Release the offset sphere joints from the differential using BL tool 18G 1240 or it is possible to withdraw the joints using a tyre lever pivoted against the end cover retaining bolt, directly below the joint (item B).

3.   Take off the gear selector bellcrank cover plate from the right-hand end of the transmission casing (item C).

4.   Undo the clevis pin or nut, washer and pivot bolt (depending on age of car) holding the selector cable fork to the bellcrank lever. Slacken the fork retaining nut and unscrew the fork from the cable. Take off the fork retaining nut and slide off the two rubber ferrules. Remove the selector outer cable adjusting nut and pull the whole cable out of the transmission casing bracket (item D).

5.   When the engine hoist has been attached, as described in the main section, lift the engine so that you have just taken the weight of the power unit and no more. Take out the four nuts and bolts holding the engine mountings to the sides of the subframe (item E).

Engine strip

The following sequences show the various stages in rebuilding a Cooper 'S' 1275 engine and there are a few differences in construction/fittings between this and other 'A'-series engines. Where differences are encountered, they are pointed out in the text and illustrated where necessary with line drawings.

The engine used in this sequence belongs to a delightfully original Cooper 'S' (LDL 784F), owned by enthusiast Mr Simon Allsop of Malvern, England. The work was carried out in most impressive and efficient manner by Moss Engineering of Ledbury (see 'Specialists' in appendix). Many owners may wish to carry out their own engine rebuild after taking the major components to a reconditioner for reboring, etc. In practice, the final cost of DIY rebuilding is about the same, but some owners just want the satisfaction of rebuilding their own car's engine.

ES1.   The engine assembly was lifted bodily from the back of the author's Land-Rover by three men which is generally accepted as the number required to lift the Mini engine/gearbox unit complete.

ES2.   If you have the use of a hoist, so much the better. It's not likely to be of the travelling type like this one, but you can always bring the workbench to the engine. Alternatively, put a piece of clean hardboard on the floor and work there: it's the safest place!

'The Mini engine can just be lifted by three strong men . . .'

ES3.   Drain all the oil and water if you haven't already done so, but leave the oil filter in place to drain it when it is stripped from the block.

ES4.   Unscrew the nuts from the studs holding the oil filter body to the block . . .

ES5.   . . . and pull off the oil filter bowl assembly complete. You can now drain it easily by pouring the oil out of the top.

ES6.   Remove the studs by running both nuts onto one stud, tightening them hard against each other, then turning the bottom nut anti-clockwise. The idea is that the nuts stay tight on the stud while the stud screws out of the block.

ES7.   This is really something of an aside, but whilst at this stage, check the gearchange linkages as they can come loose and affect gearchange quality.

ES8.   Simon's car had suffered from a sloppy gearchange and the reason was found to be a loose cotter pin on this clamp allowing the linkage to move around on a splined shaft. Simple retightening solved the problem.

ES9.   Back to the engine, the Moss Engineering mechanic removed the bolts holding the radiator support to the thermostat housing.

ES10.   Then he removed the top hose from the thermostat housing . . .

ES11.   . . . and the bottom hose from the radiator itself.

ES12.   The radiator was finally released by undoing the two bolts securing the bottom radiator mounting to the engine mounting plate area . . .

ES13.   . . . and the radiator lifted away. (Note. The nuts on the bottom bolts, see plate ES12, are really difficult to get at when the engine is in the car, so tack-weld them in place so that they act as captive nuts: it makes any future removal so much simpler!)

Clutch removal

This section is complemented by the 'Clutch change with engine in car' section: the two sections should be read together if the clutch is to be changed with the engine in the car.

ES14.   Here, the clutch slave cylinder and the starter motor are already out of the way. First step now is to remove the nine bolts holding the flywheel housing cover in place.

ES15.   It's a very good idea to put all nuts and bolts back where they came from after the parts have been removed (not practicable if the engine is to be reconditioned), into boxes or even into plastic bags which are labelled for identification. It is also good practice to wash all nuts and bolts in paraffin before re-using them.

ES16.   If the flywheel cover sticks in place, DON'T use a screwdriver to lever it off or it could easily be damaged. Instead, tap it along its joints with a soft-faced hammer.

ES17.   BEFORE GOING ANY FURTHER TAKE CAREFUL NOTE OF THE FOLLOWING: every component of the clutch assembly has the letter 'A' stamped onto one part of it and these 'A' marks must always be placed in line when reassembling the clutch so that it stays in balance. Much more importantly, the 'A's and the timing marks on the flywheel MUST ALL BE POSITIONED AT THE TOP BEFORE ANY CLUTCH DISMANTLING IS CARRIED OUT. The reasons why will become clear!

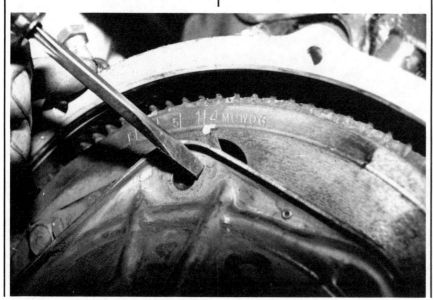

ES18. Take out the release bearing thrust plate by first removing the circlip which holds it in place, then lifting it out.

ES19. Next, remove the three bolts holding the diaphragm spring housing in place and take off the housing.

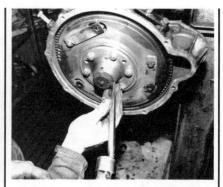

ES20. The large bolt which holds the flywheel in place is held tight by a tab washer: knock it back with a chisel.

ES21. Now get an assistant to jam the flywheel by holding a lever or large screwdriver against the starter ring and up against the clutch housing where the starter motor fits, so that the flywheel cannot turn. If the engine has been split from the gearbox, it may be better to put a block of wood between the crank and the block to stop the crank turning. The clutch flywheel must be removed with the engine upright and the 'A' and timing marks uppermost, as already described.

ES22. The bolt, tab washer and keyed washer beneath can now be taken out. The flywheel is on a tapered shaft and will almost certainly be very tightly in place.

ES23. Now screw the large bolt back in a few turns (if the type of puller you are using pushes on the bolt) and fit the flywheel puller into place.

ES24. Again, the flywheel has to be locked and the puller tightened, and tightened . . . The flywheel might eventually fly off with some force, so stand out of the way and, if you can, leave the large centre bolt loosely in place (but don't screw it fully home, of course!). If you find that the puller is straining very hard with no effect, take off the socket spanner and give the end of the puller stud a couple of good cracks with a hammer. Repeat this periodically.

ES25. Eventually, the flywheel will come off (usually with a loud 'crack'), exposing the clutch plate beneath.

ES26. The pressure plate, indicated here by the screwdriver, can also be lifted away but when reassembling do remember to line up all the 'A's as described earlier.

ES27. This is the primary gear thrust washer, which sits behind the flywheel. With the flywheel timing marks uppermost, the opening in the 'C' of the washer faces downwards holding it securely in place.

ES28.   If the flywheel was removed without aligning the 'A' marks, the C-washer can fall out of its location and jam in this groove in the flywheel. At its worst, this could present the very nasty situation where the flywheel cannot possibly come off as it is jammed solid by the misplaced washer.

ES29.   Examine the faces of the flywheel and pressure plate to see whether they have been badly scored by a worn-out clutch, or even cracked/split, which will mean that they are ready for renewal.

Stripping clutch housing, transfer gears & oil pump

Some engines have a breather fitted to the top of the flywheel housing and in this case it must be unbolted before proceeding further.

ES30.   Two bolts hold the outer flange of the clutch casing in place at the top, bolting into the cylinder block.

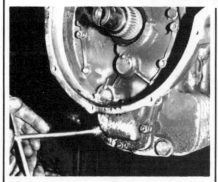

ES31.   At the bottom, there are nuts on studs holding the outer flange of the casing to the gearbox casing.

ES32.   Five bolts and three nuts hold the casing in place from inside. First, knock back the tab washers and then undo the nuts and bolts.

ES33.   Lift off the strap-type tab washers and keep them for re-use, or, if the tabs have become brittle and broken from previous renewal, obtain new ones. Don't take any chances!

ES36.   The crankshaft primary gear and the phosphor bronze thrust washer behind it can now be pulled off.

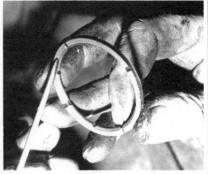

ES37.   Examine the surface of the phosphor bronze thrust washer for scoring and renew if necessary. Reassemble with the radial grooves outwards and the taper nearest the block.

ES34.   Again, it is thoroughly bad practice to lever the casing away, especially since oil leaks could result from the marks made in the soft aluminium by whatever you use for levering. Instead, tap the casing away (if you don't want to damage your hammer handle, interpose a block of hardwood).

ES35.   The casing can then be lifted away. Be ready to catch or wipe up the oil spillage that is bound to occur. If the oil seal is not to be renewed (a false economy) wrap thin tin foil or adhesive tape around the primary gear splines so that the oil seal is not damaged.

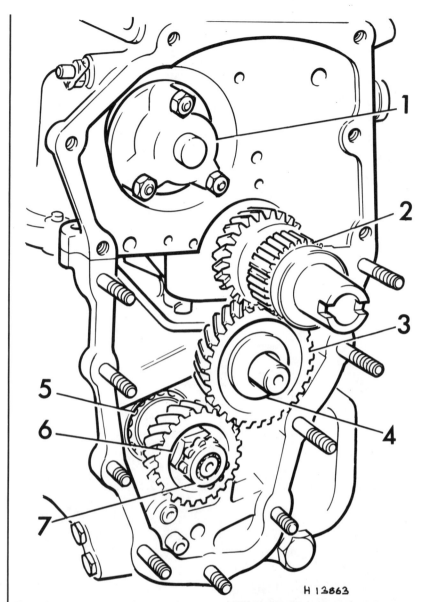

Figure 21. End view of the transfer gears with the flywheel housing removed

1 Oil pump
2 Crankshaft primary gear
3 Idler or transfer gear
4 Thrust washer
5 First motion shaft
6 First motion shaft gearwheel
7 Roller bearing

H 13863

ES39. The idler gear has a long shaft on one side with a shorter one on the other. *WHEN REASSEMBLING PLACE THE LONGER SHAFT IN THE BLOCK* or, when the clutch housing is tightened up, the shaft will punch a neat hole in it!

ES40. All the traces of old gasket can be cleaned away from the mating faces of gearbox and block/clutch housing.

ES38. The idler gear can be removed and the thrust washers, which will probably be stuck to each side of it as the surface tension of the oil, prised off.

ES41. After knocking back the locking tabs on the oil pump . . .

ES42. . . . the retaining bolts can be removed . . .

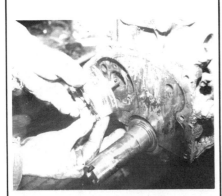

ES43. . . . and the pump body removed. Mini oil pumps are notorious for wearing relatively quickly, probably because of the oil being shared by the engine and gearbox allows small metal particles to enter the pump workings.

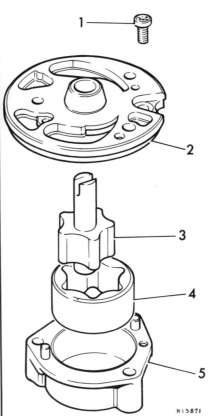

H13871

Figure 22. Oil pump (slotted drive type) components

1 Screw   4 Outer rotor
2 Cover   5 Body
3 Inner rotor and shaft

Two of the pumps fitted to Minis, the Burman and the Hobourn Eaton, shown in Figures 22 and 23, can be dismantled, examined and rebuilt, but a third type, the Concentric (Engineering) pump is a sealed unit and must be renewed if worn. The slotted-drive-type pump was fitted to 850, 1000, 1100 and 1275 'S' models, while the spline-drive-type pump was fitted to all other 1275 Minis apart from a handful of Clubman 1275 GTs which used the 'S' pump. (Note: the Cooper 'S' pump is a special pump giving higher delivery pressure.)

Cam follower removal

Most 1275cc Minis had a block casting with no access to the cam followers. These Minis' cam followers are removed after the head is removed, by turning the engine upside down and rocking it, until the cam followers slide out.

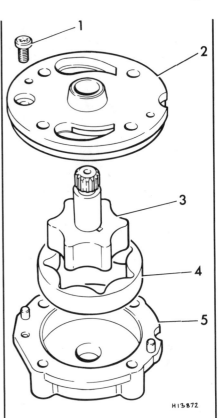

H13872

Figure 23. Oil pump (splined drive type) components

1 Screw   4 Outer rotor
2 Cover   5 Body
3 Inner rotor and shaft

Where access is available through side plates, the cam followers are taken out as shown in the following sequence.

ES44. The closed circuit breather, when fitted, sits about here, on the inlet manifold — this one has, of course, been removed. A piece of rubber pipe leads to . . .

ES45. . . . one of the side plates. The side plates are taken off after removing the central bolt that holds each in place.

ES48. After inspecting the face of the cam follower for pitting (pitted cam followers should be renewed), Moss Engineering like to 'label' each one numerically with its correct position – you should do the same.

Splitting engine from gearbox

The engine and gearbox are held together by a series of bolts. The following shots are taken with the engine tipped upside-down on Moss Engineering's one-off engine stand: it's the otherwise unidentifiable mechanical object in the foreground of many of the following shots.

ES46. Actually, it's not always quite that simple! If yours sticks, DON'T lever it off but push against the edge with a chisel as shown.

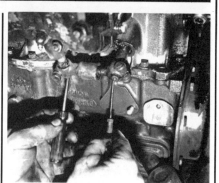

ES50. On the gearchange side, two of the bolts are concealed behind the gearchange mechanism. Their positions are pointed out here by the two screwdrivers.

ES47. The cam followers are then taken out by slipping a finger into the top of the cam follower rather like a thimble and pulling the cam follower out.

ES49. The line of bolts on the front of the engine are easy to see and easy to get at.

ES51. Another concealed bolt sits behind the engine front plate at the fan end of the engine. The screwdriver indicates its position.

ES52. The engine and gearbox tend to 'stick' all along the joint of the gasket. Once again, nothing must be forced between the two joint faces, but there is an ideal fulcrum point at the front of the engine where a good strong lever can be placed on the crank pulley and lifted upwards against the engine mounting plate.

ES53. With the seal broken, the complete gearbox can be lifted away leaving the engine looking more like an orthodox unit with the sump removed. The gearbox, with its aluminium casing, is quite easy for one person to lift.

Cylinder head removal and stripdown

ES54. First the rocker box is removed by undoing the two special nuts and washers that hold it in place. If it sticks, tap it free with a soft-faced hammer.

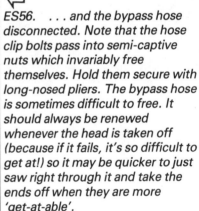

ES55. The bottom hose is released from the stub on the water pump . . .

ES56. . . . and the bypass hose disconnected. Note that the hose clip bolts pass into semi-captive nuts which invariably free themselves. Hold them secure with long-nosed pliers. The bypass hose is sometimes difficult to free. It should always be renewed whenever the head is taken off (because if it fails, it's so difficult to get at!) so it may be quicker to just saw right through it and take the ends off when they are more 'get-at-able'.

ES57. Undo the head nuts, working from the ends inwards (the order is not nearly as critical as with aluminium heads). Cooper 'S' models, and a tiny handful of 1275GTs, have two extra head studs as shown here. If the whole stud unscrews instead of the nut, there is no problem. Just take the nut off the stud when it is out of the engine and then replace the stud. (If you try screwing the whole thing back in, the nut may start to run down the stud again before the stud has sufficient threads in the block for security.)

ES58. Next, undo the four nuts that hold the valve rocker shaft trunnions in place . . .

ES59. . . . and lift off the rocker shaft assembly in one piece. Note the positions of any special washers that might be fitted.

ES60. After tapping the head upwards (just above the water pump at the front and on a casting projection at the rear) with a soft-faced hammer, the head comes free from the block and lifts away. Lift it off the studs evenly to prevent jamming.

ES61. Using the same double-nut technique as shown in photo ES6, the studs in the top of the block can be unscrewed.

ES62. Now take the opportunity to minutely examine the surfaces of the old gasket and those of the block and head to see if any leakage has taken place. Look especially hard between the bores and also look for discoloration indicating 'pathways' between the bores and water jacket.

ES63. The colour of the valves indicates well the state of tune of the engine. Because this head came from a twin-carburettor car, both extremes of carburettor setting can be seen, (although they shouldn't, of course!). The valves on the left-hand side tend towards whiteness, which means that the carburettor on that end was set to give a very weak mixture, while the valves on the right are too dark, indicating over-richness.

ES64. Before removing the valves each was 'popped' with a centre punch with 1, 2, 3, or 4 dots to show from which cylinder it came (1 is always the front of the engine). On final reassembly the valves can then be put back into the guides to which they belong, without the risk of over-tightness or looseness.

ES65. Before using a valve spring compressing tool to free the valve springs (there are several types on sale at accessory shops), tap each spring cap in turn to prevent it from 'sticking' to the top of the valve when the spring compressor is used.

Three types of valve spring assembly (Figure 24) have been used for the Mini. The spring clip around the cotters on early models can be removed with pliers or a screwdriver before the valve spring compressor is used.

ES66. As well as the parts shown in Figure 24, the Cooper 'S' also has a valve seal and another collar at the base of the spring to locate the twin springs correctly.

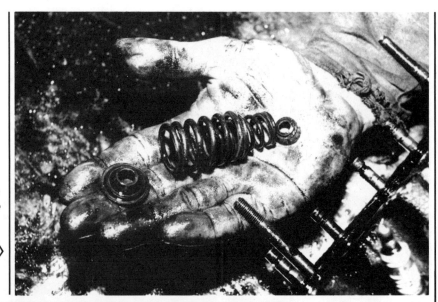

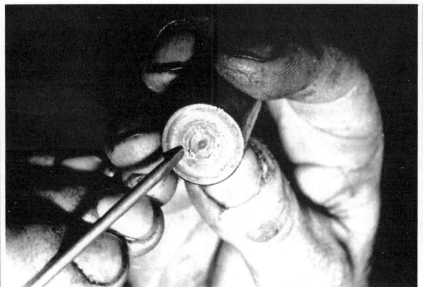

ES67. With springs removed, the valves are pulled straight out.

ES68. Examine the faces and the edges of the valves for pitting and burning and also the valve seals in the head. Slightly pitted valves and seats can be recut before lapping with fine grinding paste. Alternatively, if the seats are very bad, it is a standard procedure for a specialist company like Moss Engineering to cut out the valve seats completely and insert new ones.

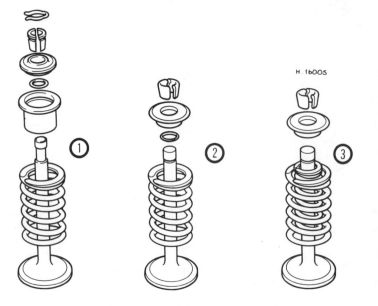

H.16005

Figure 24.   Mini valve assemblies

1 Early type 2 Later type 3 Cooper 'S' type

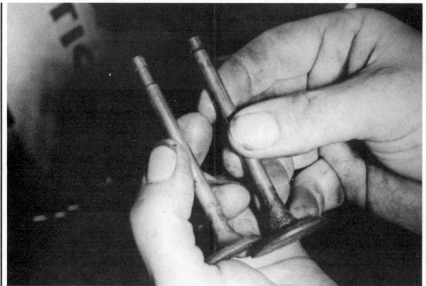

ES69. Different types and lengths of valves were used on different Mini engines, so always take your old ones along as patterns when buying new. If you're intending to retain the valves and valve guides, push the valves into the guides from the 'wrong' end and see if there is any sideways movement. If there is, consider renewing the valve guides, too.

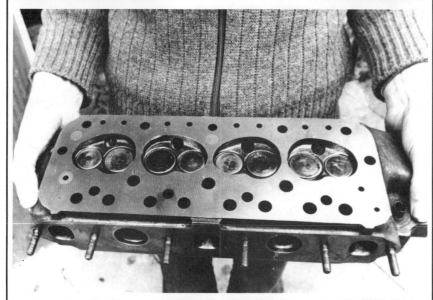

ES70. A reconditioned head, refaced to make sure that its surface is true, is the perfect way of complementing an engine with a rebuilt lower half. Of course, you may wish to tune the car which means, with the A-series engine, that now is the time! See the chapter on 'modifications' for details.

Distributor drive removal

ES71. The distributor is held in place by the clamp plate shown here. The plate can be removed separately, as in this case, by slackening the pinch bolt and pulling the distributor out, or the plate and distributor can be removed together by taking out the two bolts that screw into the distributor housing.

ES72. Just one bolt holds the distributor housing.

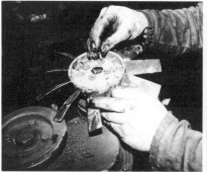

ES75. Take off the fan by removing the four bolts that hold it in place.

ES78. Take out the bolts that hold the water pump to the block . . .

ES73. After the bolt's removal, the housing pulls out of the block.

ES76. Then lift off the fan pulley from the water pump.

ES79. . . . and lever the water pump free. Again, do not push a lever between the mating surfaces.

ES74. To remove the distributor drive, screw a 5/16in bolt into it and pull out with a clockwise twist, or it can be removed with a large screwdriver in the slotted top face.

ES77. Replace the securing bolts in the water pump flange for safe keeping.

ES80. Next, the crank pulley is removed. First, knock back the large tab washer . . .

Engine block strip

ES81. . . . and undo the crank pulley nut. Place a wooden wedge between the crank and the side of the block to lock the crank: be prepared to exert a good deal of force to free the nut.

ES83. The ring of bolts holding the timing cover can be removed . . .

ES85. Behind the cover, on the crank nose is an oil thrower which will now be free to be lifted away.

ES82. Tap the pulley free with a soft-faced hammer.

ES84. . . . and the cover lifted off, again, tapping it free if necessary.

ES86. Once again, the crank is locked, then the camshaft timing gear tab washer is knocked back and the nut removed.

ES87. When reassembling − or to check the accuracy of the valve timing when dismantling if a problem is suspected − attempt to line up the dimples on each of the timing cogs with the centre of each. If they will not line up, the timing has been incorrectly set and the engine will not run properly − if it runs at all!

ES88.   Nothing is now holding the timing chain and sprockets down, so remove them together by easing both sprockets up and off at the same time with a pair of screwdrivers.

ES89.   Three bolts hold the camshaft end-plate in place.

ES90.   When it is removed, check the white metal on its inner face to see whether it has worn through: it also acts as a thrust bearing.

ES91.   The camshaft can be removed now, or after the engine front plate has been removed. Here the front plate is taken off first. Where Duplex (twin) timing gear is used, the front plate is held in place with Allen screws to provide extra clearance for the space chain. The majority of cars (including 1275GT) use a single timing chain system and here standard bolts are normally used. Remove them all . . .

ES92.   . . . then tap the front plate off the block to free it.

ES93.   The camshaft can now be pulled forwards out of the engine block, wriggling the camshaft lobes carefully clear of the white metal bearings in which the camshaft runs in the majority of Minis.

ES95.   Before the connecting rods are removed, the bearing caps must be marked with a sharp chisel as shown, or a centre punch, so that there is no risk of muddling them; each one is matched only to its own particular con-rod.

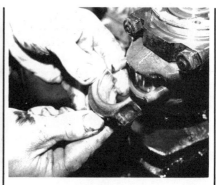

ES97.   The caps pull off, although they may stick a little at first because of the surface tension of oil, or the shell inside might stick to the crank. Both will pull away without too much trouble.

ES94.   Examine the peaks of the camshaft lobes for wear, which will mean that a new or a re-profiled camshaft is necessary.

Crank and piston removal

ES96.   Some models use tab washers to lock the retaining nuts and these must be bent back before the nuts are removed.

ES98.   As you remove each cap, inspect the shell bearing carefully for signs of grooving or, fatally for the bearing, signs of the supporting metal, which is of a reddish colour, showing through.

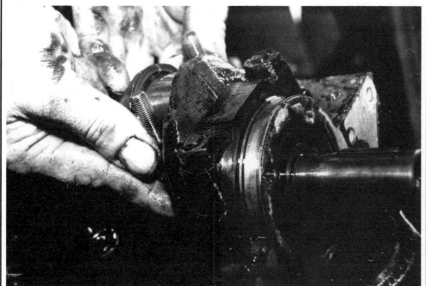

ES99.   To avoid a trapped thumb or bent nails, push the con-rod off the crank by pushing down on the outside of the bearing trunnion rather than on the threaded studs, which seems at first to be the logical thing to do.

ES100. With the con-rod free of the crank, push the piston up the bore. It usually binds on the unworn top of the bore (which is of course marginally narrower than the worn part of the bore in which it normally moves) and has to be pushed or lightly hammered upwards with a hammer handle.

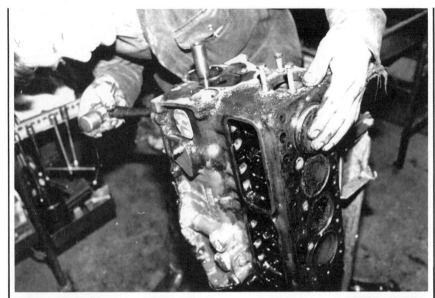

ES101. Once the piston rings are out of the bore, the piston and rod is free to be removed.

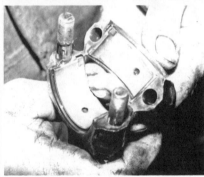

ES102. Before taking the next piston out, be sure to reassemble the cap onto the con-rod you've just removed, to make sure that nothing gets mixed up.

ES103. Undo the nuts or bolts that hold the main bearing caps, after first knocking back the tab washers if they are fitted. On 'S' engines, it is necessary to use a thin-walled socket (you can often 'cheat' and use a 14mm socket) because there is little space inside the reinforced bearing cap.

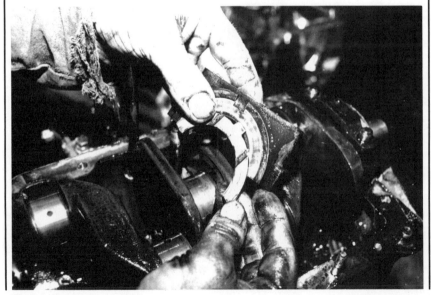

ES104. Each side of the centre cap is a thrust washer which prevents the crank from moving backwards and forwards when the clutch is used. Check both washers in the same way as a shell bearing to see whether there is any surface wear.

ES105.   Each cap can be levered upwards with a pair of stout screwdrivers.

ES106.   The crank is then free to be lifted out of the engine.

ES107.   Specialists such as Moss Engineering have the equipment and the knowledge to know how much wear is too much. After checking all the crank journals visually for signs of scoring, they are measured from several angles to check for wear and concentricity.

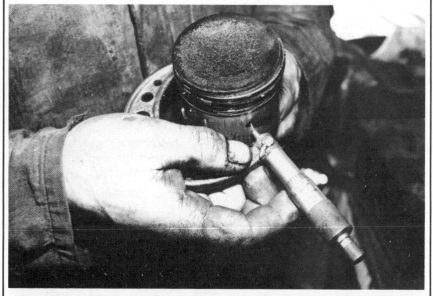

ES108.   Believe it or not, pistons can go seriously out of true. Although they are not usually checked, it is wise to do so.

ES109.   Clearly the bores can wear and here an internal micrometer with a clock dial to give measurements is being used. It is inserted held upright, the gauge is set to zero and the gauge moved up and down and around. The spring loaded anvils push against the side of the bore and measure any plus or minus discrepancies.

Before reassembling, it would be wise to dismantle the oil pump and check for scoring and to renew it if in any doubt. Fill the pump with oil before refitting it to the engine. Examine the timing chain for wear – look for grooving on the rollers –

and check the sprocket for slightly concave shaped teeth, instead of perfectly straight sided teeth, in which case they will require renewal. If there is any hint of wear, especially if the engine has covered 60,000 miles, or more, it is sensible to renew the timing chain in any case. At the very least, renew the rubber tensioner rings (where fitted) which are recessed into the outsides of the camshaft gearwheel.

Before refitting the rocker shaft, remove the plugs from its ends and clean it out — remember that it acts as the oil passage for the valve gear — and clean out its oil holes too. If the shaft shows any wear ridges, renew the shaft.

Check the rocker bushes for wear by gripping the rockers one by one and attempting to lever each sideways. If it is very loose, the rocker bushes wil need renewal (but do not mix forged and pressed steel type rockers — keep to the same type). Check the ends of the rockers for any cracking or pitting and if wear is apparent, replace the rocker.

When reassembling the engine, ensure that all oilways are clear, including those through the crank journals, and thoroughly lubricate all bearing surfaces as reassembly is carried out. Always use new spring washers, and new gaskets: a torque wrench is essential.

Reassembly is *not* necessarily the

reverse of dismantling, and unless you are fully familiar with the engine is best carried out with the aid of *Haynes Mini Owners Workshop Manual,* where piston ring positions, timing gear alignment, order of assembly, and so on, are all given in detail.

Engine/gearbox refitting

For 'Tool box' and 'Safety' refer to 'Engine Removal' section.

ERF1.   When the engine was taken out, we used a bracket bolted to the rocker box bolts. We found that there were disadvantages in that the bolts were only just strong enough and the engine came out too upright, allowing the differential to foul on the bulkhead. Therefore, before refitting the engine, a simple mild-steel strap was made up as shown and bolted down to two of the cylinder head studs.

ERF2.   So that no debris could fall into the cylinders, the spark plug holes were blanked off with masking tape. An alternative would have been to use a set of old spark plugs because it wouldn't have mattered if they had been accidentally broken during fitting.

ERF3.   The fanbelt had been fitted to the bottom pulley before the engine was lifted — normal access is particularly poor on Cooper 'S' models with a damper on the front pulley.

ERF4.　The engine was located on its mountings and bolted down. The left-hand mounting is indicated by the screwdriver here: the right-hand mounting is identical, but on the other side.

ERF5.　Next, from beneath the car, the gearchange extension was bolted back into place. Note how the front of the car is supported securely by axle stands.

ERF6.　Viewed from the back of the block, between engine and bulkhead, the inboard universal joints can be seen: they must be connected up too.

ERF7.　If you forget to reconnect the earthing strap from engine to body on those models where it is fitted, your first attempted start-up will probably be accompanied by curls of smoke and a groaning starter motor as it attempts to earth itself through the throttle and choke cables. Cable outers have been known to melt!

ERF8.　At the 'front' of the engine, the water pump went on next . . .

ERF9.　. . . followed by the radiator with its hoses already in place.

ERF10.   Then the fan was refitted after first lifting the fanbelt onto its pulleys. Note that the radiator shroud has been left off at this stage.

ERF11.   Among the ancillaries refitted/reconnected at this stage was the oil cooler, the hose connections of which must be nipped up nice and tight to prevent leakage.

ERF12.   Similarly the oil pressure gauge pipe union (where fitted) must be tightened up: over-tightening can lead to a stripped thread and it is also easy to cross this thread if you are not careful. If your car has an electrically operated oil pressure gauge/warning light you will simply need to remove the electrical connection at this stage. See checklist at the end of this section for a brief reminder of everything that has to be connected up and refitted.

ERF13.   After bolting the clutch slave cylinder back onto the engine, the clutch return spring can be clipped back on.

ERF14.   If the clutch return stop needs adjustment it should be carried out before the spring is fitted. With the lever pulled away from the engine there should be just enough clearance between the lever and the head of the stop to insert a 0.020in (twenty thou.) feeler gauge.

ERF15.   The throwout stop should only need resetting after a clutch overhaul. Slacken the locknut and stop and unscrew them as far as they will go. Have an assistant pump the clutch pedal then hold it down. Screw in the stop and lockout until the stop contacts the flywheel cover then, release the clutch pedal, screw the stop in one more flat (NOT one more turn) and then retighten the locknut.

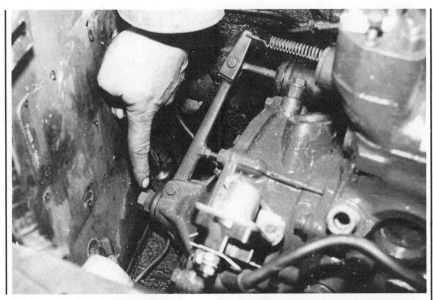

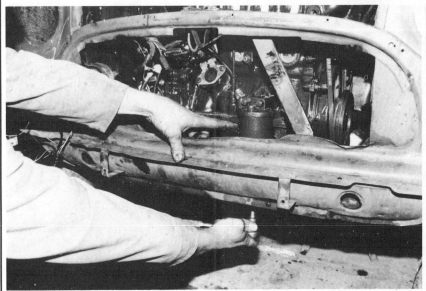

ERF18.   Whichever type of manifold is being fitted, it helps enormously to disconnect the engine tie bar, not forgetting to undo the bottom tie bar on later cars if necessary . . .

ERF16.   When refitting a rebuilt engine, it is vital to use a new oil filter and new air filters. Note how the filter is so much easier to refit with the grille out of the way. Remember to renew the sealing ring in the head of the filter assembly if your car is fitted with this type.

ERF17.   Fitting the exhaust manifold in place is always a difficult affair, but with this 3-branch Cooper 'S' manifold or with a non-standard tubular manifold, it can be a real problem. Insert it from beneath, if necessary raising the front of the car on ramps or axle stands.

ERF19. . . . which enables you to pull the engine forwards a little whilst manoeuvring the manifold.

ERF22. From underneath the car, the assembly was temporarily clamped together . . .

ERF24. The inlet manifold was then offered up, but there were more problems in store!

ERF20. Many non-genuine manifolds are difficult to fit because of being poorly made. The one we fitted was soundly built but the tailpiece at the bottom had a bend that was nowhere near sharp enough. It was adjusted as much as possible without kinking the pipe, then the front of the exhaust pipe was cut through . . .

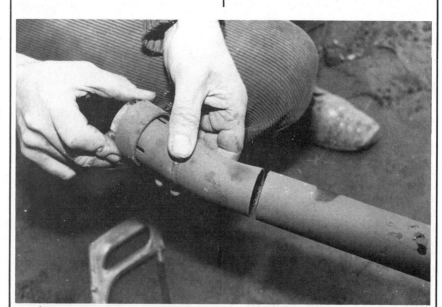

ERF21. . . . and the pipe turned to the correct angle.

ERF23. . . . and the pipe tacked together with the SIP MIG before the system was taken off again so that the pipe could be properly seam welded all the way round. Shield from heat, petrol lines and any other flammable items.

ERF25. The new exhaust manifold's flanges were too large to accommodate the inlet manifold's, so they were ground off by the whisker necessary in situ.

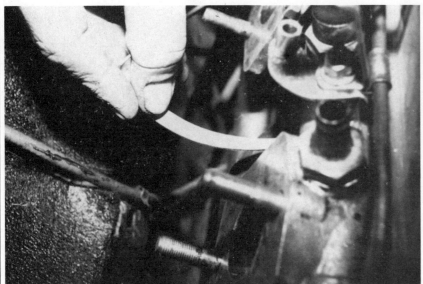

ERF26. A 'feeler gauge' was made up out of a strip of thin steel and used to check that there really was a little clearance with the inlet manifold bolted up tight. A lack of clearance could prevent the inlet manifold from seating and create an air leak which would cause weak running and possible valve and piston damage.

ERF27. Before the carburettors went back on, the float bowl tops were removed and the 'muck' scraped out of the bottom of the bowls with a screwdriver before they were washed clean with fresh petrol.

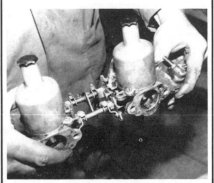

ERF28. Getting twin carbs back onto the manifold involves fitting the control shafts carefully in place between the two, ensuring that everything locates in the right place and then, with a roll on the drums, picking them both up with enough inwards pressure to keep both shafts in place.

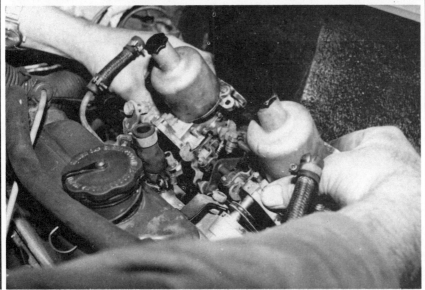

ERF29. Then the next part of the trick is to slip both carbs onto their studs still keeping the shafts in place. If you've never done it before, be prepared for a couple of frustrating practice sessions before the game is won!

ERF30.   It is essential to balance twin carbs after refitting (and periodically afterwards). Briefly, slacken one of the clamps on the throttle control rod which runs between the carbs and adjust the slow-running screw (Figure 25) until the roar/whistle into each carburettor inlet sounds at the same pitch when listened to through a piece of plastic tube, as shown. Alternatively, it is possible to buy inexpensive carburettor balancing aids which make the job much easier. When balanced, retighten the clamp, making sure that the rod opens both throttles at exactly the same time. To adjust tick-over to the desired level, screw both slow-running screws in or out by exactly the same amount. See Haynes Mini Owners Workshop Manual for fuller details of carburettor adjustment and tuning of all types.

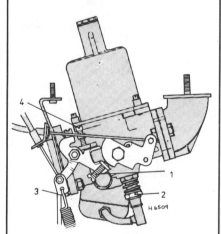

Figure 25.   Carburettor adjustment points – SU HS4

1 Fast idle adjusting screw
2 Jet adjusting nut
3 Governor control rod
   (automatic transmission)
4 Throttle adjusting screw

ERF31.   After running a rebuilt engine for around 1000 miles, it is important to drain out and renew the engine oil and filter and to torque the cylinder head down to the correct figure in the correct order for cylinder head tightening, which involves starting in the centre of the head and working outwards, tightening diagonally opposite nuts in turn. Cylinder head torque figures: all Minis 50lb. ft. (although 40lb. ft. quoted by BMC for early cars, 50lb. ft. should be fine) except emission control engine (40lb. ft.) and Cooper 'S' (42lb. ft. for ten cylinder head nuts; 25lb. ft. for one bolt).

ERF32.   After checking head torque the tappet gaps must be reset to the figure given in the specification. Turn the engine until number 1 valve just starts to rock, then adjust valve number 8. Slacken the locknut, turn the adjuster screw to adjust the gap between the top of the valve and the rocker and slip a feeler gauge in of the size shown in the specification. Turn the adjuster screw until the feeler gauge is very lightly gripped and tighten the locknut. Then turn the engine again until number 2 valve rocks and work on valve number 7, then proceed in the combination of valve 3 rocks, work on 6; 4 and 5 and so on.

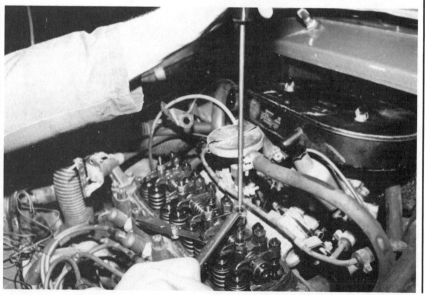

Clutch change with engine in car

One of the advantages that the Mini gave over its contemporary rivals with conventional front-to-rear engines, was the opportunity to change the clutch with the engine and gearbox still in place. Of course, now that so many cars have their engines sideways on, clutch changing has generally become much easier. Even so, this one advantage of the Mini engine layout almost makes up for so many of the car's hard-to-get-at components.

Tool Box

Jack; flywheel puller (hire from tool hire firm if necessary — you must use a robust one); usual range of screwdrivers, open-ended and socket spanners.

Safety

The biggest danger comes from the inhalation of asbestos dust from the clutch bellhousing. NEVER blow out the bellhousing. Instead wear a particle face mask, dampen the area with a garden mist sprayer, wipe all dust out with a damp rag then dispose of the rag in a sealed plastic bag. This may seem extreme, but asbestos dust is a potential killer and you can't get much more dangerous than that!

The following sequence was carried out on a Mini Clubman, but details are the same for all Minis except that access is a little better on the Clubman because of its larger engine bay. **Important: this section should be used in conjunction with the clutch removal sequence detailed under 'Engine strip' — it is incomplete on its own.**

CC1. First step is to remove air ducting on those cars where it runs along the right-hand side of the engine bay, and then remove any other ancillaries that may be in the way. Refer to 'Engine Strip' for main details but many small production changes have been made such as re-siting the horns which then had to be removed when changing the clutch, so use your common sense as to which small components will obviously be in the way. Here the starter motor has been removed after FIRST DISCONNECTING THE BATTERY and taking off the starter motor leads.

Note. It is necessary to undo the right-hand engine mounting bolts from beneath the car and jack up that end of the engine (ie the clutch end). Later Minis have a large gap between radiator and inner wing, but on all earlier cars you must remove the radiator cowl to engine support bracket.

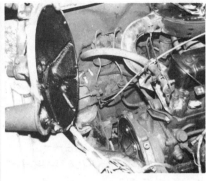

CC2. Nine bolts hold the flywheel housing cover in place and at the same time as removing them, disconnect the clutch slave cylinder pushrod.

CC3. Take out the circlip holding the release bearing thrust plate in place . . .

CC4. . . . and take out the three bolts holding the pressure plate in place.

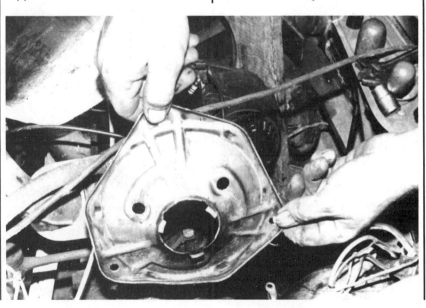

217

CC5.   Now, using the method shown in the clutch removal section of 'Engine Strip' pull the flywheel off and the clutch plate off its splines.

CC6.   With the old clutch removed, examine all the faces to check for wear (see how much depth of friction material still remains), check the steel faces for cracking and look out for dark staining of oil contamination which is the commonest reason for a juddering or slipping Mini clutch. Renew components as necessary.

Carburettor strip

In essence, all SU carburettors are constructed in the same way. The following sequence shows how to strip an HS2 carburettor, but all HS series carbs are similar. Do remember that an HS4 carburettor is fitted to all automatic Minis, all Mini 1275GTs and all other Minis from 1974 on, and has a spring mounted above the needle: take care not to drop or loose the spring and cap when removing the needle — see CS7.

CC7.   Always take the opportunity to renew the primary gear oil seal (situated behind the clutch assembly) whenever the clutch has to be removed. Claw the old one out with a screwdriver. Ideally, a special tool should be used to seat the oil seal evenly all the way round but in fact the oil seal can be fitted without the special tool if very great care is taken to tap it into place evenly using a piece of wood as a drift. It is most important to realise that this seal is very delicate, easily damaged and must be fitted evenly with no twisting. It is also essential to temporarily wrap tape over the primary gear splines to stop them damaging the new oil seal.

CS1.   Start stripping the carb by removing the float bowl top; three screws hold it down.

CS4.   Next, unscrew and remove the dashpot damper and drain out any oil found inside the dashpot by tipping the carb upside-down.

CS6.   Lift out the piston from the carb body. The needle at its base is critical to economy and smooth running. If it is worn at the base, or bent, renew it.

CS2.   Lift off the top and the float which is hinged to it.

CS5.   Two screws hold the dashpot down. Remove them and lift off the dashpot exposing the piston and spring.

CS7.   The needle is held in the bottom of the piston by means of a grub screw which fits in the hole shown. Later models incorporate a spring here too. When refitting, use the edge of a steel rule to align the shoulder at the top of the needle with the bottom face of the piston.

CS3.   The float works by pushing the valve, shown here lying on the bench, into the seating indicated by the pointing screwdriver. In case of doubt, the seat can be removed with a small socket spanner and replaced along with the valve. A leaking float is replaced by drawing out the hinge pin and replacing it.

CS8. To remove the butterfly spindle which, if worn, can allow air leaks into the carb and induce poor running, start by pushing the locking washer tabs over at the end of the butterfly spindle.

CS11. . . . and the butterfly slid out of the slotted spindle.

CS13. The jet into which the metering needle mates is removed in three moves: first, unscrew the choke arm from the block at the base of the jet . . .

CS9. With the lock washer tabs back, the retaining nut and other fittings shown are removed.

CS12. And then the spindle, with nothing retaining it, can be slid out of the carb body.

CS14. . . . next, undo the petrol feed pipe from the base of the float chamber body and carefully pull the tube and retaining nut out . . .

CS15. . . . finally, the jet simply slides out of the base of the carb.

CS10. Now, with a fine bladed screwdriver, the two screws holding the butterfly to the spindle are removed . . .

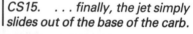

$\mathbb{6}$ Electrical Components

The following 'Tool Box' and 'Safety' notes apply generally to auto-electrical work and are relevant to every section of this chapter.

Tool Box

B.A. spanners sometimes needed for earlier cars. Engineers and long-nosed pliers. Wire cutters and cable stripper. Soldering iron and pre-fluxed solder. Selection of new electrical connectors. Insulation tape.

Safety

ALWAYS disconnect the battery before working on any electrical system. An electrical short circuit can destroy parts of the wiring system in a second or even cause a car-wrecking fire.

The vast majority of car breakdowns occur because of electrical faults, so it pays to give regular attention to your car's wiring and electrical components. This section gives an overview of some of the most important areas in the maintenance or rebuilding of a car's electrical system.

Wiring and wiring loom general

The wires used in a Mini are colour coded, so rewiring a Mini is fairly straightforward provided that a correctly colour-coded loom is used. Each lighting component already has a coded tag of wire coming from it so all you have to do is link it to the relevant part of the loom with a connector. *(See Haynes Mini Owners Workshop Manual for wiring diagrams).*

The seven basic colours are:
Brown – battery and dynamo/alternator circuits.
White – ignition.
Blue – headlamps.
Red – side and tail lamps.
Green – auxiliary (accessories, etc) circuits protected by fuse terminal 4, and only live with ignition 'on'.
Purple – other auxiliaries not wired through the ignition switch. Protected by fuse terminal 2.
Black – earth wires.
With care an older cloth covered loom can be cleaned to make it appear fresh and new. CAREFULLY remove the loom, noting the location of the clips which hold it in place and, to speed up refitting, fold a piece of masking tape double, but leaving an inch at the end single and sticky. Wrap this around the end of each wire as it is disconnected and write its location on the masking tape. Wire brush the clips and repaint them with a hammered metal finish paint. Coil the wiring loom and place it into a shallow pan with warm soapy water. SQUEEZE BUT DO NOT SCRUB the loom until it is as clean as it will get before it begins to unravel, then hang it in the garage until completely dry. PVC covered wires can be cleaned to almost new lustre by spraying a rag and the wires with aerosol carburettor cleaner, and wiping the sludge and grease from the wires.

As a rule, the wires themselves do not fail. The connectors may lose contact with the wires but the wires themselves rarely break. Any splicing or correction to the loom should be made outside the wrapping. There should be no connections within the loom itself. If changes are made in the loom, solder Lucas bullet connectors to the wires and use the black female connectors of the type used with the rest of the system.

NOTE: Prior to removing the loom from the car, remove ALL the black female connectors as they impede the free movement of the loom through the bulkhead, boot, etc. Prior to refitting the loom in the car, clean each bullet connector with fine sandpaper to ensure a good connection.

The interior light switches in the door pillars become bent and corroded so that they do not work. Remove them from the pillar and from the purple/white wire. Wire brush them so that they will make good contact to the pillar and to themselves. Straighten bent plungers with pliers.

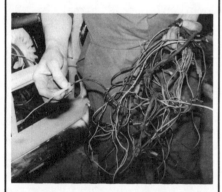

E1. You can buy new wiring looms both of the braided and plastic covered types, as advertised by specialist suppliers in magazines like Practical Classics and Thoroughbred and Classic Cars. If you decide to re-use your own loom, clean it as described earlier and be prepared to cut out and renew damaged sections and remove 'bodged' additions.

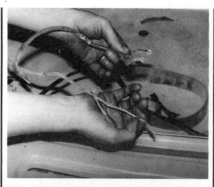

E2. Many terminals will need to be renewed. Sometimes they are corroded, where they are often hanging on by a thread of wire and exposing a dangerous section of bare cable.

E3. Some terminals can be renewed with the component in situ, either because it makes it easier to get the wiring in place or because taking the component out would be more hassle than soldering in a confined space.

E4. You really need three hands to solder bullet connectors onto the ends of wires: one to hold the wire, one the iron and one for the solder itself! Cleanliness is the key to obtaining a good soldered joint. Remember that solder will tend to be drawn towards the heat and try not to heat for so long that the wire's insulation melts.

E5. When fitting new spade-type connectors, do remember to push on the plastic insulator before soldering the spade in place!

E6. You can tape up any additions, or replacement sections, with plastic insulation tape wrapped around the wire in a spiral, each wind covering about half of the one that went before.

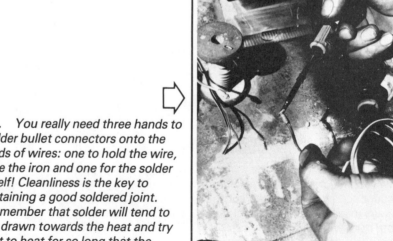

Lighting circuit trouble shooting

After rewiring the lights following a rebuild, or after renewing the wiring loom, or simply after a period of neglect, the lights can begin to give problems. Here's how to solve some of them.

Headlights

Glowing or very dim — faulty earth connection.
No illumination BUT dashpanel light indicator is on for both high and low beam — faulty earth.
High or low beam not working on one side — faulty bulb or faulty connection (blue/white = full beam; blue/red = dip beam)
Headlamp flasher not working — brown/purple wire fuse

Parking lights

One side (left or right) not working — fuse.
One light not working — probably the bulb.

Turn signals

Neither dash bulb or lights illuminate — faulty hazard switch (when fitted — switch the hazard switch on and off a few times and try again).
Lights and indicators illuminate but don't flash or flash very slowly — faulty flasher.
One side flashes properly, one side doesn't — faulty front or rear bulb.

Wire size selection

If you fit new accessories to your car, make certain that you buy the right size of wire for the job. Household wire WILL NOT do the job. Many people think that because domestic wire carries such a high voltage, it will always be strong enough for work in a car. In fact, household lighting wire, for example, would quickly melt its insulation if used to power a high-load accessory.

Always choose the correct wire by first finding out what the AMPERES (amps) rating of the accessory is. (If you're given a WATTAGE figure, divide by 12 to give amps because the Mini is on a 12 volt system.)

If the accessory rates less than 6 amps, ask your supplier for 14/0.010 cable (if he/she doesn't know what you mean, don't shop there!); if it rates between 6 amps and 18 amps, go for 28/0.012 cable. If you need more (how many spotlamps *can* you fit?), seek specialist advice and consider fitting an uprated alternator/dynamo.

Distributor identification

Distributor overhaul

Four different types of distributor have been fitted to the Mini over the years. Their type numbers and identifying serial numbers are shown in the following table. All pre-1969 Minis were fitted with the 25D4 unit. All Cooper and 'S's were also fitted with the 25D4 distributor except the MK III Cooper 'S' of 1970-71 which received the 23D4 distributor, which is similar to the more common 25D4 except that it was not fitted with a vacuum advance mechanism.

Mini model	Type	Serial Number (stamped on side of distributor body)
850 Saloon, Estate, 1969-72	25D4	41026
	or 45D4	41411
850 Van, Pick-up, 1969-72	25D4	41007
	or 45D4	41410
1000 Saloon, Estate, 1969-72	25D4	40931 or 41030
	or 45D4	41412
1000 Van, Pick-up, 1969-72	25D4	41007
	or 45D4	41410
1000 Auto, Clubman Auto, 1969-74	25D4	41134 or 41242
	or 45D4	41417
Cooper MkIII, 1969-72	23D4	40819 or 41033
Clubman 998, 1969-72	25D4	41030
	or 45D4	41412
1275GT, 1969-72	25D4	41257
	or 45D4	41419
850 Saloon and variants, 1972-74	25D4	41026 or 41569*
	or 45D4	41411 or 41570
1000 Clubman, Saloon & variants, 1972-74	25D4	41254 or 41246
	or 45D4	41212 or 41418
1275Gt, 1972-76	25D4	41257 or 41214
	or 45D4	41419
850 Saloon and variants, 1974-76	45D4	41570
All 1000 models, 1974-76	45D4	41418
Clubman 1100, 1974-76	25D4	41246
	or 45D4	41418
850 and variants, 1976-on	45D4	41417 or 41767
Clubman 1100, 1976-on	45D4	41418 or 41793
1000, all models, 1976-78	45D4	41418 or 41793
1275GT, 1976-on	45D4	41419 or 41768
1000, all models, 1978-on	45D4	41406 or 41765

* Alternative distributor fitted to some 1974 models.
As well as the 25D4/23D4 distributors, a later type, the 45D4, was fitted intermittently to some models while others are fitted with a Ducellier distributor.

Many parts of the distributor can wear and malfunction. In particular, the following points should be checked (for component identification see Figures 26, 27 and 28):

1) The vacuum advance unit perforates and no longer functions (check by releasing the pipe from the carb, suck it and look and listen for distributor base plate movement).

2) The plates holding the points wear, allowing the points to contact the distributor cam at an angle and causing the vacuum unit to work jerkily.

3) The mechanical advance screw seizes.

4) The cam develops sideplay on the distributor shaft.

5) The distributor shaft wears where it fits the body bush, which also wears.

6) The points and condenser fail.

DO1.   Wire insulation inside the distributor is inclined to disintegrate and cause a car-stopping short. Replace the wire with a new piece.

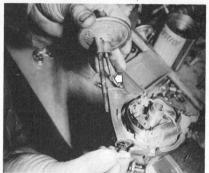

DO2.   To remove the vacuum advance on the 25D4 distributor, lever off the clip that holds the advance/retard finger nut (held in right hand here) in place, disconnect the spring from the baseplate (arrowed) and unscrew the nut completely before withdrawing the advance mechanism. Don't loose the spring from behind the knurled nut.

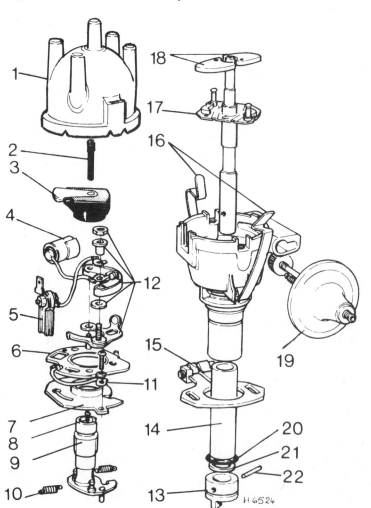

Figure 26.   Exploded view of Lucas 25D4 distributor

1	Distributor cap	12	Contact breaker
2	Brush and spring		points
3	Rotor arm	13	Driving dog
4	Condenser	14	Bush
5	Terminal and	15	Clamp plate
	lead	16	Cap retaining
6	Moving		clips
	baseplate	17	Shaft and action
7	Fixed baseplate		plate
8	Cam screw	18	Bob weights
9	Cam	19	Vacuum unit
10	Advance spring	20	O-ring oil seal
11	Earth lead	21	Thrust washer
		22	Taper pin

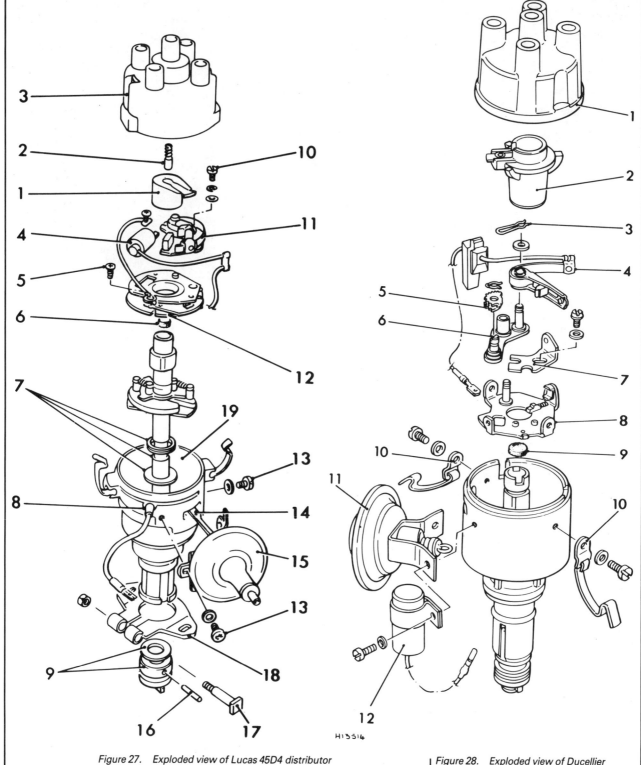

Figure 27. Exploded view of Lucas 45D4 distributor

1	Rotor	6	Felt pad	10	Contact set securing screw	14	Vacuum unit link
2	Carbon brush and spring	7	Shaft assembly with steel washer and spacer	11	Contact set	15	Vacuum unit
3	Cap			12	Baseplate	16	Parallel pin
4	Condenser (capacitor)	8	Low tension lead and grommet	13	Vacuum unit retaining screws and washers	17	Pinch bolt and nut
5	Baseplate securing screw	9	Drive dog and thrust washer			18	Lockplate
						19	Distributor body

Figure 28. Exploded view of Ducellier distributor

1	Cap	7	Fixed contact
2	Rotor	8	Baseplate
3	Rocker arm clip	9	Felt pad
4	Moving contact assembly	10	Cap retaining clips
5	Serrated cam	11	Vacuum unit
6	Eccentric D-post	12	Condenser

DO3. The Lucas distributor shaft assembly is held in place by a pin (see Figures 26 and 27) which must be driven out with a pin punch, after which the distributor components can be pulled apart. Note: when reassembling the distributor, make certain that the drive dog is offset relative to the position of the rotor arm as shown in Figure 29 or the ignition spark will occur 180° out (ie the wrong plug will fire).

DO4. When refitting the distributor, make sure that the clamp plate is not distorted, if so it can damage the distributor mounting flange, like this.

Figure 29. Correct relative positions of drive dog and rotor arm

1 Offset drive dog tongues   2 Rotor arm

Horn general

H1. So that the horn works from the centre of the steering column (earlier cars) without getting its wiring in a twist, it operates from a slip ring (A) and a contact (B) which bears on the slip ring. The contact is connected to a feed wire; the slip ring is connected to the piece of wire shown here sticking out of the top of the column. Make sure that the contact spring has sufficient life in it to hold the contact in place and that neither contact nor slip ring are dirty and thus preventing the flow of current.

HS2. The horn button (removed here) pushes down on the contact to which the wire (shown sticking out of the top of the column in the previous photo) is fitted. This action creates a complete circuit which sounds the horn. If you're not sure whether the horn or switch is faulty, put a test lamp in place of the horn and see if it lights up when the horn is 'sounded' (ignition on).

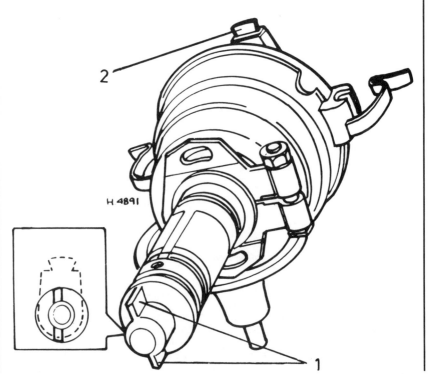

H 4891

7 Modifications

The subject of tuning the Mini for performance is worth a book in itself and, not surprisingly, several have been written on the subject. For those who want to squeeze every last ounce of power out of their Mini, or who want to get as much as they possibly can out of their existing engine, David Vizard's book *Tuning BL's A-Series Engine* (Haynes/Foulis autumn 1984) is without doubt the definitive work on the subject.

If all you want is a quicker Mini at reasonable cost, then the following section is for you! So many cars have been built using variations of the A-series engine, and so many of these engines are very easy to fit or part-fit into the Mini, that it doesn't really make sense to look much further than a breaker's yard for a quick and easy performance boost, provided of course that you can find what you want in good condition and don't have to spend a small fortune on reconditioning it.

Buying a second-hand engine

The cardinal rule about buying an engine from a car breaker is: NEVER buy without hearing the engine running first. If no cooling system is fitted because someone else has bought the radiator, that's not much good to you either. You need to take a can of petrol with you, top-up the water and the oil too, if it is desperately low and warm the engine up thoroughly. Since you're unlikely to be able to drive the car around, thorough warming up without any engine load could take somewhat longer than on the road but do it anyway. Keep an eye on the temperature gauge though, because you don't want to overdo it especially because standing engines often seize their thermostats.

Once the engine is warm, try to carry out as many of the checks detailed in the 'Buying' section as possible, particularly with regard to the state of the coolant and the oil, engine rattles and a smoking exhaust.

Assuming that you found a good second-hand engine — and that's not unlikely because the tough old Austin/Morris 1100/1300 engine, for instance, was quite capable of outliving the rust-prone bodywork that was wrapped round it — you should do one of two things with it. Either clean it and fit it without touching a thing except plugs, points, oil filter and fresh oil; or strip it right down and replace bearing shells, piston rings, regrind the valves, replace the gaskets and consider fitting a new oil pump. Even if a used engine seems OK it will live much longer if given that sort of preventative maintenance but, if the engine needs more than that, you really shouldn't have bought it in the first place! Of course, if you can persuade the breaker's yard people to let you take off the sump and a couple of bearing caps and take off the head for closer inspection, you could learn a great deal more about the condition of the engine, but they are not likely to be too enthusiastic.

Note that every yard 'guarantees' its engines. They usually mean that if there is something wrong with it, you can take it back — but then what? Sometimes you will get your money back (you want it in writing!) but often all it means is that you will get another engine in place of the one you have taken. But what if there is nothing there that is suitable? Suffice it to say that most scrapyard 'punters' seem to be out for all they can get and the yard owners generally fight fire with fire, so don't expect the Marks and Spencer touch!

There is actually another good way of finding a second-hand engine and that is through the local newspaper. Look out for advertisements from private owners 'breaking' a car and if that doesn't bring the desired results, try placing a couple of 'Wanted' ads in the same newspapers. You may find that you have to take a whole car doing it this way but the price is usually rock-bottom, and you end up with a lot more spares — you also usually make someone's parents or wife very happy . . .

Which engine to transplant?

The 848cc engine was available through most of the Mini's production years but since it's the bottom of the pile as far as performance is concerned, it's a total non-starter in the race for more speed. However, if you want to swap one 848cc engine for another, and you are not too worried about originality, then the later the better as far as the replacement engine is concerned — see 'Production modifications' in the appendices for details of changes.

The 997cc and 970cc and 1071cc engines were made in such small numbers that anything I have

said about buying second-hand can be instantly ignored! If you need one of these engines because your Cooper or 'S' has got the wrong unit and you come across one then, provided that the price is right, don't worry too much about the condition — go for it!

The 998 unit is one of the commonest engines around and it gives a small increase in power over the 848cc engine, the smaller engine giving 34bhp to the larger unit's 38bhp. This is a tiny increase which will not really justify the hassle of an engine swap. There is the further problem in that the 998cc unit was used only in the Mini range, so the range of tuning goodies which can be adapted from other more sporting cars is actually non-existent. Tuning companies may well stock tuned heads, hotter cams and better carburettors for 998 engines and special exhaust manifolds are certainly available, but by now the whole package is starting to look somewhat expensive when compared with the original modest outlay on the engine, so it would certainly be more cost-effective to look upwards to the next engine size.

1098cc engines were used in the Mini and Clubman but they are far, far more common in the Austin/Morris range of cars. It also happens that 1100s have rotted out in large numbers creating a source of good, useable engine-gearbox units, although it must be remembered that the model has not been built since 1971, so even this source of engines is thinning out.

Later 1100 engines are mated to a gearbox that is potentially much better than your existing 'box if yours is an earlier Mini — check the production changes listed in the appendices and assume that changes to the 1100 model's gearbox would have been similar. Quite apart from the fact that it gives 48bhp in standard form (admittedly not exciting but around 40% more than the standard 848cc engine), the biggest 'plus' of this engine is that the head, carbs and cam from an MG1100, a Sprite or Midget 1098cc are an easy swap.

MG and A-H Sprite 1098 engines give around 55bhp which is starting to get interesting because that is exactly the same output as the first Mini Coopers in both 997 and 998 forms. The MG head may not be very easy to find, primarily because Mini owners tend to snatch whole engine units and fit them to their cars as soon as they become available, but Midget/Sprite individual parts should be much easier to find. Specialists such as *Spridgebits* of Birmingham (see list of suppliers in appendix) have parts left over from owners of 'their' cars who are uprating their cars from 1098 to 1275cc!

If 55bhp is not enough for you, there is still one other engine to go for and that is the 1275cc unit fitted to the Mini Clubman and to the Austin/Morris 1300 and 1300GT range. The standard 1300 engine gives around 55bhp and quite a lot of torque as well; the GT version an extra 13bhp which is getting close to Cooper 'S' figures at a fraction of the cost of buying and fitting a host of expensive equipment to a smaller engine. Don't forget that you can tune the standard 1300 engine in the same way that the 1100 engine can be tuned, by fitting head, carburettors and cam from a 1275 Sprite or Midget. 1300GT engines and also the Riley Kestrel 1275cc units (but not the first ones, before April 1968) used a higher compression cylinder head than Sprites and Midgets and there could well have been valve size differences, too.

Clues to engine identification

If the engine prefix (see P.248 on) is missing, these clues could be helpful.

850 engine

— Casting no. '12 1456', '2A 628' or '2A 629' on head beneath rocker cover (but could also be 998).
— Casting no. or plate riveted to back of block stating '850'.

– Measure bore – 62.9mm is correct.

998 engine

– Casting no. '12A 1456' '2A 628' or '2A 629' stamped on back of head (but could also be 850).
– Casting no. or plate riveted to back of block stating '998'.
– Measure bore – 64.6mm is correct.

997 Cooper

– Casting no. or plate riveted to back of block stating '1000'.
– Measure bore – 62.4mm is correct.

998 Cooper

– Number '12G 295' or '12G 206' cast in head.

1098 '1100' engine

– engine mountings on front plate.
– temperature gauge connection in cylinder head.

1300/1300GT engine

– No removable tappet covers.
– temperature gauge connection in cylinder head.
– engine mountings on front plate.

Mini 1275GT engine

– No removable tappet covers.
– Engine mountings in standard Mini location.
– Could have head secured by 8 studs + 1 bolt or 9 studs.

1275 'S' engine

– Head secured by 8 studs + 1 bolt or 9 studs.
– Removable tappet covers fitted; stroke – 81.3mm.

1071 'S' engine

– Removable tappet covers.
– 8 studs + 1 bolt or 9 stud head fixing.
– stroke – 68.26mm.

970 'S' engine

– Removable tappet covers.
– 8 stud + 1 bolt or 9 stud head fixing.
– stroke – 61.91mm

Note. The 1275GT MkIV Sprite head has 9 studs. The 1300GT, MG1300 MkII, late Cooper 'S' have 11 head studs.

Priority modifications for engine performance

As already explained, the simplest and easiest way to make a Mini go faster is to fit one of the bigger engines to it. You must, at the same time, consider the problems of stopping the car, cornering and cooling and these will be dealt with later in this chapter. However, you may not want to just throw your existing engine out; you may want to retain it but simply make it a little more powerful. Once again, there is a wide selection of alternatives available and for the sake of simplicity, I'm going to assume that you have an 848cc or 948cc engine fitted. If it's a 1098 or 1275, the range of bolt-on goodies has already been mentioned (ie ex-Sprite, Midget or MG1100/1300).

Both of the smaller Mini engines benefit most of all from a change of cylinder head. The 948cc Sprite MkII/Midget MkI head would offer a real improvement, always assuming you could find one, but the 1098 'Spridget' head would be better still. In each case you would have to measure the volume of the combustion chamber and calculate the compression ratio before working out how much to have skimmed from the head in order to obtain a compression ratio that is not so low that you are losing lots of potential performance.

The second improvement in the priority list comes from fitting a larger carburettor or carburettors. Twin carbs from a Cooper, Sprite MG or a tuning firm would be fine

but a larger single SU carb and matching manifold from one of the automatic Minis or 1100/1300s proves to be virtually as efficient as twin carbs without the attendant hassle of regular re-tuning. You hear a lot about the virtues of Weber carbs and other similar twin-choke set ups. I'm not going to consider any of them here because, although they can offer benefits they are expensive, difficult to set up correctly, especially on a non-standard engine where there is not already a body of published data to help you get the initial setting-up right and, worst of all from the starting premise of this section, they are nowhere near as easy to get hold of cheaply and second-hand as twin or larger SUs.

The third most profitable area for improvement is the exhaust system and especially the manifold, where a good quality long-centre-branch manifold can make a real difference to power output, though not an especially large one when used by itself.

The Mini has a tendency to smoke front wheels.

Fourth in the list comes a change of cam. Different specialists swear by different cams, each of which has a different characteristic and causes the engine to have various attributes. (Unfortunately, every cam is a compromise and for every plus-point, it also has a counterbalancing minus-point, so you have to make up your own mind about which set of characteristics you are looking for or are prepared to live with.) Probably the best thing you can do when choosing a cam is to read all the literature so that you know a bit about the subject, find a good dealer and talk to him about what your needs are.

There is a great deal more that can be done to an engine such as lightening some of the moving parts, strengthening others, changing the oil feed system and so on, but most if not all are entirely superfluous for normal road use and in any case cost a great deal of money. It's an unfortunate fact of engine tuning that the further you go down the road, the more you come up against the law of diminishing returns: the more you do, the more it costs and the less additional effect it has on your engine's performance! If you really are interested in tuning to esoteric levels, you are thinking beyond the intentions of this book and you really need to get hold of a serious tuning book such as the one mentioned at the start of this chapter.

Swapping heads? Caution!

While stud positions are the same for all heads (even those with more stud holes will fit even if they won't bolt down properly), the 1275cc head's eight water passages do not line up with the passages on non-1275 cars and, moreover, there is not enough room for the valves to open when some, if not all, of the 1275 heads are placed upon smaller capacity cylinder blocks.

Gearbox and final drive ratios

In general, the later the 'box, the better and stronger it is, with perhaps the *crème de la crème* of production 'boxes being the 1300GT

gearbox which is all-synchro and has closer ratios than any of the others, other than Cooper boxes, of course.

Alteration of the final drive (differential) ratio can be achieved by a swap and is most useful if you have added significantly to your car's power output. There have been three ratios in common use and a fourth less common. The 850 Mini used a 3.765:1 ratio; the 1300 used 3.647:1 and the later Cooper 'S' used 3.444:1. 998s were produced with any of these ratios, and it would seem that some early 1275 GTs were fitted with a very low 4.133:1 ratio.

The best way of finding which ratio is best for the job is simply to 'suck it and see' — try out the final drive ratio you have and if it feels too low, as though you want to change up although you already *are* in top gear, swap it for the next one up. You can only tell which ratio is which for certain by carefully counting the teeth on the crownwheel and dividing it by the number of teeth on the pinion. You will get one of the figures shown.

If you have taken the final drive from another Mini, try to buy the speedometer as well so the speed readings are correct. Otherwise, apply to Smiths Industries or one of the specialists advertising in the motoring press to have your own speedometer recalibrated.

Cooling system

1275 engines generally are more prone to overheating than the smaller units so try to get hold of the right radiator/fan set-up for these units and make sure that the system is thoroughly flushed through and working efficiently. You may want to try fitting a 'cooler' thermostat which is OK, but don't be lulled into thinking that an electric fan will make the cooling system more efficient, it won't!

Fitting an alternator/Negative earth conversion

There are great benefits to be gained from swapping an older Mini's dynamo for an alternator, especially if the car is used through the winter months when modern accessories create a heavy drain on the battery. Changing to negative earth from the old positive earth system can also be useful, especially if you want to fit a modern radio or radio/cassette of the negative earth type. (A negative earth radio *can* be fitted to a positive earth car but it is essential to completely insulate the unit from the car's bodywork and to fit a non-earthing type of aerial such as those which fit across the windscreen.) It is not necessary to change any of the positive earth car's electrical equipment in order to change to negative earth (other than those detailed at the end of this section), and the wipers won't park on the wrong side, or anything like that!

Tool box

AF spanners; engineer's pliers (use two pairs for parting stubborn bullet connectors); jumper wire; wire strippers; soldering equipment.

Safety

Follow usual safety precautions when working on a car's electrical system. Be especially certain that the battery is disconnected before working on anything electrical.

1.   Disconnect the battery, clean all posts and clamps and renew the connection from the earth strap to the body. (This prevents the inefficiency that develops in old, frayed earth straps.)

NE1. While the clamps are being looked at, replace the Lucas 'cap' style terminals with 'wrap around' style clamps. The Lucas terminal ends match the battery posts and since the positive is larger than the negative will no longer be of any use.

DO NOT cut the old terminal ends from the wire in case they then become too short, but melt them off (place a suitable receptacle beneath) with a small propane torch. *Beware of a naked flame used near the fuel tank. Disconnect the cables and do the job outside the boot.*

Replace the battery 180° from its old alignment and connect the power cables, clamping them up tight. Be certain to use the proper battery fixing clamp as excessive bouncing will take years off the life of your battery.

2.   Examine the ignition coil. The WHITE wire must now be connected to the ' + ' or 'CB' terminal; the WHITE & BLACK wire (distributor to coil) must now be connected to the ' − ' or 'SW' terminal. ('CB' = contact breaker; 'SW' = switch; reversed in this new application.) The coil functions well with wires connected wrongly but it runs with a few percentage points drop in efficiency).

3.   *If you are not fitting an alternator:* Polarise the dynamo. Remove the BROWN/GREEN wire from the 'F' (Field) terminal on the dynamo (the smaller spade). Use a jumper wire and make a momentary connection between this spade terminal and the 'live' post of the starter solenoid (the post with the BROWN wire).

You should aim to flick a couple of good sparks on the dynamo terminal with the end of the wire: this procedure reverses the magnetic field in the dynamo. Reconnect the BROWN/GREEN wire to the generator and start up the engine. The ignition light should act as before − (ON when ignition is on; ON at very low rpm; OFF above around 1000 rpm and OFF when ignition is off). **WARNING** if the ignition light remains ON when the ignition is OFF, disconnect the BROWN wires from the started solenoid *straight away* and re-check your work.

4.   Check the heater operation. Turn the ignition and heater blower on and judge the amount of air being blown. Then reverse the wires at the heater motor (swap the bullet connectors round) and check again. Use whichever gives the greatest amount of air movement.

5.   Place a warning label, taken from a newer Mini or hand lettered under the bonnet and near the battery with the legend: 'WARNING − This vehicle wired negative earth'.

6.   *Fitting an alternator in place of a dynamo:* assuming that a second-hand alternator will be obtained from a breaker's yard, the physical fitting is straightforward. Obtain the alternator mounting and adjusting plates with the alternator, together with the plug that fits into the back of it. Also buy a new fanbelt to suit the age of car from which the alternator was taken because the alternator pulley is likely to be of a different size to that of the original dynamo.

7.   Swap the dynamo mounting and adjustment brackets for the alternator brackets and bolt the alternator in place with the new fanbelt correctly adjusted. (About 0.5 inch of fanbelt deflection halfway between alternator and crankshaft pulleys.)

8.   Use a wiring diagram from the *Haynes Mini Owners Workshop*

Manual to connect up the wires to the alternator plug; disconnect both ends of each of the redundant dynamos wires and tape them neatly out of the way, preferably back to the wiring loom, in such a way that there are no bare ends capable of causing an electrical short-circuit.

Footnote. The following components are polarity sensitive. *Clock.* Most modern car clocks have transistorised rectification and so cannot be polarity changed, the only option is to fit a later unit of the correct negative earth polarity. *Electronic ignition.* Again, the polarity of these units cannot be converted. Either revert to conventional ignition or up-date the equipment, unless the equipment was built to be switchable. *Ammeter.* This will simply read back-to-front until the cables are reversed on the rear of the instrument. *Air horns.* There are many different types but they can be damaged. Consult the makers for specific instructions. *Windscreen washers (electric).* It will probably be necessary to swap the connections on the impeller motor. *Rev. Counter.* It is possible to carry out a rather complex conversion. Either seek the assistance of an auto-electrician or swap for a later type.

Brakes, suspension and wheels

Most standard Mini brakes are fine for everyday motoring with a useful reserve for light tuning. The two exceptions to this are the early Mini brakes with single leading shoes (see production modification section of appendices for change points) which are barely adequate even for the least powerful cars, and the disc brakes fitted to the early Mini Coopers which can also be pretty frightening, especially in view

231

of the extra power these models had on tap.

Before you consider up-rating the brakes (and if the engine is made significantly faster it would be, to put it bluntly, extremely stupid not to do so), check that the existing brake drums are in good condition. Mini brake drums are prone to becoming oval and also to scoring, both of which make them less efficient. (Actually even new drums can be oval! – have them checked.) Lightly scored or slightly out-of-true drums can be skimmed by any good machine shop, but check the cost first; it can sometimes be cheaper to buy new.

There are several possible ways of uprating Mini brakes including: fitting later brakes to an early car; fitting harder linings and a brake booster; or changing to disc brakes.

Brake swaps

If you are considering changing the brakes in order to keep up with an engine swap, your guide as to which brakes to fit will be the car from which the engine came or, in the case of the early Cooper whose brakes were awful anyway, a car with similar performance. Later-type non-dual circuit drum brakes are excellent substitutes for any of the early brakes and can be fitted by buying second-hand breakers yard backplates and drums and fitting them with new wheel and master cylinders and brake shoes. They bolt straight onto 850 Minis but if an older-type Cooper is to be modified, you will have to fit 850 Mini hubs as well. It is always a good idea to renew the rear brake limiter valve at the same time.

Cooper S and 1275GT discs have to be fitted with drive flanges, hubs, calipers and constant velocity joints from the same models so they can often by quite an expensive proposition. Although all Austin/Morris 1100 and 1300 saloons used disc brakes, sadly they will not fit the Mini because these models have different sized constant velocity joints and larger 12 inch wheels, so they just won't go on to a Mini.

Servo

Fitting a servo will NOT improve the efficiency of your brakes! Many people think it does, but it only makes the pedal feel lighter and the effort needed to stop the car less. If your car's brakes fade after several heavy applications, fitting a servo will not make the slightest difference: it only makes it less of an effort for your right leg to take the brakes to the limit. However, if you want to give your braking leg a rest, but bearing in mind what has been said about the inferiority of early brakes, fit one by all means. A scrapyard servo should cost very little, perhaps less than the cost of a new tyre – but make sure you get all the 'plumbing' that comes with it and be prepared to recondition it too.

You *can* go a stage further and improve your brakes in conjunction with fitting a servo. Harder brake linings will stop the car more often before starting to fade but can take a lot more pedal pressure to operate, so much so that to fit very hard linings with no other modifications would be downright dangerous. Fit a servo, too, and you've got the best of both worlds. It can often be useful to fit harder linings such as Ferodo AM4 to the front while fitting the same or possibly the standard linings to the rear.

Shock absorbers

Harder shock absorbers undoubtedly improve the handling of a Mini but can make the ride intolerable. You have to decide what you want. The same effect can be obtained by fitting stiffer Hydrolastic units to Hydrolastic Minis but in view of the amount of work required to fit them, you've *got* to be serious!

Suspension lowering

Lowering a Mini's suspension makes it look meaner, corner better and can cost nothing. What more could you want – originality? Take a look at the sections of this book on suspension overhaul and decide whether you want to lower and by how much (1 inch is usually plenty to achieve the desired effect) then see how to take out the suspension 'trumpets' or struts. Lowering is achieved by removing metal from the narrow end of the strut in the ratio of: ⅛in. from the end of the strut lowers the car by about ⅝in. If you take much off the struts, you will have to buy special shortened shock absorbers to cope with the decreased distance between the mounting pins. Also, if you lower the suspension a great deal, check carefully that no brake pipe chaffing or wheel rubbing can take place.

Wheels

There is no doubt that wider wheels make the Mini corner better in dry conditions because there is always more rubber in contact with the road. Before doing anything else, however, if you have an early Mini with thin gauge wheel centres (see production changes in appendices for change points) strongly consider throwing them away and fitting later, similar but stronger wheels. (Early wheel centres were about 0.080in. thick, while later ones are about 0.120in.).

There are so many different types of wheel on the accessory market that it is impossible to give specific recommendations but you should check the following points before buying:
1)   Are widened steel wheels from a reputable manufacturer? The chance of collapse may be slim, but is it worth taking!
2)   Never buy second-hand alloy wheels. They all deteriorate dangerously over a period of time no matter how well they are looked after and, in any case, you can't know how they have been treated.
3)   Make certain that the wheels and tyres you want don't foul on the bodywork or suspension without modification (for this reason Cooper 'S' wheels cannot be fitted to other models: they foul the suspension arms and shockers).
4)   If the wheels extend beyond the bodywork, you must fit wheelarch extensions to stay legal.

Well, zur, I overheard you sayin' you couldn't afford a Range Rover, what with buyin' your missus a brand new Mayfair an' all, so I reckoned as you'd be pleased if I turned 'im into a Mayfair County for 'ee . . .

T1. Hotter cams and bigger valves, are ways of making a quicker Mini, but changing the cam by itself will give little or no improvement to most Mini engines and fitting bigger valves may actually be more trouble and more expensive than fitting a better head complete — second-hand, of course.

T2. For those determined to carry out their tuning to the furthest possible degree, the Mini Spares Centre even stocks blank, unmachined cranks which can be machined to the owner's specification.

T3. When you strip an engine down for tuning or even just for a normal rebuild, it is well worth having the crank and flywheel balanced by a specialist because it adds a great deal to the smooth running and ultimate reliability of the engine.

T4. In combination with head modifications, better carburation and an improved inlet manifold, an exhaust manifold such as this can play an important role in speeding the flow of gases through an engine.

T5. Stiffer shock absorbers certainly improve the Mini's roadholding but they can make an already stiff suspension almost unbearable over some surfaces. Perhaps the best solution is to fit Spax adjustable shock absorbers, which can be adjusted to give a softer or a firmer ride at the turn of a screwdriver.

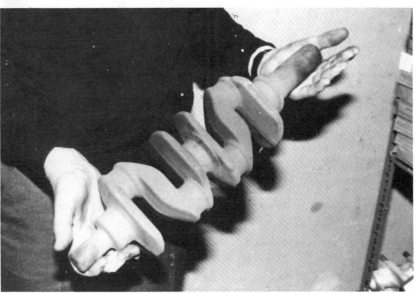

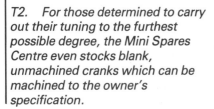

T6. The Mini tuning, modification and customising accessories currently available would probably require another book of this size to catalogue. This one, offered by the Mini Spares Centre, gives a quieter timing drive.

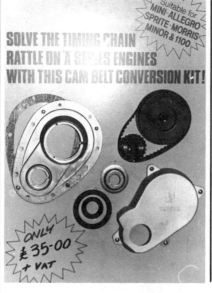

T7. This chapter recommends that larger and more powerful engines and improved cylinder heads can come cheaply from second-hand sources. The 1100/1300 range is a rich source of such parts. A GT model such as this, would provide an excellent engine for a Mini.

T8. Without a doubt, one of the fastest non-Cooper transverse engines and one of the best gearboxes can both be found in the 1300GT. This is the legend to look for.

Accessories – general

AC1. There can be no car in the world that is better catered for in terms of accessories. Every motorists' shop large or small carries a great range of 'goodies' for Minis, some of them made just for the car and some of a more universal nature. In the Midlands, the Midland Mini Centre specialises in the cars (thanks due to them for help with the photographs in this section) while in the South, Keith Dodd's Mini Spares Centre, a somewhat larger set-up, is located in North London.

Wheels and spacers

AC2. Probably the classic Mini wheels are these Minilites. The company that makes them has gone out of business so, unless someone else starts to produce them, excellent second-hand examples are bound to be worth a premium. Beware of the dangers noted earlier in this chapter when it comes to buying second-hand wheels. There is a vast range of Mini wheels on the market. The Midland Mini Centre recommends two basic 'ideal' wheel/tyre combinations for the Mini: 145 × 10 tyres on 3 ½ or 4 ½ inch wheels or 165 × 70 × 10 on 4 ½ to 6 inch wheels. 5 inch wheels generally require the use of spats to stay legal although it depends on the amount of offset which the manufacturer puts into his wheels. They do not recommend the use of wheels over 6 inches in width for road use.

AC3. Wheel spacer kits give a wider track but of course, they put more stress on the wheel bearings. It is really vital to use a heavier-duty hub-bearing kit. These fit easily to the rears, but they are so difficult to fit to the front that . . .

AC4. . . . owners frequently go the whole hog and fit Cooper discs to the front at the same time. The specialists mentioned can usually supply them new or second-hand.

AC5.   An alternative route to
increased brake efficiency is to fit
Minifin aluminium brake drums.
These conduct the heat away a lot
more quickly than cast iron drums
and give a real boost to brake
efficiency. Two different types give
a choice of two different increases
in track.

AC6.   Obviously, aluminium is
unsuitable as a brake drum friction
surface and so a steel ring is shrunk
into the drum.

Body modifications

You can buy all sorts of body
modification packages for Minis
(but interestingly spoilers, which are
often seen fitted to larger cars are
only occasionally sold for Minis, it
seems).

AC7.   Wheel arch extensions are
much more popular. This BL part
comes from the limited edition Minis
and, naturally enough, is an
excellent component. It is fitted by
drilling holes and screwing into the
bodywork.

AC8. These aluminium extensions are just as easy to fit but don't look quite as smart. All wheel arch extensions tend to look silly when used with standard size wheels and tyres!

AC9. You can even buy these rubber mud-shields to go up inside the wings and prevent corrosion-forming mud from splashing up into the wing area – an excellent accessory for the conscientious owner.

AC10. Some folk like to fit a second fuel tank for which task you need: a Cooper 'S' tank; a length of steel pipe to go between the two tanks behind the seat; a tee-piece to join the second tank into the original tank's fuel line; an extra grommet for the hole that has to be cut in the rear body for the filler pipe and an adaptation of a standard tank strap for holding the new one in place. Non-standard right-hand tank kits are available from the specialists.

AC11. Heated rear screens can be provided by buying one with the elements let into the glass, as was original equipment on some models, (second-hand screens should therefore be readily available) . . .

AC12. . . . or by buying one of the stick-on heated rear screen elements. In either case, if you're refitting a screen, see the relevant section of this book.

Interior

AC13.   There are countless numbers of steering wheels available, from normal size down to ridiculously small. They are easy to fit provided that you have the right sized spanner to undo the fixing nut.

AC14.   You can modify the spartan Mini dashboard in a number of ways: this ABS moulding just fits straight on, held in place by a couple of self-tapping screws.

AC15.   These rather plush real-wood-veneer dashes are available for just about every model and really do look very attractive when properly slotted into place: again there's very little which is complex about their fitting.

AC16.   The basic Mini is certainly not over-endowed with instrumentation! A new dash is an ideal place to fit one of the many accessory instruments you can buy: tachometers being among the most popular.

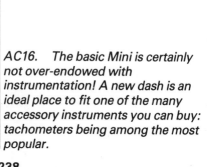

AC17.   These 'Restall' seats were very expensive twenty years ago but are among the best Mini aftermarket seats ever made. Find good used ones if you can . . .

AC18.   Two kinds of Cooper seat shown here are the standard, back-acheing offering on the left, and the fairly rare 'factory-recliners' on the right. Either type can be hard to find nowadays, but there is a wide range of styles, and prices, in the new aftermarket seats currently available.

AC19.   Roll-over bars are fairly popular accessories among the true racers and the 'go-faster' fraternity. They usually bolt down according to the manufacturer's instructions and so are fairly easy to fit.

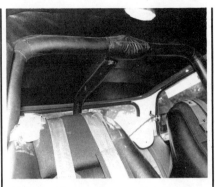

AC20.   You can buy padded roll-over bars too, but the better ones are rather expensive.

Sundries

AC21.   Earlier cars often suffer from damp splashing onto the ignition. A good solution is to fit a splash guard from a later car, or bought new through Austin-Rover Unipart.

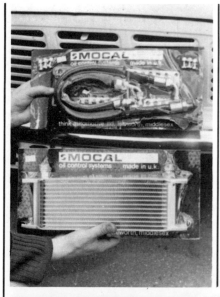

AC22.   If you think you can squeeze an oil cooler behind the dash, it's a useful accessory to have, especially with a Mini that develops extra power, and it's a very straightforward item to fit — apart from the lack of room, that is!

AC23.   Spax adjustable shock absorbers probably provide the best solution for someone who wants hard suspension on occasions, perhaps for the odd autotest, but prefers more bearable 'soft' suspension for everyday use.

AC24.   Mini owners have always loved to bolt 'goodies' to their cars. This one was fitted with a black grille and wheelarch extensions from a later model, smart wide wheels, heavy duty nudge bars, spotlamps and a sliding fabric sunroof.

Appendices

1 Workshop Procedures ~ Safety First

Professional motor mechanics are trained in safe working procedures. However enthusiastic you may be about getting on with the job in hand, do take the time to ensure that your safety is not put at risk. A moment's lack of attention can result in an accident, as can failure to observe certain elementary precautions.

There will always be new ways of having accidents, and the following points do not pretend to be a comprehensive list of all dangers; they are intended rather to make you aware of the risks and to encourage a safety-conscious approach to all work you carry out on your vehicle.

Essential DOs and DON'Ts

DON'T rely on a single jack when working underneath the vehicle. Always use reliable additional means of support, such as axle stands, securely placed under a part of the vehicle that you know will not give way.

DON'T attempt to loosen or tighten high-torque nuts (e.g. wheel hub nuts) while the vehicle is on a jack; it may be pulled off.

DON'T start the engine without first ascertaining that the transmission is in neutral (or 'Park' where applicable) and the parking brake applied.

DON'T suddenly remove the filler cap from a hot cooling system — let it cool down first, cover it with a cloth and release the pressure gradually first, or you may get scalded by escaping coolant.

DON'T attempt to drain oil until you are sure it has cooled sufficiently to avoid scalding you.

DON'T grasp any part of the engine, exhaust or catalytic converter without first ascertaining that it is sufficiently cool to avoid burning you.

DON'T inhale brake lining dust — it is injurious to health.

DON'T allow any spilt oil or grease to remain on the floor — wipe it up straightaway, before someone slips on it.

DON'T use ill-fitting spanners or other tools which may slip and cause injury.

DON'T attempt to lift a heavy component which may be beyond your capability — get assistance.

DON'T rush to finish a job, or take unverified short cuts.

DON'T allow children or animals in or around an unattended vehicle.

DO wear eye protection when using power tools such as drill, sander, bench grinder etc, and when working under the vehicle.

DO use a barrier cream on your hands prior to undertaking dirty jobs — it will protect your skin from infection as well as making the dirt easier to remove afterwards; but make sure your hands aren't left slippery.

DO keep loose clothing (cuffs, tie etc) and long hair well out of the way of moving mechanical parts.

DO remove rings, wristwatch etc, before working on the vehicle — especially the electrical system.

DO ensure that any lifting tackle used has a safe working load rating adequate for the job.

DO keep your work area tidy — it is only too easy to fall over articles left lying around.

DO get someone to check periodically that all is well, when working alone on the vehicle.

DO carry out work in a logical sequence and check that everything is correctly assembled and tightened afterwards.

DO remember that your vehicle's safety affects that of yourself and others. If in doubt on any point, get specialist advice.

IF, in spite of following these precautions, you are unfortunate enough to injure yourself, seek medical attention as soon as possible.

Fire

Remember at all times that petrol (gasoline) is highly flammable. Never smoke, or have any kind of naked flame around, when working on the vehicle. But the risk does not end there — a spark caused by an electrical short-circuit, by two metal surfaces contacting each other, or even by static electricity built up in your body under certain conditions can ignite petrol vapour, which in a confined space is highly explosive.

Always disconnect the battery earth (ground) terminal before working on any part of the fuel system, and never risk spilling fuel on to a hot engine or exhaust.

It is recommended that a fire extinguisher of a type suitable for fuel and electrical fires is kept handy in the garage or workplace at all times. Never try to extinguish a fuel or electrical fire with water.

Fumes

Certain fumes are highly toxic and can quickly cause unconsciousness

and even death if inhaled to any extent. Petrol (gasoline) vapour comes into this category, as do the vapours from certain solvents such as trichloroethylene. Any draining or pouring of such volatile fluids should be done in a well ventilated area.

When using cleaning fluids and solvents, read the instructions carefully. Never use any materials from unmarked containers — they may give off poisonous vapours.

Never run the engine of a motor vehicle in an enclosed space such as a garage. Exhaust fumes contain carbon monoxide which is extremely poisonous; if you need to run the engine, always do so in the open air or at least have the rear of the vehicle outside the workplace.

If you are fortunate enough to have the use of an inspection pit never drain or pour petrol, and never run the engine, while the vehicle is standing over it; the fumes, being heavier than air, will concentrate in the pit with possibly lethal results.

The battery

Never cause a spark, or allow a naked light, near the vehicle battery. It will normally be giving off a certain amount of hydrogen gas, which is highly explosive.

Always disconnect the battery earth (ground) terminal before working on the fuel or electrical systems.

If possible, loosen the filler plugs or cover when charging the battery from an external source. Do not charge at an excessive rate or the battery may burst.

Take care when topping up and when carrying the battery. The acid electrolyte, even when diluted, is very corrosive and should not be allowed to contact the eyes or skin.

If you ever need to prepare electrolyte yourself, always add the acid slowly to the water, and never the other way round. Protect against splashes by wearing rubber gloves and goggles.

Mains electricity

When using an electric power tool, inspection light etc. which works from the mains, always ensure that the appliance is correctly connected to its plug and that, where necessary, it is properly earthed (grounded). Do not use such appliances in damp conditions and, again, beware of creating a spark or applying excessive heat in the vicinity of fuel or fuel vapour.

Ignition HT voltage

A severe electric shock can result from touching certain parts of the ignition system, such as the HT leads, when the engine is running or being cranked, particularly if components are damp or the insulation is defective. Where an electronic ignition system is fitted, the HT voltage is much higher and could prove fatal.

Compressed gas cylinders

There are serious hazards associated with the storage and handling of gas cylinders and fittings, and standard precautions should be strictly observed in dealing with them. Ensure that cylinders are stored in safe conditions, properly maintained and always handled with special care and make constant efforts to eliminate the possibilities of leakage, fire and explosion.

The cylinder gases that are commonly used are oxygen, acetylene and liquid petroleum gas (LPG). Safety requirements for all three gases are:
Cylinders must be stored in a fire resistant, dry and well ventilated space, away from any source of heat or ignition and protected from

ice, snow or direct sunlight. Valves of cylinders in store must always be kept uppermost and closed, even when the cylinder is empty. Cylinders should be handled with care and only by personnel who are reliable, adequately informed and fully aware of all associated hazards. Damaged or leaking cylinders should be immediately taken outside into the open air, and the supplier should be notified. No one should approach a gas cylinder store with a naked light or cigarette. Care should be taken to avoid striking or dropping cylinders, or knocking them together. Cylinders should never be used as rollers. One cylinder should never be filled from another. Every care must be taken to avoid accidental damage to cylinder valves. Valves must be operated without haste, never fully opened hard back against the back stop (so that other users know the valve is open) and never wrenched shut but turned just securely enough to stop the gas. Before removing or loosening any outlet connections, caps or plugs, a check should be made that the valves are closed. When changing cylinders, close all valves and appliance taps, and extinguish naked flames, including pilot jets, before disconnecting them. When reconnecting ensure that all connections and washers are clean and in good condition and do not overtighten them. Immediately a cylinder becomes empty, close its valve.

Safety requirements for acetylene: Cylinders must always be stored and used in the upright position. If a cylinder becomes heated accidentally or becomes hot because of excessive backfiring, immediately shut the valve, detach the regulator, take the cylinder out of doors well away from the building, immerse it in or continuously spray it with water, open the valve and allow the gas to escape until the cylinder is empty.

Safety requirements for oxygen: No oil or grease should be used on valves or fittings. Cylinders with convex bases should be used in a stand or held securely to a wall.

Safety requirements for LPG: The store must be kept free of combustible material, corrosive material and cylinders of oxygen.

Dangerous liquids and gases

Because of flammable gas given off by batteries when on charge, care should be taken to avoid sparking by switching off the power supply before charger leads are connected or disconnected. Battery terminals should be shielded, since a battery contains energy and a spark can be caused by any conductor which touches its terminals or exposed connecting straps.

When internal combustion engines are operated inside buildings the exhaust fumes must be properly discharged to the open air. Petroleum spirit or mixture must be contained in metal cans which should be kept in a store. In any area where battery charging or the testing of fuel injection systems is carried out there must be good ventilation and no sources of ignition. Inspection pits often present serious hazards. They should be of adequate length to allow safe access and exit while a car is in position. If there is an inspection pit, petrol may enter it. Since petrol vapour is heavier than air it will remain there and be a hazard if there is any source of ignition. All sources of ignition must therefore be excluded. Special care should be taken when any type of lifting equipment is used. Lifting jacks are for raising vehicles; they should never be used as supports while work is in progress. Jacks must be replaced by adequate rigid supports before any work is begun on the vehicle. Risk of injury while

working on running engines, eg, adjusting the timing, can arise if the operator touches a high voltage lead and pulls his hand away on to a projection or revolving part.

Work with plastics

Work with plastic materials brings additional hazards into workshops. Many of the materials used (polymers, resins, adhesives and materials acting as catalysts and accelerators) readily produce very dangerous situations in the form of poisonous fumes, skin irritants, risk of fire and explosions.

Jacks and axle stands

Any jack, especially the factory jack for the Mini, is made for lifting the car, not for supporting it. NEVER even consider working under your car using only a jack to support the weight of the car. Jacks are for lifting; axle stands are available from many discount stores and all auto parts stores. These stands are absolutely essential if you plan to work under your car. Simple triangular stands (fixed or adjustable) will suit almost all of your working situations. Drive-on ramps are very limiting because of their design and size.

When jacking the car from the front, leave the gearbox in neutral and the brake off until you have placed the axle stands under the frame. Then put the car into gear and/or engage the handbrake and lower the jack. Obviously DO NOT put the car in gear if you plan to turn over the engine! Leaving the brake on or leaving the car in gear while jacking the front of the car will necessarily cause the jack to tip. This is unavoidable when jacking the car on one side and the use of the handbrake in this case is recommended.

Excellent jacking points are; the front cross member (never the engine's sump); the centre of the differential; under either leaf spring; under the doors at the frame; or with the factory jack, the jack tubes. If the car is older and if it shows signs of weakening at the jack tubes while using the factory jack, it is best to purchase a good scissors jack or pneumatic jack (depending on your budget).

Welding and bodywork Repairs

It is so useful to be able to weld when carrying out restoration work and yet there is a good deal that could go dangerously wrong for the uninformed — in fact more than could be covered here. *For safety's sake* you are strongly recommended to seek tuition in whatever branch of welding you wish to use, from your local evening institute or through an adult education class. In addition, all of the information and instructional material produced by the suppliers of materials and equipment you will be using must be studied carefully. You may have to ask your stockist for some of this printed material if it is not made available at the time of purchase.

In addition, it is strongly recommended that *The Car Bodywork Repair Manual*, published by Haynes, is purchased and studied before carrying out any welding or bodywork repairs. Consisting of 292 pages and around 1,000 illustrations, and written by the author of this book, *The Car Bodywork Repair Manual* picks the brains of specialists from a variety of fields and covers arc, MIG and gas welding; panel beating and accident repair; rust repair and treatment; paint spraying; glass-fibre work, filler; lead loading; interiors; and much more besides. Alongside a number of car bodywork projects, the book describes in detail how to carry out each of the techniques involved in car bodywork repair with safety notes where necessary. As such, it is the ideal complement to this book.

Workshop safety — summary

1) Always have a fire extinguisher at arm's length whenever working on the fuel system — under the car, or under the bonnet.
2) NEVER use a torch near the petrol tank.
3) Keep your inspection lamp FAR AWAY from any source of dripping petrol (gasoline), for example while removing the fuel pump.
4) NEVER use petrol (gasoline) to clean parts. Use paraffin (kerosene) or white (mineral) spirits.
5) NO SMOKING!
   If you do have a fire, DON'T PANIC. Use the extinguisher effectively by directing it at the base of the fire.

2 Tools & Working Facilities

Introduction

A selection of good tools is a fundamental requirement for anyone contemplating the maintenance and repair of a motor vehicle. For the owner who does not possess any, their purchase will prove a considerable expense, offsetting some of the savings made by doing-it-yourself. However, provided that the tools purchased are of good quality, they will last for many years and prove an extremely worthwhile investment.

To help the average owner to decide which tools are needed to carry out the various tasks detailed in this manual, we have compiled three lists of tools under the following headings: Maintenance and minor repair, Repair and overhaul, and Special. The newcomer to practical mechanics should start off with the 'Maintenance and minor repair' tool kit and confine himself to the simpler jobs around the vehicle.

Then, as his confidence and experience grows, he can undertake more difficult tasks, buying extra tools as, and when, they are needed. In this way a 'Maintenance and minor repair' tool kit can be built up into a 'Repair and overhaul' tool kit over a considerble period of time without any major cash outlays. The experienced do-it-yourselfer will have a tool kit good enough for most repairs and overhaul procedures and will add tools from the 'Special' category when he feels the expense is justified by the amount of use these tools will be put to.

Maintenance and minor repair tool kit

The tools given in this list should be considered as a minimum requirement if routine maintenance, servicing and minor repair operations are to be undertaken.

We recommend the purchase of combination spanners (ring one end, open-ended the other); although more expensive than open-ended ones, they do give the advantage of both types of spanner.

Combination spanners − $7/16$, $1/2$, $9/16$, $5/8$, $11/16$, $3/4$, $13/16$, $15/16$ in. AF
Combination spanners − 5, 6, 8, 10 and 12 mm
Adjustable spanner − 9 inch
Engine sump/gearbox/rear axle drain plug key (where applicable)
Spark plug spanner (with rubber insert)
Spark plug gap adjustment tool
Set of feeler gauges
Brake adjuster spanner (where applicable)
Brake bleed nipple spanner
Screwdriver − 4 in. long × $1/4$ in. dia. (plain)
Screwdriver − 4 in. long × $1/4$ in. dia. (crosshead)
Combination pliers − 6 inch
Hacksaw, junior
Tyre pump

Tyre pressure gauge
Grease gun (where applicable)
Oil can
Fine emery cloth (1 sheet)
Wire brush (small)
Funnel (medium size)

Repair and overhaul tool kit

These tools are virtually essential for anyone undertaking any major repairs to a motor vehicle, and are additional to those given in the Basic list. Included in this list is a comprehensive set of sockets. Although these are expensive they will be found invaluable as they are so versatile — particularly if various drives are included in the set. We recommend the $\frac{1}{2}$ square-drive type, as this can be used with most proprietary torque wrenches. If you cannot afford a socket set, even bought piecemeal, then inexpensive tubular box spanners are a useful alternative.

The tools in this list will occasionally need to be supplemented by tools from the Special list.

Sockets (or box spanners) to cover range in previous list
Reversible ratchet drive (for use with sockets)
Extension piece, 10 inch (for use with sockets)
Universal joint (for use with sockets)
Torque wrench (for use with sockets)
'Mole' wrench — 8 inch
Ball pein hammer
Soft-faced hammer, plastic or rubber
Screwdriver — 6 in. long × $^5/_{16}$ in. dia. (plain)
Screwdriver — 2 in. long × $^5/_{16}$ in. square (plain)
Screwdriver — 1 $\frac{1}{2}$ in. long × $^1/_4$ in. dia. (crosshead)
Screwdriver — 3 in. long × $^1/_8$ in. dia. (electrician's)
Pliers — electrician's side cutters

Pliers — needle noses
Pliers — circlip (internal and external)
Cold chisel — $^1/_2$ inch
Scriber (this can be made by grinding the end of a broken hacksaw blade)
Scraper (This can be made by flattening and sharpening one end of a piece of copper pipe)
Centre punch
Pin punch
Hacksaw
Valve grinding tool
Steel rule/straightedge
Allen keys
Selection of files
Wire brush (large)
Axle stands
Jack (strong scissor or hydraulic type)

Special tools

The tools in this list are those which are not used regularly, are expensive to buy, or which need to be used in accordance with their manufacturer's instructions. Unless relatively difficult mechanical jobs are undertaken frequently, it will not be economic to buy many of these tools. Where this is the case, you could consider clubbing together with friends (or a motorists' club) to make a joint purchase, or borrowing the tools against a deposit from a local garage or tool hire specialist.

The following list contains only those tools and instruments freely available to the public, and not those special tools produced by the vehicle manufacturer specially for its dealer network.

Valve spring compressor
Piston ring compressor
Ball joint separator
Universal hub/bearing puller
Impact screwdriver
Micrometer and/or vernier gauge
Carburettor flow balancing device (where applicable)
Dial gauge
Stroboscopic timing light

Dwell angle meter/tachometer
Universal electrical multi-meter
Cylinder compression gauge
Lifting tackle
Trolley jack
Light with extension lead

Buying tools

For practically all tools, a tool factor is the best source since he will have a very comprehensive range compared with the average garage or accessory shop. Having said that, accessory shops often offer excellent quality goods at discount prices, so it pays to shop around.

Remember, you don't have to buy the most expensive items on the shelf, but it is always advisable to steer clear of the very cheap tools. There are plenty of good tools around, at reasonable prices, so ask the proprietor or manager of the shop for advice before making a purchase.

Care and maintenance of tools

Having purchased a reasonable tool kit, it is necessary to keep the tools in a clean and serviceable condition. After use, always wipe off any dirt, grease and metal particles using a clean, dry cloth, before putting the tools away. Never leave them lying around after they have been used. A simple tool rack on the garage or workshop wall, for items such as screwdrivers and pliers is a good idea. Store all normal spanners and sockets in a metal box. Any measuring instruments, gauges, meters etc., must be carefully stored where they cannot be damaged or become rusty.

Take a little care when the tools are used. Hammer heads inevitably become marked and screwdrivers lose the keen edge on their blades from time-to-time. A little timely attention with emery cloth or a file will soon restore items like this to a good serviceable finish.

Working facilities

Not to be forgotten when discussing tools, is the workshop itself. If anything more than routine maintenance is to be carried out, some form of suitable working area becomes essential.

It is appreciated that many an owner mechanic is forced by circumstance to remove an engine or similar item, without the benefit of a garage or workshop. Having done this, any repairs should always be done under the cover of a roof.

Wherever possible, any dismantling should be done on a clean flat workbench or table at a suitable working height.

Any workbench needs a vice: one with a jaw opening of 4 in. (100mm) is suitable for most jobs. As mentioned previously, some clean, dry storage space is also required for tools, as well as the lubricants, cleaning fluids, touch-up paints and so on which soon become necessary.

Another item which may be required, and which has a much more general usage, is an electric drill with a chuck capacity of at least $5/16$ in. (8mm). This, together with a good range of twist drills, is virtually essential for fitting accessories such as wing mirrors and reversing lights.

Last, but not least, always keep a supply of old newspapers and clean, lint-free rags available, and try to keep any working areas as clean as possible.

Spanner jaw gap comparison table

Jaw gap (in.)	Spanner size
0.250	$1/4$ in. AF
0.275	7 mm AF
0.312	$5/16$ in. AF
0.315	8 mm AF
0.340	$11/32$ in. AF/$1/8$ in. Whitworth
0.354	9 mm AF
0.375	$3/8$ in. AF
0.393	10 mm AF
0.433	11 mm AF
0.437	$7/16$ in. AF
0.445	$3/16$ in. Whitworth/$1/4$ in. BSF
0.472	12 mm AF
0.500	$1/2$ in. AF
0.512	13 mm AF
0.525	$1/4$ in. Whitworth/$5/16$ in. BSF
0.551	14 mm AF
0.562	$9/16$ in. AF
0.590	15 mm AF
0.600	$5/16$ in. Whitworth/$3/8$ in. BSF
0.625	$5/8$ in. AF
0.629	16 mm AF
0.669	17 mm AF
0.687	$11/16$ in. AF
0.708	18 mm AF
0.710	$3/8$ in. Whitworth/$7/16$ in. BSF
0.748	19 mm AF
0.750	$3/4$ in. AF
0.812	$13/16$ in. AF
0.820	$7/16$ in. Whitworth/$1/2$ in. BSF
0.866	22 mm AF
0.875	$7/8$ in. AF
0.920	$1/2$ in. Whitworth/$9/16$ in. BSF
0.937	$15/16$ in. AF
0.944	24 mm AF
1.000	1 in. AF
1.010	$9/16$ in. Whitworth/$5/8$ in. BSF
1.023	26 mm AF
1.062	$1 1/16$ in. AF/27 mm AF
1.100	$5/8$ in. Whitworth/$11/16$ in. BSF
1.125	$1 1/8$ in. AF
1.181	30 mm AF
1.200	$11/16$ in. Whitworth/$3/4$ in. BSF
1.250	$1 1/4$ in. AF
1.259	32 mm AF
1.300	$3/4$ in. Whitworth/$7/8$ in. BSF
1.312	$1 5/16$ in. AF
1.390	$13/16$ in. Whitworth/$15/16$ in. BSF
1.417	36 mm AF
1.437	$1 7/16$ in. AF
1.480	$7/8$ in. Whitworth/1 in. BSF
1.500	$1 1/2$ in. AF
1.574	40 mm AF/$15/16$ in. Whitworth
1.614	41 mm AF
1.625	$1 5/8$ in. AF
1.670	1 in. Whitworth/$1 1/8$ in. BSF
1.687	$1 11/16$ in. AF
1.811	46 mm AF
1.812	$1 13/16$ in. AF
1.860	$1 1/8$ in. Whitworth/$1 1/4$ in. BSF
1.875	$1 7/8$ in. AF
1.968	50 mm AF
2.000	2 in. AF
2.050	$1 1/4$ in. Whitworth/$1 3/8$ in. BSF
2.165	55 mm AF
2.362	60 mm AF

Specifications

Engine data — Mini 850 (all models) & Elf Hornet Mk I

Type	8MB
Number of cylinders	4
Bore	2.478 in. (62.94 mm)
Stroke	2.687 in. (68.26 mm)
Capacity	51.7 in³ (848 cc)
Firing order	1, 3, 4, 2
Compression ratio	8.3:1
Valve operation	Overhead by pushrod
Bmep	128 lb/in² (9 kg/cm²) at 2900 rev/min
Torque	44 lb ft (6.08 kg m) at 2900 rev/min
BHP (PUDD)	35 @ 5500 rev/min

Engine data — Mini 850 Automatic (as above, except —)

Type	8AH
Compression ratio	9:1
Torque	44 lb ft (6.08 kg m) at 2500 rev/min
Bhp (DIN)	37 @ 5250 rev/min

Engine data — Mini 1000 (except Cooper) & Elf/Hornet Mk II & III

Type	9WR, 99H
Bore	2.543 in. (64.588 mm)
Stroke	3.00 in. (76.2 mm)
Capacity	60.96 in³ (998 cc)
Compression ratio	8.3:1
Bmep	130 lb/in² (9.14 kg/cm²) at 2700 rev/min
Torque	52 lb ft (7.28 kg m) at 2700 rev/min
Bhp (DIN)	36 @ 4600 rev/min

Engine data — Mini Cooper 997

Type	9F
Bore	2.458 in. (62.43 mm)
Stroke	3.20 in. (81.28 mm)
Capacity	60.87 in³ (997 cc)
Compression ratio:	
High compression	9:1
Low compression	8.3:1
Bmep: High compression	134 lb/in² (9.42 kg/cm²) at 3500 rev/min
Low compression	129 lb/in² (9.07 kg/cm²) at 3500 rev/min
Torque: High compression	54 lb ft (7.46 kg m) at 3600 rev/min
Low compression	53 lb ft (7.32 kg m) at 3500 rev/min
Bhp (DIN): High compression	55 @ 6000 rev/min

Engine data — Mini Cooper 998

Type	9FA
Bore	2.543 in. (64.588 mm)
Stroke	3.00 in. (76.2 mm)
Capacity	60.96 in³ (998 cc)
Compression ratio:	
High	9:1
Low	7.8:1
Bmep: High compression	142 lb/in² (10 kg/cm²) at 3000 rev/min
Low compression	135 lb/in² (9.5 kg/cm²) at 3000 rev/min
Torque: High compression	57 lb ft (7.88 kg m) at 3000 rev/min
Low compression	56 lb ft (7.74 kg m) at 2000 rev/min
Bhp (DIN):	
High compression	53.8 @ 5800 rev/min
Low compression	50.2 @ 5900 rev/min

Engine data – Mini Cooper 'S' (all models)

Type	970 = 9F
	1071 – 10F
	1275 = 12F
Bore (all models)	2.780 in (70.6 mm)
Stroke: 970 cc	2.4375 in (61.91 mm)
1071 cc	2.687 in. (68.26 mm)
1275 cc	3.2 in (81.33 mm)
Capacity: 970 cc	59.1 in³ (970 cc)
1071 cc	63.35 in³ (1071 cc)
1275 cc	77.9 in³ (1275 cc)
Compression ratio: 970cc	10:1
1071 cc	9.0:1
1275 cc	9.75:1
Bmep: 970 cc	142 lb/in² (9.98 kg/cm²) at 4500 rev/min
1071 cc	143 lb/in² (10.05 kg/cm²) at 4500 rev/min
1275 cc	153 lb/in² (10.76 kg/cm²) at 3000 rev/min
Torque: 970 cc	57 lb ft (7.88 kg m) at 5000 rev/min
1071 cc	62 lb ft (8.58 kg m) at 4500 rev/min
1275 cc	79 lb ft (10.92 kg m) at 3000 rev/min
Bhp (DIN): 970 cc	64 @ 6500 rev/min
1071 cc	67.5 @ 6500 rev/min
1275 cc	76.1 @ 6000 rev/min

Engine data – Mini 1275 GT

Type	12H
Bore	2.78 in. (70.61 mm)
Stroke	3.2 in. (81.28 mm)
Capacity	77.8 in³ (1274.86 cm³)
Compression ratio:	
High compression	8.8:1
Low compression	8.3:1
Bmep	130 lb/in² (9.14 kg/cm²) at 2500 rev/min
Torque	84 lb ft (9.2 kg m) at 2500 rev/min
Bhp (DIN)	57 @ 5500 rev/min

Engine data – Mini Clubman 1100

Type	
Bore	2.543 in. (64.588 mm)
Stroke	3.296 in. (83.73 mm)
Capacity	66.96 in³ (1098 cc)
Compression ratio	8.5:1
Bmep	127 lb/in² (8.85 kg/cm²) at 2700 rev/min
Torque	56 lb ft (7.7 kg m) at 2700 rev/min
Bhp (DIN)	44.6 @ 5000 rev/min

Engine data general — all models

Firing order	1-3-4-2 (Cyl. 1 nearest radiator)
Oil pressure (hot):	
Running	60 psi: (1275 Cooper 'S' pressure can rise to 90 psi)
Idling	15 psi

General mechanical specifications — all models (except Cooper)

Please note that in the main, these specifications relate to original models. See your vehicle's handbook and 'Production Modifications' in these appendices for later specification changes.

Fuel system
Carburetter, S.U. Type HS2
Jet, 0.090 in. bore
Needles: standard, EB; rich, M; weak, GG
Pump, S.U. electric
Delivery pressure, 2 to 3 psi

Ignition system
Plugs type, Champion N.5
Plug gap, 0.025 in.
Distributor point gap, 0.014-0.016 in.

Gearbox
Ratios:
   top, 1.0 to 1
   third, 1.412 to 1
   second, 2.172 to 1
   first, 3.627 to 1
   reverse, 3.627 to 1

Cooling system
Thermostat setting, 72°C

Differential
Ratio 3.765 to 1

Steering
Type, rack-and-pinion
Turns, lock to lock, 2¼
Camber 1° to 3° positive
Castor, 3°
King-pin inclination, 9° 30'
Toe-out, $^1/_{16}$ in.

Rear suspension
Toe-in, ⅛ in.
Camber, 1° positive

Electrical system
Type, 12-volt, positive earth
Starter, Lucas Type M35G
Dynamo, Lucas Type C40
Cut-out:
   cut-in voltage, 12.7 to 13.3
   drop-off voltage, 8.5 to 11.0

Brakes
Drum size, 7 in. dia.
Lining dimensions, 6.25 in. by 1.25 in.
Lining material, Mintex M.32

Tyres	Size, 5.20 by 10
	Pressures: Front 24 psi
	Rear: 22 psi

Capacities

Power unit, 8 ½ pints
Cooling system, 5 ½ pints
Petrol tank:
   Saloon, 5 ½ gallons
   Van, 6 gallons
   Traveller, 6 ½ gallons

Dimensions

Saloon:
   wheelbase, 6 ft. 8 in.
   length, 10 ft. 0 ¼ in.
   width, 4 ft. 7 ½ in.
   height, 4 ft. 5 in.
   clearance (ground), 6⅜ in.
   weight, 1,330 lb.
Van and Traveller:
   wheelbase, 7 ft.
   length, 10 ft. 9 in.
   width, 4 ft. 7 ½ in.
   height, 4 ft. 6 ½ in. (Trav. 4 ft. 5 ½ in.)
   clearance (ground), 6⅜ in.
   weight, 1,334 lb. (Trav. 1,456 lb.)

General mechanical specifications — Cooper (as above, except —)

Fuel system

Carburetters, Twin S.U. Type HS2
Needle, GZ standard
Pump, S.U. electric

Gearbox

Ratios:
   top, 1.0 to 1
   third, 1.356 to 1
   second, 1.915 to 1

first, 3.20 to 1
reverse, 3.20 to 1

Brakes

Front: disc size, 7 in. dia.
Rear: drum size, 7 in. dia.

General mechanical specifications — Cooper 'S' (as given under previous two section headings, except —)

Fuel system

Needles:
   970 cc, AN
   1071 cc, H6
   1275 cc, M

Ignition system	Plugs type, Champion N9Y
	Timing (static):
	   970 cc, 12° BTDC
	   1071 cc, 3° BTDC
	   1275 cc, 2° BTDC

Gearbox	Ratios:
	   top, 1:1
	   third, 1.357:1
	   second, 1.916:1
	   first and reverse, 3.200:1
	Optional Ratios:
	   top, 1:1
	   third, 1.242:1
	   second, 1.78:1
	   first and reverse, 2.57:1

Final drive	Ratio, standard:
	   970 cc and 1.071 cc, 3.765:1
	   1275 cc, 3.444:1
	Optional Ratios — all models:
	   3.939:1; 4.133:1; 4.267:1

Brakes	Front: disc size, 7 ½ in. dia. Pad material: DA6 Power assisted by vacuum servo

Wheels & tyres	Wheel size:
	   standard, 3.50B × 10
	   optional, 4.5J × 10
	Tyres:
	   standard, Dunlop SP or C41
	   optional, Dunlop 5.00L × 10
	Tyre pressures:
	   front, 28 psi; rear, 26 psi

Production Modifications

There have been hundreds of production changes made to the dozens of Mini variants in the car's quarter century of production, and it really isn't possible to detail *every* one. Even so, this is one of the most complete catalogue of changes yet published in any book.

Date	Chassis number (where available). Austin given first, where applicable	Modification
1959		
August	101	Austin Seven/Morris Mini Minor announced.
–	4232/4093	Radiator cowl split for ease of access.
–	5488/5537	Pivoting quadrant fitted to handbrake cable on radius arm.
–	10151/11670	Castor angle altered from 1.5 to 3 degrees.
December		Interior trim improved on Austins – standard from body no. 9146, De Luxe from 10549.
1960		
January	10502	Improved window catches.
February	(Morris only, 14215 Austin no. not available)	Improved trim with padding around instrument cluster, and in door and side panels. Improved telescopic dampers, fuel tank with drain plug, improved window catches.
March	19126	Countryman first built.
April	26590/24831	Driveshafts changed from square section splines to involute, shorter with modified flanges.
May		Mini Van announced.

Date	Chassis number (where available). Austin given first, where applicable	Modification
September October General	19101 (Austin only) 58698	Countryman/Traveller announced with wood framing. Improvements as to Morris from February 1960. Other changes in 1960: improved air cleaners, changes to clutch stop, larger front wheel bearings, cranked gear lever, improved damper mountings, primary gear oil seal improved (engine 16490/17450), rigid foam introduced into sills, seatbelt anchorages fitted, distributor shield fitted behind grille.
1961		
April		Mini Pick-up introduced.
May	123291/70376	Aluminium suspension trumpets fitted.
August	– /69834	16-blade (quieter) fan fitted, grille plated instead of painted.
August	138301	Mini Cooper MkI 997cc produced.
September	125538/75533	Super announced (produced from June). Extra bars in grille, duo-tone paint, lever-type door handles, 3 instruments in grille, key start ignition.
Autumn		Stronger wheels fitted.
October	156851	Riley Elf/Wolseley Hornet introduced with extended tail fins, bigger boot, improved trim and larger brakes.
1962		
January	197021 (Saloon); 201201 (Super); 197104 (Countryman)	Austin Seven now known as 'Mini'. Larger brake wheel cylinders fitted. Plastic oil-filler cap on engine.
March	226055/116623	Cloth upholstery replaced by Vyanide on Saloon.
October	307125/148817 308939	De Luxe and Super replaced by Super De Luxe model. All-metal Traveller introduced on home market (export only from April 1961). Synchro and gearbox in general largely improved.
End of year	Engine 8A-M-UH-452359	Oil feed to end of crank deleted.
1963		
Jan/February	369601/367151	MkII Elf/Hornet with larger and much stronger engine, 2-leading brake shoes.
March	346017/382183 3844101/384601 186267 (Mor.)	Better brakes fitted to Cooper – twin leading front shoes. Cooper 'S' 1071 introduced. More powerful heater – body no. 087448 (Aus.).
May	197219 (Mor.)	Improved sliding window catch – body no. 091678 (Aus.)
End 1963		Much stronger 848cc engine introduced.
1964		
January	489222/487907 502447/502482	Final 997 Cooper produced. 998 Cooper introduced.
March	563570/550980	Cooper 'S' 1071 discontinued.
April	551501/552501	Cooper 'S' 1275 introduced.

Date	Chassis number (where available). Austin given first, where applicable	Modification
June	549501/550501	Cooper 'S' 970cc introduced.
September	640203/296257 (Saloon)	All Saloons and Coopers with Hydrolastic suspension, starter/ignition switch, courtesy lights, oil filter warning light, diaphragm spring clutch, 2-leading shoe front brakes, closer ratio and stronger gearbox fitted to all models.

1965

January	549992/550980	Cooper 'S' 970 discontinued.
October	798693/361001	Automatic transmission option on De Luxe
November		Reclining seats option on Cooper/Cooper 'S'.

1966

January		Safety bosses fitted to door handles, all models, sealed beam headlamps fitted. 1275 'S' fitted with twin tanks and oil cooler from body no. 47681.
October	930221/927473	MkIII Elf/Hornet introduced with concealed door hinges, winding windows, remote gearlever, fresh air vents, push-button exterior door handles.

1967

October	1068051 (Std) 1068001 (De L)/ 507001/ (Std) 507934 (De L)	MkII introduced with thicker grille surround, rectangular rear lights, wider rear window, combined stalk switch on steering column, etc. Super De Luxe with remote gearchange. Saloon, De L. Countryman and Traveller 'Mini 1000' introduced with 998cc engine and remote gearchange.

1968

September	Engine prefix 8-AM-WE-H (Saloon) 9 FX-XE-H (Cooper)	All-synchro gearbox fitted.

1969

August	1337993/1337528	Riley Elf/Wolseley Hornet discontinued.
October	101 (Saloon); 576 (Estate); 107 (1275 GT);	Clubman range announced, GT with rev. counter Hydrolastic on Saloons and GT.
	1359152	Countryman discontinued.
November	1368676	Traveller discontinued.
	112 (850 Sal.); 601 (1000 Sal.)	BL Mini introduced with 'MINI' badges, B.L. badges on wings, Austin and Morris names dropped. Larger doors with concealed hinges, wind up windows, rubber suspension replaces Hydrolastic again, mechanical fuel pump.
	1370956	Mini-Cooper 998 discontinued.

Date	Chassis number (where available). Austin given first, where applicable	Modification
December	1372023/711800 (850); 1367106/713901 (1000)	Final Austin/Morris Minis built.
1970		
March	1375331 X/ADI 34127	Final Austin Mini-Cooper 1275 'S' MkII. MkIII MINI-Cooper 'S' 1275, still with Hydrolastic suspension.
1971		
February	Engine 12H 389SH6091	1275 GT final drive ratio changed from 3.65 to 3.44.
June	Commission no. S20S-48645A 458987	Clubman Saloon changed from Hydrolastic to rubber suspension. Mini-Cooper 'S' MkIII discontinued.
During year		Radiator cowling removed.
1972		
December		Alternator fitted to all models.
1973		
January	Commission no. D20S 59998A	New rod-change gearbox and revised floor pressing.
May	Commission no. D20S 703 04A	New driveshaft with plunging CV inboard joints (except Clubman)
July		New driveshafts fitted to Clubman.
1974		
February		Inertia reel seatbelts fitted as standard.
April		Heater standard on 850 (!)
May		SUHS4 carburettor, revised manifold and timing.
July		12 inch roadwheels fitted to Clubman GT with larger disc brakes and larger fuel tank.
1974		
October		Special edition Mini with special trim. Clubman available with 1098cc engine.
1976		
January		Limited edition 1000, fitted with reclining seats and face-level vents.

Date	Chassis number (where available). Austin given first, where applicable	Modification
May		Twin-stalk controls, new subframe mountings (quieter), face vents on 1000. Softer rear spring settings and dampers except 1275GT, Estate and LCVs (all models).
1977		
August		Matt black grille fitted to all models, 1000 with reclining front seats. Denovo 'run-flat' tyres fitted as standard to Clubman (already fitted as optional extras to other Clubman models).
1980		
September		850 discontinued. City 'base' level and HL 'de-luxe' introduced.
October		Metro introduced.
1982		
April		Compression ratio of 10.3:1 (was 8.3:1), higher gearing — all models suffixed 'E' for economy (ie: Metro 'A + ' engine fitted).
September		More luxurious 'Mayfair' model introduced replacing HLE saloons. City E specification uprated, including heated rear windscreen, reversing lamps, etc.
1984		
August		All models on 12 inch wheels and front disc brakes. 25th 'Anniversary' model launched.

5 Colour Schemes

In the first 2 years, all Morris Minis were finished in Clipper Blue, Cherry Red or Old English White, whilst all Austin Minis were finished in Tartan Red, Farina Grey or Speedwell Blue. There was a very limited choice of trim and all standard models had grey cloth trim whereas De Luxe models had vinyl trim.

Rose Metallic and Silver Metallic were only used on 20th Anniversary Minis along with special Tartan seats.

The famous Cooper colour scheme — Tartan Red with a white roof — was never a production colour scheme but was only used on 'works' competition cars. Coopers in red had black roofs as standard.

Riley Elf and Wolseley Hornets were painted in traditional Riley and Wolseley colours. In 1961, only duotones were available at first with Grey upholstery, but after a few months there were colour co-ordinated interiors. In 1969, only monotone paint colours were available.

Body Colour and BMC Paint Code	Seats	Seat piping	Liners	Headlining	Door seals	Rubber mats
Austin/Morris Mini	*Standard Saloon MkI*					
El Paso Beige (BG17)	Satin Beige	Satin Beige	Satin Beige	Pale Grey	Natural rubber	Dark Grey
Sandy Beige (BG15)	Tartan Red	Tartan Red	Tartan Red	Pale Grey	Natural rubber	Dark Grey
Black (BK1)	Cumulus Grey	Cumulus Grey	Cumulus Grey	Pale Grey	Natural rubber	Dark Grey
Black (BK1)	Satin Beige	Satin Beige	Satin Beige	Pale Grey	Natural rubber	Dark Grey

Body Colour and BMC Paint Code	Seats	Seat piping	Liners	Headlining	Door seals	Rubber mats
Black (BK1)	Tartan Red	Tartan Red	Tartan Red	Pale Grey	Natural rubber	Dark Grey
Bermuda Blue (BU40) White (WT2)	Cumulus Grey	Cumulus Grey	Cumulus Grey	Pale Grey	Natural rubber	Dark Grey
Clipper Blue (BU14)	Silver Grey	Pale Grey	Silver Grey	Pale Grey	Grey Flock	Dark Grey
Clipper Blue (BU14)	Silver Grey	Black	Silver Grey	Pale Grey	Grey Flock	Dark Grey
Island Blue (BU5)	Cumulus Grey	Cumulus Grey	Cumulus Grey	Pale Grey	Natural rubber	Dark Grey
Speedwell Blue (BU1)	Grey Cloth	Farina Grey	Grey Cloth	Pale Grey	Grey	Dark Grey
Surf Blue (BU35)	Grey Cloth	Farina Grey	Grey Cloth	Pale Grey	Natural rubber	Dark Grey
Surf Blue (BU35)	Powder Blue	Powder Blue	Powder Blue	Pale Grey	Natural rubber	Dark dark
Almond Green (GN37)	Grey Cloth	Powder Blue	Powder Blue	Pale Grey	Natural rubber	Dark Grey
Almond Green (GN37)	Cumulus Grey	Cumulus Grey	Cumulus Grey	Pale Grey	Natural rubber	Dark Grey
Almond Green (GN37)	Satin Beige	Satin Beige	Satin Beige	Pale Grey	Natural rubber	Dark Grey
Almond Green (GN37)	Porcelain Green	Porcelain Green	Porcelain Green	Pale Grey	Natural rubber	Dark Grey
Farina Grey (GR11)	Grey Cloth	Farina Grey	Grey Cloth	Pale Grey	Grey	Dark Grey
Smoke Grey (BU15)	Grey Cloth	Farina Grey	Grey Cloth	Pale Grey	Natural rubber	Dark Grey
Smoke Grey (BU15)	Dark Grey	Dark Grey	Dark Grey	Pale Grey	Natural rubber	Dark Grey
Smoke Grey (BU15)	Blue Grey	Blue Grey	Blue Grey	Pale Grey	Natural rubber	Dark Grey
Tweed Grey (GR4)	Cumulus Grey	Cumulus Grey	Cumulus Grey	Pale Grey	Natural rubber	Dark Grey
Tweed Grey (GR4)	Satin Beige	Satin Beige	Satin Beige	Pale Grey	Natural rubber	Dark Grey
Tweed Grey (GR4)	Tartan Red	Tartan Red	Tartan Red	Pale Grey	Natural rubber	Dark Grey

Body Colour and BMC Paint Code	Seats	Seat piping	Liners	Headlining	Door seals	Rubber mats
Maroon B (RD23)	Cumulus Grey	Cumulus Grey	Cumulus Grey	Pale Grey	Natural rubber	Dark Grey
Maroon B (RD23)	Satin Beige	Satin Beige	Satin Beige	Pale Grey	Natural rubber	Dark Grey
Cherry Red (RD4)	Silver Grey	Pale Grey	Silver Grey	Pale Grey	Grey Flock	Dark Grey
Cherry Red (RD4)	Silver Grey	Black	Silver Grey	Pale Grey	Grey Flock	Dark Grey
Tartan Red (RD9)	Grey Cloth	Farina Grey	Grey Cloth	Pale Grey	Grey	Dark Grey

Austin/Morris Mini Standard Saloon MkI

Body Colour and BMC Paint Code	Seats	Seat piping	Liners	Headlining	Door seals	Rubber mats
Tartan Red (RD9)	Grey Cloth	Farina Grey	Grey Cloth	Pale Grey	Natural rubber	Dark Grey
Tartan Red (RD9)	Cumulus Grey	Cumulus Grey	Cumulus Grey	Pale Grey	Natural rubber	Dark Grey
Tartan Red (RD9)	Satin Beige	Satin Beige	Satin Beige	Pale Grey	Natural rubber	Dark Grey
Tartan Red (RD9)	Tartan Red	Tartan Red	Tartan Red	Pale Grey	Natural rubber	Dark Grey
White (WT2)	Fitted with any trim colour applicable to Austin and Morris Standard Saloon Mk I			Pale Grey	Natural rubber	Dark Grey
Old English White (WT3)	Silver Grey	Pale Grey	Silver Grey	Pale Grey	Grey Flock	Dark Grey
Old English White (WT3)	Silver Grey	Black	Silver Grey	Pale Grey	Grey Flock	Dark Grey
Old English White (WT3)	Grey Cloth	Farina Grey	Grey Cloth	Pale Grey	Natural rubber	Dark Grey
Old English White (WT3)	Porcelain Green	Porcelain Green	Porcelain Green	Pale Grey	Natural rubber	Dark Grey
Old English White (WT3)	Satin Beige	Satin Beige	Satin Beige	Pale Grey	Natural rubber	Dark Grey
Old English White (WT3)	Tartan Red	Tartan Red	Tartan Red	Pale Grey	Natural Rubber	Dark Grey
Fiesta Yellow (YL11)	Grey Cloth	Farina Grey	Grey Cloth	Pale Grey	Natural rubber	Dark Grey
Fiesta Yellow (YL11)	Powder Blue	Powder Blue	Powder Blue	Pale Grey	Natural rubber	Dark Grey

Body Colour and BMC Paint Code	Seats	Seat piping	Liners	Headlining	Door seals	Carpets
De Luxe Saloon MkI						
Clipper Blue (BU14)	Grey Flock /Blue Grey	Blue Grey	Blue Grey	Pale Grey	Natural rubber	Blue
Speedwell Blue (BU1)	Grey Flock /Spanish Blue	Farina Grey	Grey Flock	Pale Grey	Natural rubber	Blue
Surf Blue (BU35)	Grey Flock /Powder Blue	Powder Blue	Powder Blue	Pale Cream	Natural rubber	Powder Blue
Surf Blue (BU35)	Powder Blue	Powder Blue	Powder Blue	Pale Cream	Natural rubber	Powder Blue
Almond Green (GN35)	Grey Flock /Porcelain Green	Porcelain Green	Porcelain Green	Pale Cream	Natural rubber	Cumulus Grey
Almond Green (GN35)	Grey Flock /Porcelain Green	Porcelain Green	Porcelain Green	Pale Cream	Grey Flock	Dark Grey
Almond Green (GN35)	Porcelain Green	Porcelain Green	Porcelain Green	Pale Grey	Natural rubber	Cumulus Grey
Farina Grey GR11)	Grey Flock /Spanish Blue	Farina Grey	Grey Flock	Pale Grey	Grey Flock	Blue
Farina Grey (GR11)	Grey Flock /Spanish Red	Farina Grey	Grey Flock	Pale Grey	Grey Flock	Tartan Red
Smoke Grey (BU15)	Grey Flock /Dark Grey	Dark Grey	Dark Grey	Pale Grey	Natural rubber	Cumulus Grey
Smoke Grey (BU15)	Grey Flock /Dark Grey	Dark Grey	Dark Grey	Pale Grey	Grey Flock	Dark Grey
Smoke Grey (BU15)	Blue Grey	Blue Grey	Blue Grey	Pale Grey	Natural rubber	Blue
De Luxe Saloon MkI						
Cherry Red (RD4)	Green Flock /Red	Red	Red	Pale Grey	Grey Flock	Cherry Red
Tartan Red (RD9)	Grey Flock /Spanish Red	Farina Grey	Grey Flock	Pale Grey	Grey Flock	Tartan Red
Tartan Red (RD9)	Grey Flock /Tartan Red	Tartan Red	Tartan Ted	Pale Grey	Grey Flock	Tartan Red

262

Body Colour and BMC Paint Code	Seats	Seat piping	Liners	Headlining	Door seals	Carpets
Tartan Red (RD9)	Tartan Red	Tartan Red	Tartan Red	Pale Grey	Natural rubber	Tartan Red
Old English White (WT3)	Grey Flock /Blue Grey	Blue Grey	Blue Grey	Pale Grey	Grey Flock	Blue
Old English White (WT3)	Grey Flock /Red	Red	Red	Pale Grey	Grey Flock	Cherry Red
Old English White (WT3)	Grey Flock /Tartan Red	Tartan Red	Tartan Red	Pale Grey	Grey Flock	Tartan Red
Old English White (WT3)	Tartan Red	Tartan Red	Tartan Red	Pale Grey	Natural rubber	Tartan Red
Fiesta Yellow (YL11)	Grey Flock /Powder Blue	Powder Blue	Powder Blue	Pale Grey	Grey Flock	Powder Blue
Fiesta Yellow (YL11)	Powder Blue	Powder Blue	Powder Blue	Pale Grey	Natural rubber	Powder Blue

Super De Luxe Saloon MkI

Body Colour and BMC Paint Code	Seats	Seat piping	Liners	Headlining	Door seals	Carpets
El Paso Beige (BG17)	Satin Beige	Satin Beige	Satin Beige	Pale Grey	Natural rubber	Hazelnut
Sandy Beige (BG15)	Tartan Red	Tartan Red	Tartan Red	Pale Grey	Natural rubber	Cherokee Red
Black (BK1)	Cumulus Grey	Cumulus Grey	Cumulus Grey	Pale Grey	Natural rubber	Cumulus Grey
Black (BK1)	Satin Beige	Satin Beige	Satin Beige	Pale Grey	Natural rubber	Satin Beige
Black (BK1)	Tartan Red	Tartan Red	Tartan Red	Pale Grey	Natural rubber	Tartan Red
Black (BK1)	Tartan Red	Tartan Red	Tartan Red	Pale Grey	Natural rubber	Cherokee Red
Bermuda Blue (BU40) + White (WT2)	Cumulus Grey	Cumulus Grey	Cumulus Grey	Pale Grey	Natural rubber	Cumulus Grey
Island Blue (BU8) Old English White (WT3)	Gold Brocade/ Grey/ Cumulus Grey	Cumulus Grey	Gold Brocade/ Grey/	Pale Grey	Natural rubber	Cumulus Grey

Body Colour and BMC Paint Code	Seats	Seat piping	Liners	Headlining	Door seals	Carpets
Island Blue (BU8)	Cumulus Grey	Cumulus Grey	Cumulus Grey	Pale Grey	Natural rubber	Cumulus Grey
Surf Blue (BU35) Old English White (WT3)	Silver Brocade Grey/ Powder Blue	Powder Blue	Silver Brocade Grey	Pale Grey	Natural rubber	Powder Blue
Surf Blue (BU35) Old English White (WT3)	Gold Brocade Grey/ Powder Blue	Powder Blue	Gold Brocade Grey	Pale Grey	Natural rubber	Blue
Surf Blue (BU35) Old English White (WT3)	Gold Brocade Grey/ Powder Blue	Powder Blue	Gold Brocade Grey	Pale Grey	Natural rubber	Powder Blue
Surf Blue (BU35)	Powder Blue	Powder Blue	Powder Blue	Pale Grey	Natural rubber	Powder Blue
Almond Green (GN37) Old English White (WT3)	Dove Grey/ Porcelain Green	Porcelain Green	Dove Grey	Pale Grey	Natural rubber	Cumulus Grey
Almond Green (GN37) Old English White (WT3)	Dove Grey/ Porcelain Green	Porcelain Green	Dove Grey	Pale Grey	Natural rubber	Porcelain Green
Almond Green (GN37)	Cumulus Grey	Cumulus Grey	Cumulus Grey	Pale Grey	Natural rubber	Cumulus Grey
Almond Green (GN37)	Porcelain Green	Porcelain Green	Porcelain Green	Pale Grey	Natural rubber	Almond Green
Almond Green (GN37)	Porcelain Green	Porcelain Green	Porcelain Green	Pale Grey	Natural rubber	Cumulus Grey
Almond Green (GN37)	Satin Beige	Satin Beige	Satin Beige	Pale Grey	Natural rubber	Satin Beige
Smoke Grey (BU15) Old English White (WT3)	Dove Grey/ Dark Grey	Dark Grey	Dark Grey	Pale Grey	Natural rubber	Cumulus Grey
Smoke Grey (BU15) Old English White (WT3)	Dove Grey/ Dark Grey	Dark Grey	Dark Grey	Pale Grey	Natural rubber	Grey
Smoke Grey (BU15)	Blue Grey	Blue Grey	Blue Grey	Pale Grey	Natural rubber	Blue
Tweed Grey (GR4)	Cumulus Grey	Cumulus Grey	Cumulus Grey	Pale Grey	Natural rubber	Cumulus Grey
Tweed Grey (GR4)	Satin Beige	Satin Beige	Satin Beige	Pale Grey	Natural rubber	Satin Beige

Body Colour and BMC Paint Code	Seats	Seat piping	Liners	Headlining	Door seals	Carpets
Tweed Grey (GR4)	Tartan Red	Tartan Red	Tartan Red	Pale Grey	Natural rubber	Tartan Red
Maroon B (RD23)	Cumulus Grey	Cumulus Grey	Cumulus Grey	Pale Grey	Natural rubber	Cumulus Grey
Maroon B (RD23)	Satin Beige	Satin Beige	Satin Beige	Pale Grey	Natural rubber	Satin Beige
Maroon B (RD23)	Satin Beige	Satin Beige	Satin Beige	Pale Grey	Natural rubber	Hazelnut
Tartan Red (RD9) Black (BK1)	Gold Brocade Grey/Tartan Red	Tartan Red	Gold Brocade Grey	Pale Grey	Natural rubber	Tartan Red
Tartan Red (RD9) Black (BK1)	Gold Brocade Grey/Tartan Red	Tartan Red	Gold Brocade Grey	Pale Grey	Natural rubber	Cherokee Red
Tartan Red (RD9)	Cumulus Grey	Cumulus Grey	Cumulus Grey	Pale Grey	Natural rubber	Cumulus Grey
Tartan Red (RD9)	Satin Beige	Satin Beige	Satin Beige	Pale Grey	Natural rubber	Satin Beige
Tartan Beige (RD9)	Tartan Red	Tartan Red	Tartan Red	Pale Grey	Natural rubber	Tartan Red
Tartan Red (RD9)	Tartan Red	Tartan Red	Tartan Red	Pale Grey	Natural rubber	Cherokee Red
White (WT2)	Fitted with any trim colour applicable to Austin & Morris Super De Luxe Saloons MkI.					

Super De Luxe Saloon MkI

Body Colour and BMC Paint Code	Seats	Seat piping	Liners	Headlining	Door seals	Carpets
Old English White (WT3) Black (BK1)	Gold Brocade Grey/Tartan Red	Tartan Red	Gold Brocade Red	Pale Grey	Natural rubber	Tartan Red
Old English White (WT3) Black (BK1)	Gold Brocade Grey/Tartan Red	Tartan Red	Gold Brocade Red	Pale Grey	Natural rubber	Cherokee Red
Old English White (WT3)	Porcelain Green	Porcelain Green	Porcelain Green	Pale Grey	Natural rubber	Almond Green

Body Colour and BMC Paint Code	Seats	Seat piping	Liners	Headlining	Door seals	Carpets
Old English White (WT3)	Satin Beige	Satin Beige	Satin Beige	Pale Grey	Natural rubber	Satin Beige
Old English White (WT3)	Tartan Red	Tartan Red	Tartan Red	Pale Grey	Natural rubber	Tartan Red
Old English White (WT3)	Tartan Red	Tartan Red	Tartan Red	Pale Grey	Natural rubber	Cherokee Red
Fiesta Yellow (YL11) Old English White (WT3)	Gold Brocade Grey/Powder Blue	Powder Blue	Gold Brocade Grey	Pale Grey	Natural rubber	Blue
Fiesta Yellow (YL11) Old English White (WT3)	Gold Brocade Grey/Powder Blue	Powder Blue	Gold Brocade Grey	Pale Grey	Natural rubber	Powder Blue
Fiesta Yellow (YL11)	Powder Blue	Powder Blue	Powder Blue	Pale Grey	Natural rubber	Powder Blue

Austin/Morris Mini Cooper Standard & 'S'

Body Colour and BMC Paint Code	Seats	Seat piping	Liners	Headlining	Door seals	Carpets
Island Blue (BU8) Old English White (WT3)	Gold Brocade Grey/ Cumulus Grey	Cumulus Grey	Gold Brocade	Pale Cream	Natural rubber	Cumulus Grey
Surf Blue (BU35) Old English White (WT3)	Silver Brocade Grey/ Powder Blue	Powder Blue	Silver Brocade Grey	Pale Cream	Natural rubber	Powder Blue
Surf Blue (BU35) Old English White (WT3)	Gold Brocade Grey/ Powder Blue	Powder Blue	Gold Brocade Grey	Pale Cream	Natural rubber	Powder Blue
Almond Green (GN37) Old English White (WT3)	Dove Grey/ Porcelain Green	Porcelain Green	Dove Grey	Pale Cream	Natural rubber	Grey
Almond Green (GN37) Old English White (WT3)	Dove Grey/ Porcelain Green	Porcelain Green	Dove Grey	Pale Cream	Natural rubber	Cumulus Grey
Smoke Grey (BU15) Old English White (WT3)	Dove Grey/ Dark Grey	Dark Grey	Dove Grey	Pale Cream	Natural rubber	Grey
Smoke Grey (BU15) Old English White (WT3)	Dove Grey/ Dark Grey	Dark Grey	Dove Grey	Pale Cream	Natural rubber	Cumulus Grey

Body Colour and BMC Paint Code	Seats	Seat piping	Liners	Headlining	Door seals	Carpets
Tweed Grey (GR4) Old English White (WT3)	Dove Grey/ Dark Grey	Dark Grey	Dove Grey	Pale Cream	Natural rubber	Cumulus Grey
Tartan Red (RD9) Black (BK1)	Gold Brocade Grey/ Tartan Red	Tartan Red	Gold Brocade Grey	Pale Cream	Natural rubber	Tartan Red
Old English White (WT3) Black (BK1)	Gold Brocade	Tartan Red	Gold Brocade Grey	Pale Cream	Natural rubber	Powder Blue
Fiesta Yellow (YL11) Old English White (WT3)	Silver Brocade Grey/ Powder Blue	Powder Blue	Silver Brocade Grey	Pale Cream	Natural rubber	Powder Blue
Fiesta Yellow (YL11) Old English White (WT3)	Gold Brocade Grey/ Powder Blue	Powder Blue	Gold Brocade Grey	Pale Cream	Natural rubber	Powder Blue

Austin Mini Countryman & Morris Mini Traveller MkI

Clipper Blue (BU14)	Grey Flock/ Spanish Blue	Spanish Blue	Spanish Blue	Pale Grey	Spanish Blue	Blue
Clipper Blue (BU14)	Grey Flock/ Spanish Blue	Farina Grey	Spanish Blue	Pale Grey	Spanish Blue	Blue
Island Blue (BU8)	Cumulus Grey	Cumulus Grey	Cumulus Grey	Pale Grey	Natural rubber	Cumulus Grey
Speedwell Blue (BU1)	Grey Flock/ Spanish Blue	Spanish Blue	Grey Flock	Pale Grey	Spanish Blue	Blue
Surf Blue (BU35)	Grey Flock/ Powder Blue	Powder Blue	Powder Blue	Pale Grey	Natural rubber	Powder Blue
Surf Blue (BU35)	Powder Blue	Powder Blue	Powder Blue	Pale Grey	Natural rubber	Powder Blue
Almond Green (GN37)	Grey Flock/ Porcelain Green	Porcelain Green	Porcelain Green	Pale Grey	Natural rubber	Cumulus Grey
Almond Green (GN37)	Grey Flock/ Porcelain Green	Porcelain Green	Porcelain Green	Pale Grey	Natural rubber	Dark Grey

Body Colour and BMC Paint Code	Seats	Seat piping	Liners	Headlining	Door seals	Carpets
Almond Green (GN37)	Porcelain Green	Porcelain Green	Porcelain Green	Pale Grey	Natural rubber	Cumulus Grey
Farina Grey (GR11)	Grey Flock/ Spanish Red	Spanish Red	Grey Flock	Pale Grey	Tartan Red	Tartan Red
Farina Grey (GR11)	Grey Flock/ Spanish Red	Spanish Red	Grey Flock	Pale Grey	Spanish Blue	Blue
Smoke Grey (BU15)	Grey Flock/ Dark Grey	Dark Grey	Dark Grey	Pale Grey	Natural rubber	Dark Grey
Smoke Grey (BU15)	Grey Flock/ Dark Grey	Dark Grey	Dark Grey	Pale Grey	Natural rubber	Cumulus Grey
Smoke Grey (BU15)	Blue Grey	Blue Grey	Blue Grey	Pale Grey	Natural rubber	Blue
Tweed Grey (GR4)	Blue Grey	Blue Grey	Blue Grey	Pale Grey	Natural rubber	Blue
Cherry Red (RD4)	Grey Flock/ Spanish Red	Spanish Red	Spanish Red	Pale Grey	Tartan Red	Tartan Red
Cherry Red (RD4)	Grey Flock/ Spanish Red	Farina Grey	Spanish Red	Pale Grey	Tartan Red	Tartan Red
Tartan Red (RD9)	Grey Flock/ Spanish Red	Spanish Red	Grey Flock	Pale Grey	Tartan Red	Tartan Red
Tartan Red (RD9)	Grey Flock/ Tartan Red	Tartan Red	Tartan Red	Pale Grey	Natural rubber	Tartan Red
Tartan Red (RD9)	Tartan Red	Tartan Red	Tartan Red	Pale Grey	Natural rubber	Tartan Red
Tartan Red (RD9)	Tartan Red	Tartan Red	Tartan Red	Pale Grey	Natural rubber	Cherokee Red
Old English White (WT3)	Grey Flock/ Spanish Blue	Spanish Blue	Spanish Blue	Pale Grey	Spanish Blue	Blue
Old English White (WT3)	Grey Flock/ Spanish Blue	Farina Grey	Spanish Blue	Pale Grey	Spanish Blue	Blue
Old English White (WT3)	Grey Flock/ Spanish Red	Spanish Red	Spanish Red	Pale Grey	Tartan Red	Tartan Red
Old English White (WT3)	Grey Flock/ Spanish Red	Farina Grey	Spanish Red	Pale Grey	Tartan Red	Tartan Red
Old English White (WT3)	Grey Flock	Tartan Red	Tartan Red	Pale Grey	Natural rubber	Tartan Red

Body Colour and BMC Paint Code	Seats	Seat piping	Liners	Headlining	Door seals	Carpets
Old English White (WT3)	Tartan Red	Tartan Red	Tartan Red	Pale Grey	Natural rubber	Tartan Red
Fiesta Yellow (YL11)	Grey Flock/ Powder Blue	Powder Blue	Powder Blue	Pale Grey	Natural rubber	Powder Blue
Fiesta Yellow (YL11)	Powder Blue	Powder Blue	Powder Blue	Pale Grey	Natural rubber	Powder Blue

Riley Elf Saloon MkI

Body Colour and BMC Paint Code	Seats	Seat piping	Liners	Headlining	Door seals	Carpets
Florentine Blue (BU7) Old English White (WT3)	Grey/ Powder Blue	Powder Blue	Grey/ Powder Blue	Pale Cream	Natural rubber	Powder Blue
Florentine Blue (BU7) Old English White (WT3)	Powder Blue	Powder Blue	Powder Blue	Pale Cream	Natural rubber	Powder Blue
Cumberland Green (GN35) Old English White (WT3)	Grey/ Porcelain Green	Porcelain Green	Grey/ Porcelain Green	Pale Cream	Natural rubber	Porcelain Green
Porcelain Green (GN35) Old English White (WT3)	Porcelain Green	Porcelain Green	Porcelain Green	Pale Cream	Natural rubber	Porcelain Green
Birch Grey (GR3) Old English White (WT3)	Grey/ Powder Blue	Powder Blue	Grey/ Powder Blue	Pale Cream	Natural rubber	Powder Blue
Birch Grey (GR3) Old English White (WT3)	Powder Blue	Powder Blue	Powder Blue	Pale Cream	Natural rubber	Powder Blue
Birch Grey (GR3) Old English White (WT3)	Grey/ Porcelain Green	Porcelain Green	Grey/ Porcelain Green	Pale Cream	Natural rubber	Powder Blue
Birch Grey (GR3) Old English White (WT3)	Porcelain Green	Porcelain Green	Porcelain Green	Pale Cream	Natural rubber	Powder Blue
Birch Grey (GR3) Old English White (WT3)	Grey/ Cardinal Red	Cardinal Red	Grey/ Cardinal Red	Pale Cream	Natural rubber	Cardinal Red
Birch Grey (GR3) Old English White (WT3)	Cardinal Red	Cardinal Red	Cardinal Red	Pale Cream	Natural rubber	Cardinal Red
Yukon Grey (GR7) Birch Grey (GR3)	Grey/ Powder Blue	Powder Blue	Grey/ Powder Blue	Pale Cream	Natural rubber	Powder Blue
Yukon Grey (GR7) Birch Grey (GR3)	Powder Blue	Powder Blue	Powder Blue	Pale Cream	Natural rubber	Powder Blue
Yukon Grey (GR7) Birch Grey (GR3)	Grey/ Cardinal Red	Cardinal Red	Grey/ Cardinal Red	Pale Cream	Natural rubber	Powder Blue

Body Colour and BMC Paint Code	Seats	Seat piping	Liners	Headlining	Door seals	Carpets
Yukon Grey (GR7) Birch Grey (GR3)	Cardinal Red	Cardinal Red	Cardinal Red	Pale Cream	Natural rubber	Powder Blue
Yukon Grey (GR7) Birch Grey (GR3)	Grey/ Dove Grey	Dove Grey	Grey/ Dove Grey	Pale Cream	Natural rubber	Powder Blue
Yukon Grey (GR7) Birch Grey (GR3)	Dove Grey	Dove Grey	Dove Grey	Pale Cream	Natural rubber	Dove Grey
Damask Red (RD5) Whitehall Beige (BG4)	Grey/ Cardinal Red	Cardinal Red	Grey/ Cardinal Red	Pale Cream	Natural rubber	Cardinal Red
Damask Red (RD5) Whitehall Beige (BG4)	Cardinal Red	Cardinal Red	Cardinal Red	Pale Cream	Natural rubber	Cardinal Red
Chartreuse Yellow (YL2) Florentine Blue (BU5)	Grey/ Powder Blue	Powder Blue	Grey/ Powder Blue	Pale Cream	Natural rubber	Powder Blue
Chartreuse Yellow (YL2) Florentine Blue (BU5)	Powder Blue	Powder Blue	Powder Blue	Pale Cream	Natural rubber	Powder Blue

Riley Elf MkII

Body Colour and BMC Paint Code	Seats	Seat piping	Liners	Headlining	Door seals	Carpets
Arianca Beige (BG13) Pale Ivory (YL1)	Cardinal Red	Cardinal Red	Cardinal Red	Pale Cream	Natural rubber	Cardinal Red
Florentine Blue (BU7)	Powder Blue	Powder Blue	Powder Blue	Pale Cream	Natural rubber	Powder Blue or Blue
Cumberland Green (GN35) Old English White (WT3)	Porcelain Green	Porcelain Green	Porcelain Green	Pale Cream	Natural rubber	Porcelain or Almond Green
Birch Grey (GL3) Old English White (WT3)	Porcelain Green	Porcelain Green	Porcelain Green	Pale Cream	Natural rubber	Powder Blue or Blue
Birch Grey (GL3) Old English White (WT3)	Porcelain Green	Porcelain Green	Porcelain Green	Pale Cream	Natural rubber	Porcelain or Almond Green
Birch Grey (GL3) Old English White (WT3)	Cardinal Red	Cardinal Red	Cardinal Red	Pale Cream	Natural rubber	Cardinal Red
Yukon Grey (GR7) Birch Grey (GR3)	Powder Blue	Powder Blue	Powder Blue	Pale Cream	Natural rubber	Powder Blue or Blue
Yukon Grey (GR7) Birch Grey (GR3)	Cardinal Red	Cardinal Red	Cardinal Red	Pale Cream	Natural rubber	Cardinal Red
Yukon Grey (GR7) Birch Grey (GR3)	Dove Grey	Dove Grey	Dove Grey	Pale Cream	Natural rubber	Cumulus Grey
Damask Red (RD5) Beige (BG4)	Cardinal Red	Cardinal Red	Cardinal Red	Pale Cream	Natural rubber	Cardinal Red

Body Colour and BMC Paint Code	Seats	Seat piping	Liners	Headlining	Door seals	Carpets
Chartreuse Yellow (YL2) Florentine Blue (BU7)	Powder Blue	Powder Blue	Powder Blue	Pale Cream	Natural rubber	Powder Blue

Wolseley Hornet Saloon MkI

Body Colour and BMC Paint Code	Seats	Seat piping	Liners	Headlining	Door seals	Carpets
Whitehall Beige (BG4) Florentine Blue (BU7)	Grey/ Powder Blue	Powder Blue	Grey/ Powder Blue	Pale Cream	Natural rubber	Powder Blue
Whitehall Beige (BG4) Florentine Blue (BU7)	Powder Blue	Powder Blue	Powder Blue	Pale Cream	Natural rubber	Powder Blue
Iris Blue (BU12) Old English White (WT3)	Grey/ Dove Grey	Dove Grey	Grey/ Dove Grey	Pale Cream	Natural rubber	Cumulus Grey
Iris Blue (BU12) Old English White (WT3)	Dove Grey	Dove Grey	Dove Grey	Pale Cream	Natural rubber	Cumulus Grey
Island Green (GN6) Old English White (WT3)	Grey/ Dove Grey	Dove Grey	Grey/ Dove Grey	Pale Cream	Natural rubber	Cumulus Grey
Island Green (GN6) Old English White (WT3)	Dove Grey	Dove Grey	Dove Grey	Pale Cream	Natural rubber	Cumulus Grey
Birch Grey (GR3) Yukon Grey (GR7)	Grey/ Powder Blue	Powder Blue	Grey/ Powder Blue	Pale Cream	Natural rubber	Powder Blue
Birch Grey (GR3) Yukon Grey GR7)	Powder Blue	Powder Blue	Powder Blue	Pale Cream	Natural rubber	Powder Blue
Birch Grey (GR3) Yukon Grey (GR7)	Grey/ Cardinal Red	Cardinal Red	Grey/ Cardinal Red	Pale Cream	Natural rubber	Cardinal Red
Birch Grey (GR3) Yukon Grey (GR7)	Cardinal Red	Cardinal Red	Cardinal Red	Pale Cream	Natural rubber	Cardinal Red
Birch Grey (GR3) Yukon Grey (GR7)	Grey/ Dove Grey	Dove Grey	Grey/ Dove Grey	Pale Cream	Natural rubber	Cumulus Grey
Birch Grey (GR3) Yukon Grey (GR7)	Dove Grey	Dove Grey	Dove Grey	Pale Cream	Natural rubber	Cumulus Grey
Yukon Grey (GR7) Old English White (WT3)	Grey/ Cardinal Red	Cardinal Red	Grey/ Cardinal Red	Pale Cream	Natural rubber	Cardinal Red
Yukon Grey (GR7) Old English White (WT3)	Cardinal Red	Cardinal Red	Cardinal Red	Pale Cream	Natural rubber	Cardinal Red
Yukon Grey (GR7) Old English White (WT3)	Grey/ Powder Blue	Powder Blue	Grey/ Powder Blue	Pale Cream	Natural rubber	Powder Blue
Yukon Grey (GR7) Old English White (WT3)	Powder Blue	Powder Blue	Powder Blue	Pale Cream	Natural rubber	Powder Blue

Body Colour and BMC Paint Code	Seats	Seat piping	Liners	Headlining	Door seals	Carpets
Yukon Grey (GR7) Old English White (WT3)	Grey/ Porcelain Green	Porcelain Green	Grey/ Porcelain Green	Pale Cream	Natural rubber	Porcelain Green
Yukon Grey (GR7) Old English White (WT3)	Porcelain Green	Porcelain Green	Porcelain Green	Pale Cream	Natural rubber	Porcelain Green
Pale Ivory (YL1) Damask Red (RD5)	Grey/ Cardinal Red	Cardinal Red	Grey/ Cardinal Red	Pale Cream	Natural rubber	Cardinal Red
Pale Ivory (YL1) Damask Red (RD5)	Cardinal Red	Cardinal Red	Cardinal Red	Pale Cream	Natural rubber	Cardinal Red

Wolseley Hornet Saloon MkII

Body Colour and BMC Paint Code	Seats	Seat piping	Liners	Headlining	Door seals	Carpets
Whitehall Beige (BG4) Florentine Blue (BU7)	Powder Blue	Powder Blue	Powder Blue	Pale Cream	Natural rubber	Powder Blue or Blue
Iris Blue (BU12) Old English White (WT3)	Dove Grey	Dove Grey	Dove Grey	Pale Cream	Natural rubber	Cumulus Grey
Glen Green (GN40) Spruce Green (GN13)	Porcelain Green	Porcelain Green	Porcelain Green	Pale Cream	Natural rubber	Almond Green
Island Green (GN6) Old English White (WT3)	Dove Grey	Dove Grey	Dove Grey	Pale Cream	Natural rubber	Cumulus Grey
Island Green (GN6) Old English White (WT3)	Porcelain Green	Porcelain Green	Porcelain Green	Pale Cream	Natural rubber	Almond Green
Birch Grey (GR3) Yukon Grey (GR7)	Powder Blue	Powder Blue	Powder Blue	Pale Cream	Natural rubber	Powder Blue or Blue
Birch Grey (GR3) Yukon Grey (GR7)	Cardinal Red	Cardinal Red	Cardinal Red	Pale Cream	Natural rubber	Cardinal Red
Birch Grey (GR3) Yukon Grey (GR7)	Dove Grey	Dove Grey	Dove Grey	Pale Cream	Natural rubber	Cumulus Grey
Yukon Grey (GR7) Old English White (WT3)	Powder Blue	Powder Blue	Powder Blue	Pale Cream	Natural rubber	Powder Blue or Blue
Yukon Grey (GR7) Old English White (WT3)	Porcelain Green	Porcelain Green	Porcelain Green	Pale Cream	Natural rubber	Porcelain or Almond Green
Pale Ivory (YL1) Damask Red (RD5)	Cardinal Red	Cardinal Red	Cardinal Red	Pale Cream	Natural rubber	Cardinal Red
Maroon B (RD23) Toga White (WT5)	Dove Grey	Dove Grey	Dove Grey	Pale Cream	Natural rubber	Cumulus Grey
Toga White (WT5) Damask Red (RD5)	Cardinal Red	Cardinal Red	Cardinal Red	Pale Cream	Natural rubber	Cardinal Red
Toga White (WT5) Damask Red (RD5)	Dove Grey	Dove Grey	Dove Grey	Pale Cream	Natural rubber	Cumulus Grey

Body Colour and BMC Paint Code	Seats	Seat piping	Liners	Headlining	Door seals	Rubber Mats
Austin/Morris Standard Saloon MkII						
El Paso Beige (BG17)	Sandy Beige	Sandy Beige	Sandy Beige	Pale Cream	Natural rubber	Dark Grey
Sandy Beige (BG15)	Tartan Red	Tartan Red	Tartan Red	Pale Cream	Natural rubber	Dark grey
Bermuda Blue (BU40) White (WT2)	Cumulus Grey	Cumulus Grey	Cumulus Grey	Pale Cream	Natural rubber	Dark Grey
Island Blue (BU6)	Cumulus Grey	Cumulus Grey	Cumulus Grey	Pale Cream	Natural rubber	Dark Grey
Almond Green (GN37)	Satin Beige	Satin Beige	Satin Beige	Pale Cream	Natural rubber	Dark Grey
Tartan Red (RD9)	Tartan Red	Tartan Red	Tartan Red	Pale Cream	Natural rubber	Dark Grey
White (WT2)	Fitted with any trim colour applicable to Austin & Morris Standard Saloon MkII			Pale Cream	Natural rubber	Dark Grey
Snowberry White (WT4)	Black	Black	Black	Pale Cream	Natural rubber	Dark Grey

Body Colour and BMC Paint Code	Seats	Seat piping	Liners	Headlining	Door seals	Carpets
Austin & Morris Super De Luxe Saloon MkII						
El Paso Beige (BG17)	Satin Beige	Satin Beige	Satin Beige	Pale Cream	Natural rubber	Arianca Beige
Sandy Beige (BG15)	Tartan Red	Tartan Red	Tartan Red	Pale Cream	Natural rubber	Cherokee Red
Bermuda Blue (BU40) White (WT2)	Cumulus Grey	Cumulus Grey	Cumulus Grey	Pale Cream	Natural rubber	Cumulus Grey
Island Blue (BU8)	Cumulus Grey	Cumulus Grey	Cumulus Grey	Pale Cream	Natural rubber	Cumulus Grey
Almond Green (GN37)	Satin Beige	Satin Beige	Satin Beige	Pale Cream	Natural rubber	Arianca Beige
Tartan Red (RD9)	Tartan Red	Tartan Red	Tartan Red	Pale Cream	Natural rubber	Cherokee Red
White (WT2)	Fitted with any trim colour applicable to Austin & Morris Super De Luxe Saloon MkII			Pale Cream	Natural rubber	
Snowberry White (WT4)	Black	Black	Black	Pale Cream	Natural rubber	Black

Body Colour and BMC Paint Code	Seats	Seat piping	Liners	Headlining	Door seals	Carpets
Austin/Morris Mini Cooper Standard & 'S' MkII						
El Paso Beige (BG17) + Snowberry White (WT4)	Black	Black	Black	Pale Cream	Natural rubber	Black
Sand Beige (BG15) Snowberry White (WT4)	Black	Black	Black	Pale Cream	Natural rubber	Black
Island Blue (BU8) Snowberry White (WT4)	Black	Black	Black	Pale Cream	Natural rubber	Black
Almond Green (GN37) Snowberry White (WT4)	Black	Black	Black	Pale Cream	Natural rubber	Black
Tartan Red (RD9) Black (BK1)	Black	Black	Black	Pale Cream	Natural rubber	Black
Snowberry White (WT4) Black (BK1)	Black	Black	Black	Pale Cream	Natural rubber	Black
Austin Mini Countryman & Morris Mini Traveller MkII						
El Paso Beige (BG17)	Satin Beige	Satin Beige	Satin Beige	Pale Cream	Natural rubber	Arianca Beige
Sandy Beige (BG3)	Tartan Red	Tartan Red	Tartan Red	Pale Cream	Natural rubber	Cherokee Red
Island Blue (BU8)	Cumulus Grey	Cumulus Grey	Cumulus Grey	Pale Cream	Natural rubber	Cumulus Grey
Almond Green (GN37)	Satin Beige	Satin Beige	Satin Beige	Pale Cream	Natural rubber	Arianca Beige
Tartan Red (RD5)	Tartan Red	Tartan Red	Tartan Red	Pale Cream	Natural rubber	Cherokee Red
Snowberry White (WT4)	Black	Black	Black	Pale Cream	Natural rubber	Black
Austin & Morris Mini Van & Pick-Up MkI & II						**Rubber mats**
Whitehall Beige (BG4)	Tan	Tan	Tan	Pale Cream	Natural rubber	Dark Grey
Persian Blue (BU39)	Arizona Beige	Arizona Beige	Arizona Beige	Pale Cream	Natural rubber	Dark Grey
Everglade Green (GN42)	Arizona Beige	Arizona Beige	Arizona Beige	Pale Cream	Natural rubber	Dark Grey
Cumulus Grey (GR29)	Arizona Beige	Arizona Beige	Arizona Beige	Pale Cream	Natural rubber	Dark Grey

Body Colour and BMC Paint Code	Seats	Seat piping	Liners	Headlining	Door seals	Rubber mats
Damask Red (RD5)	Arizona Beige	Arizona Beige	Arizona Beige	Pale Cream	Natural rubber	Dark Grey
Snowberry White (WT4)	Arizona Beige	Arizona Beige	Arizona Beige	Pale Cream	Natural rubber	Dark Grey
Willow Green (GN33)	Tan	Tan	Tan	Pale Cream	Natural rubber	Dark Grey
Tweed Grey (GR4)	Tan	Tan	Tan	Pale Cream	Natural rubber	Dark Grey
Marigold (YL7)	Tan	Tan	Tan	Pale Cream	Natural rubber	Dark Grey
White (WT2)	Tan	Tan	Tan	Pale Cream	Natural rubber	Dark Grey

Riley Elf MkIII

Body Colour and BMC Paint Code	Seats	Seat piping	Liners	Headlining	Door seals	Carpets
Arianca Beige (BG13) Pale Ivory (YL1)	Cardinal Red	Cardinal Red	Cardinal Red	Pale Cream	Natural rubber	Cardinal Red
Florentine Blue (BU7) Old English White (WT3)	Powder Blue	Powder Blue	Powder Blue	Pale Cream	Natural rubber	Blue
Persian Blue (BN39) Snowberry White (WT4)	Powder Blue	Powder Blue	Powder Blue	Pale Grey	Blue	Reef Blue
Fawn Brown (RD24) Pale Ivory (YL1)	Cardinal Red	Cardinal Red	Cardinal Red	Pale Cream	Cardinal Red	Cardinal Red
Fawn Brown (RD24) Pale Ivory (YL1)	Mushroom	Mushroom	Mushroom	Pale Cream	Mushroom	Mushroom
Birch Grey (GR3) Old English White (WT3)	Cardinal Red	Cardinal Red	Cardinal Red	Pale Cream	Natural rubber	Cardinal Red
Birch Grey (GR3) Snowberry White (WT4)	Cardinal Red	Cardinal Red	Cardinal Red	Pale Cream	Cardinal Red	Cardinal Red
Yukon Grey (GR7) Birch Grey (GR3)	Cardinal Red	Cardinal Red	Cardinal Red	Pale Cream	Natural rubber	Cardinal Red
Yukon Grey (GR7) Snowberry White (WT4)	Cardinal Red	Cardinal Red	Cardinal Red	Pale Cream	Cardinal Red	Cardinal Red
Damask Red (RD5) Whitehall Beige (BG4)	Cardinal Red	Cardinal Red	Cardinal Red	Pale Cream	Cardinal Red	Cardinal Red
Cumberland Green (GN35) Old English White (WT3)	Porcelain Green	Porcelain Green	Porcelain Green	Pale Cream	Natural rubber	Almond Green
Cumberland Green (GN35) Snowberry White (WT4)	Porcelain Green	Porcelain Green	Porcelain Green	Pale Cream	Almond Green	Almond Green

Body Colour and BMC Paint Code	Seats	Seat piping	Liners	Headlining	Door seals	Carpets
Peony Red (RD29) Whitehall Beige (BG4)	Cardinal Red	Cardinal Red	Cardinal Red	Pale Cream	Cardinal Red	Cardinal Red
Sable (RD30) Pale Ivory (YL1)	Cardinal Red	Cardinal Red	Cardinal Red	Pale Cream	Cardinal Red	Cardinal Red
Snowberry White (WT4)	Black	Black	Black	Pale Cream	Black	Black

Wolseley Hornet MkIII

Body Colour and BMC Paint Code	Seats	Seat piping	Liners	Headlining	Door seals	Carpets
Everglade Green (GN42) Snowberry White (WT4)	Porcelain Green	Porcelain Green	Porcelain Green	Pale Cream	Almond Green	Almond Green
Glen Green (GN40) Spruce Green (GN13)	Porcelain Green	Porcelain Green	Porcelain Green	Pale Cream	Natural rubber or Almond Green	Almond Green
Birch Grey (GR3) Yukon Grey (GR7)	Cardinal Red	Cardinal Red	Cardinal Red	Pale Cream	Cardinal Red	Cardinal Red
Cumulus Grey (GR29) Yukon Grey (GR7)	Cardinal Red	Cardinal Red	Cardinal Red	Pale Cream	Cardinal Red	Cardinal Red
Maroon B (RD23) Toga White (WT5)	Dove Grey	Dove Grey	Dove Grey	Pale Cream	Natural rubber	Cumulus Grey
Maroon B (RD23) Snowberry White (WT4)	Dove Grey	Dove Grey	Dove Grey	Pale Cream	Cumulus Grey	Cumulus Grey
Snowberry White (WT4)	Black	Black	Black	Pale Cream	Black	Black
Snowberry White (WT4) Trafalgar Blue (BU37)	Dove Grey	Dove Grey	Dove Grey	Pale Cream	Cumulus Grey	Cumulus Grey
Snowberry White (WT4) Damask Red (RD5)	Cardinal Red	Cardinal Red	Cardinal Red	Pale Cream	Cardinal Red	Cardinal Red
Snowberry White (WT4) Peony Red (RD29)	Cardinal Red	Cardinal Red	Cardinal Red	Pale Cream	Cardinal Red	Cardinal Red
Toga White (WT5) Damask Red (RD5)	Cardinal Red	Cardinal Red	Cardinal Red	Pale Cream	Natural rubber	Cardinal Red
Toga White (WT5) Trafalgar Blue (BU37)	Dove Grey	Dove Grey	Dove Grey	Pale Cream	Natural rubber	Cumulus Grey

Body Colour + Paint Code + VIN Paint Code	Model	Seats	Carpets/Mats	Liners	Door seals
Mini From September 1969					
Antelope (BLVC7)	850 De Luxe	Icon Red	Black	Icon Red	Icon Red
	850 De Luxe	Black	Black	Black	Black
	1000	Icon Red	Icon Red		
	Clubman Estate	Black	Black	Black	Black
	1275GT	Black	Black	Black	Black
	Van *Pick Up	Black	Black	Black	Black
Aqua (BLVC60) JMA	850 De Luxe	Black	Black	Black	Black
	850 De Luxe	Navy	Black	Navy	Navy
	1000	Black	Black	Black	Black
	Clubman Estate	Navy	Black	Black	Black
	1275GT	Black	Black	Black	Black
	1275GT	Navy	Navy	Navy	Navy
	Van & Pick Up	Black	Black	Black	Black
Blue Royal (BU38)	850 De Luxe	Galleon Blue	Black	Galleon Blue	Galleon Blue
	1000 Clubman Estate	Galleon Blue	Galleon Blue	Galleon Blue	Galleon Blue
Bronze Yellow (BLVC15) FMF	850 De Luxe	Black	Black	Black	Black
	850 De Luxe	Navy	Black	Navy	Navy
	1000 Clubman Estate	Black	Black	Black	Black
		Navy			
	1275GT	Black	Black	Black	Black
	1275GT	Navy	Navy	Navy	Navy
Flame Red (BLVC61) CMB	850 De Luxe	Autumn Leaf	Black	Autumn Leaf	Autumn Leaf
	850 De Luxe	Black	Black	Black	Black
	850 De Luxe	Navy	Black	Navy	Navy
	850 De Luxe	Geranium	Black	Geranium	Geranium
	1000 Clubman Estate	Autumn Leaf	Brown	Autumn Leaf	Autumn Leaf
		Black	Black	Black	Black
		Navy	Navy	Navy	Navy
		Geranium	Geranium	Geranium	Geranium
	1275GT	Black	Black	Black	Black
	1275GT	Geranium	Geranium	Geranium	Geranium
	1275GT	Navy	Navy	Navy	Navy
	Van & Pick Up	Navy or	Black	Navy	Black
		Black	Black	Black	Black
Glacier White (BLVC59) NMA	850 De Luxe	Black	Black	Black	Black
	850 De Luxe	Icon Red	Black	Icon Red	Icon Red
	850 De Luxe	Navy	Black	Navy	Navy
	850 De Luxe	Geranium	Black	Geranium	Geranium
	850 De Luxe	Autumn Leaf	Black	Autumn Leaf	Autumn Leaf
	850 De Luxe	Ochre	Black	Ochre	Ochre
	850 De Luxe	Sorrel	Black	Sorrel	Sorrel
	850 De Luxe	Regal	Black	Regal	Regal
	1000 Clubman	Regal	Navy	Regal	Regal

	Model	Seats	Carpets/Mats	Liners	Door seals
	Estate	Black	Black	Black	Black
		Icon Red	Icon Red	Icon Red	Icon Red
		Navy	Navy	Navy	Navy
		Geranium	Geranium	Geranium	Geranium
		Autumn Leaf	Autumn Leaf	Autumn Leaf	Autumn Leaf
		Ochre	Ochre	Ochre	Ochre
		Sorrel	Sorrel	Sorrel	Sorrel
		Regal/Navy	Navy	Regal	Regal
		Orange	Safari	Orange	Orange
	1275GT	Black	Black	Black	Black
		Navy	Navy	Navy	Navy
		Ochre	Ochre	Ochre	Ochre
		Autumn Leaf	Autumn Leaf	Autumn Leaf	Autumn Leaf
		Geranium	Geranium	Geranium	Geranium
		Sorrel	Safari	Sorrel	Sorrel
		Regal/Navy	Black	Regal	Regal
	Van & Pick Up	Navy	Black	Navy	Black
		Black	Black	Black	Black
Blaze (BLVC16)	850 De Luxe 1000 Clubman	Navy	Black	Navy	Navy
EMA	Estate	Navy	Navy	Navy	Navy
	1275GT	Navy	Navy	Navy	Navy
Bedouin (BLVC4)	850 De Luxe 1000	Navy	Black	Navy	Navy
	Clubman Estate	Autumn Leaf	Autumn Leaf	Autumn Leaf	Autumn Leaf
Teal Blue 70	850 De Luxe	Limeflower	Black	Limeflower	Limeflower
(BLVC18)	850 De Luxe	Ochre	Black	Ochre	Ochre
JMC	1000				
	Clubman	Limeflower	Olive	Limeflower	Limeflower
	Estate	Ochre	Ochre	Ochre	Ochre
	1275GT	Limeflower	Olive	Limeflower	Limeflower
	1275GT	Ochre	Ochre	Ochre	Ochre
	Van & Pick Up	Navy	Black	Navy	Black
		Black	Black	Black	Black
Limeflower	850 De Luxe	Limeflower	Black	Limeflower	Limeflower
(BLVC20)	1000				
	Clubman	Limeflower	Olive	Limeflower	Limeflower
HMA	Estate				
	1275GT	Limeflower	Olive	Limeflower	Limeflower
Black Tulip	850 De Luxe	Geranium	Black	Geranium	Geranium
(BLVC23)	850 De Luxe	Ochre	Black	Ochre	Ochre
KMA	1000				
	Clubman	Geranium	Geranium	Geranium	Geranium
	Estate	Ochre	Ochre	Ochre	Ochre
	1275GT	Geranium	Geranium	Geranium	Geranium
	1275GT	Ochre	Ochre	Ochre	Ochre

Body Colour + Paint Code + VIN Paint Code	Model	Seats	Carpets/Mats	Liners	Door seals
Mini From September 1969					
Green Mallard (BLVC22) HMD	850 De Luxe 1000	Limeflower	Black	Limeflower	Limeflower
	Clubman Estate	Limeflower	Olive	Limeflower	Limeflower
	1275GT	Limeflower	Olive	Limeflower	Limeflower
	Van & Pick Up	Navy	Black	Navy	Black
Citron (BLVC73) FMD	850 De Luxe 1000	Navy	Black	Navy	Black
	Clubman Estate	Navy	Navy	Navy	Navy
	1275GT	Navy	Navy	Navy	Navy
Harvest Gold (BLVC19)	850 De Luxe	Olive	Black	Olive	Olive
	850 De Luxe	Navy	Black	Navy	Navy
	850 De Luxe	Sorrel	Black	Sorrel	Sorrel
	1000	Olive	Olive	Olive	Olive
	Clubman	Navy	Navy	Navy	Navy
	Estate	Sorrel	Safari	Sorrel	Sorrel
	1275GT	Olive	Olive	Olive	Olive
	1275GT	Navy	Navy	Navy	Navy
	1275GT	Sorrel	Sorrel	Sorrel	Sorrel
	1275GT	Sorrel	Safari	Sorrel	Sorrel
	Van & Pick Up	Navy	Black	Navy	Black
Aconite (BLVC95) KMB	850 De Luxe	Sorrel	Black	Sorrel	Sorrel
	850 De Luxe 1000	Navy	Black	Navy	Navy
	Clubman Estate	Sorrel	Sorrel	Sorrel	Sorrel
	1275GT	Sorrel	Sorrel	Sorrel	Sorrel
Tundra (BLVC94) HMF	850 De Luxe	Limeflower	Black	Limeflower	Limeflower
	850 De Luxe 1000	Mink	Black	Mink	Mink
	Clubman	Limeflower	Olive	Limeflower	Limeflower
	Estate	Mink	Safari	Mink	Mink
	1275GT	Limeflower	Olive	Limeflower	Limeflower
	1275GT	Mink	Safari	Mink	Mink
	Van & Pick Up	Navy	Black	Navy	Black
Mirage (BLVC11) LMF	850 De Luxe	Spanish Rose	Black	Spanish Rose	Spanish Rose
	850 De Luxe	Sorrel	Black	Sorrel	Sorrel
	850 De Luxe	Navy	Black	Navy	Navy
	1000	Spanish Rose	Spanish Rose	Spanish Rose	Spanish Rose
	Clubman	Sorrel	Sorrel	Sorrel	Sorrel
	Estate	Navy	Navy	Navy	Navy
		Sorrel	Safari	Sorrel	Sorrel
	Van & Pick Up	Navy	Black	Navy	Black

Body Colour + Paint Code + VIN Paint Code	Model	Seats	Carpets/Mats	Liners	Door seals
Bracken (BLVC93) FME	850 De Luxe	Sorrel	Black	Sorrel	Sorrel
	850 De Luxe	Navy	Black	Navy	Navy
	1000	Sorrel	Safari	Sorrel	Sorrel
	Clubman	Navy	Navy	Navy	Navy
	Estate	Sorrel	Sorrel	Sorrel	Sorrel
	1275GT	Navy	Navy	Navy	Navy
	1275GT	Sorrel	Safari	Sorrel	Sorrel
Tahiti Blue (BLVC65) JMP	850 De Luxe	Mink	Black	Mink	Mink
	850 De Luxe	Navy	Black	Navy	Navy
	850 De Luxe	Regal	Black	Regal	Regal
	850 De Luxe	Beige	Black	Beige	Beige
	1000	Regal	Navy	Regal	Regal
	Clubman	Mink	Safari	Mink	Mink
	Estate	Navy	Navy	Navy	Navy
		Mink	Mink	Mink	Mink
		Regal/Navy	Navy	Regal	Regal
		Regal/Navy	Black	Regal	Regal
	1000	Beige (striped)	Chestnut	Beige	Black
	Clubman	Beige	Chestnut	Beige	Black
	Estate	Beige	Chestnut	Beige	Black
	1100 Special	Beige	Chestnut	Beige	Black
	1275GT	Navy	Navy	Navy	Navy
	1275GT	Mink	Safari	Mink	Mink
	1275GT	Regal/Navy	Black	Regal	Regal
	1275GT	Beige (striped)	Chestnut	Beige	Black
	Van & Pick Up	Navy or Black	Black	Navy or Black	Black
Damask Red (BLVC99) CMA	850 De Luxe	Mink	Black	Mink	Mink
	850 De Luxe	Navy	Black	Navy	Navy
	1000	Navy	Navy	Navy	Navy
	Clubman	Mink	Mink	Mink	Mink
	Estate	Mink	Safari	Mink	Mink
		Mink	Triumph Brown	Mink	Mink
	1275GT	Spanish Rose	Spanish Rose	Spanish Rose	Spanish Rose
	1275GT	Navy	Navy	Navy	Navy
	1275GT	Mink	Safari	Mink	Mink
	1275GT	Mink	Triumph Brown	Mink	Mink
	Van & Pick Up	Black	Black	Black	Black
Cumulus Grey (BLVC194) LMB	Van & Pick Up	Black	Black	Black	Black
Persian Blue (BU39)	Van & Pick Up	Black	Black	Black	Black
Connaught Green (GN18)	Van & Pick Up	Black	Black	Black	Black

Body Colour + Paint Code + VIN Paint Code	Model	Seats	Carpets/Mats	Liners	Door seals
Flamenco (BLVC133) EMC	850 De Luxe	Mink	Black	Mink	Mink
	850 De Luxe	Navy	Black	Navy	Navy
	850 De Luxe	Black	Black	Black	Black
	850 De Luxe	Beige	Black	Beige	Beige
	1000	Navy	Navy	Navy	Navy
	Clubman	Mink	Mink	Mink	Mink
	Estate	Mink	Safari	Mink	Mink
		Mink	Triumph Brown	Mink	Mink

Mini From September 1969

Body Colour + Paint Code + VIN Paint Code	Model	Seats	Carpets/Mats	Liners	Door seals
Flamenco	1000	Grey (striped)	Black	Black	Black
	Clubman	Black	Black	Black	Black
	Clubman	Beige	Chestnut	Beige	Beige
	Estate	Beige	Chestnut	Beige	Beige
	Estate	Black	Black	Black	Black
	1100 Special	Black	Black	Black	Black
	1275GT	Navy	Navy	Navy	Navy
	1275GT	Mink	Safari	Mink	Mink
	1275GT	Mink	Triumph Brown	Mink	Mink
	1275GT	Grey (striped)	Black	Black	Black
	1275GT	Beige (striped)	Chestnut	Beige	Beige
	Van & Pick Up	Black	Black	Black	Black
Antique Gold (BLVC138) GMB	850 De Luxe	Sorrel	Black	Sorrel	Sorrel
	1000	Sorrel	Safari	Sorrel	Sorrel
	Clubman	Almond	Safari	Almond	Almond
	Estate	Sorrel	Triumph Brown	Sorrel	Sorrel
	1275GT	Almond	Safari	Almond	Almond
	1275GT	Almond	Triumph Brown	Almond	Almond
Lagoon Metallic (BLVC42) JMD	1275GT	Navy	Navy	Navy	Navy
	1275GT	Mink	Safari	Mink	Mink
Cosmic Blue Metallic (BLVC111) JMK	1275GT	Navy	Navy	Navy	Navy
	1275GT	Mink	Safari	Mink	Mink
Brazil Metallic (BLVC109) AMD	1275GT	Sorrel	Safari	Sorrel	Sorrel
	1275GT	Mink	Safari	Mink	Mink
	1275GT	Almond	Safari	Almond	Almond
Reynard Metallic (BLVC112) BMB	Clubman	Sorrel	Chestnut	Sorrel	Black
	1275GT	Sorrel	Safari	Sorrel	Sorrel
	1275GT	Navy	Navy	Navy	Navy
	1275GT	Sorrel (striped)	Chestnut	Sorrel	Black
Aurora Metallic (BLVC43) DMA	1275GT	Navy	Navy	Navy	Navy

Body Colour + Paint Code + VIN Paint Code	Model	Seats	Carpets/Mats	Liners	Door seals
Astral Blue Metallic (BLVC140) JMR	Clubman	Black	Black	Black	Black
	1100 Special	Black	Black	Black	Black
	1275GT	Regal/Navy	Navy	Regal	Regal
	1275GT	Grey (striped)	Black	Black	Black
Sandglow (BLVC63) AMF	850 De Luxe	Sorrel	Black	Sorrel	Sorrel
	850 De Luxe	Sorrel	Black	Sorrel	Black
	850 City	Black/Ecru	Black	Black	Black
	850 Super	Sorrel (striped)	Black	Sorrel	Black
	1000	Sorrel	Safari	Sorrel	Sorrel
	Clubman Estate	Sorrel	Triumph Brown	Sorrel	Sorrel
	1000	Sorrel (striped)	Chestnut	Sorrel	Black
	Clubman	Sorrel	Chestnut	Sorrel	Black
	1100 Special	Sorrel or Sorrel (striped)	Chestnut	Sorrel	Black
	1275GT	Sorrel (striped)	Safari	Sorrel	Sorrel
	1275GT	Sorrel	Triumph Brown	Sorrel	Sorrel
	1275GT	Sorrel	Chestnut	Sorrel	Black
	Van	Black/Ecru	Black	Black	Black
	Van & Pick Up	Black	Black	Black	Black
Russet (BLVC205) AAE	850 De Luxe	Beige	Black	Beige	Beige
	850 Super	Beige (striped)	Chestnut	Beige	Black
	1000	Beige	Chestnut	Beige	Black
	Clubman Estate	Beige	Chestnut	Beige	Black
	1100 Special	Beige	Chestnut	Beige	Black
	1100 Special	Beige (striped)	Chestnut	Beige	Black
	1275GT	Beige (striped)	Chestnut	Beige	Black
Inca Yellow (BLVC207) FAB	850 De Luxe	Black	Black	Black	Black
	850 City	Black/Ecru	Black	Black	Black
	850 Super	Beige (striped)	Black	Beige	Beige
	1000	Grey (striped)	Black	Black	Black
	Clubman Estate 1100 Special	Black	Black	Black	Black
	1275GT	Grey (striped)	Black	Black	Black

Body Colour + Paint Code + VIN Paint Code	Model	Seats	Carpets/Mats	Liners	Door seals

Mini From September 1969

Body Colour + Paint Code + VIN Paint Code	Model	Seats	Carpets/Mats	Liners	Door seals
Triumph White (BLVC206) NAB	850 De Luxe	Sorrel	Black	Sorrel	Black
	1000	Sorrel (striped)	Chestnut	Sorrel	Black
	1275GT				
	Clubman				
	Estate	Sorrel (striped)	Chestnut	Sorrel	Black
	1100 Special				
Java (BLVC208) HAB	850 De Luxe	Beige	Black	Beige	Black
	850 City	Black/Ecru	Black	Black	Black
	850 Super	Beige	Chestnut	Beige	Black
	1000	(striped)			
	1275GT				
	Clubman	Beige	Chestnut	Beige	Black
	Estate	(striped)			
	1100 special				
	Clubman	Beige	Chestnut	Beige	Black
	Estate				
	1100 Special				
	1275GT	Beige (striped)	Chestnut	Beige	Black
	Van	Black/Ecru	Black	Black	Black
	Van & Pick Up	Black/Ecru	Black	Black	Black
Vermilion Red (BLVC118) CML	850 De Luxe	Black/Ecru	Black	Black	Black
	850 City	Black/Ecru	Black	Black	Black
	850 Super	Grey (striped)	Black	Black	Black
	1000	Grey (striped)	Black	Black	Black
	Clubman	Black	Black	Black	Black
	Estate	Black	Black	Black	Black
	1100 Special	Black	Black	Black	Black
	1275GT	Grey (striped)	Black	Black	Black
Tara Green Metallic (BLVC148) HAD	850 De Luxe	Black	Black	Black	Black
	850 Super	Grey (striped)	Black	Black	Black
	1000				
	Clubman	Black	Black	Black	Black
	Estate				
	1100 Special				
	1275GT	Grey (striped)	Black	Black	Black

Body Colour + Paint Code + VIN Paint Code	Model	Seats	Carpets/Mats	Liners	Door seals
Denim Blue Metallic (BLVC249) JMY	850 De Luxe Clubman Estate 1100 Special 850 Super	Black	Black	Black	Black
	1000	Grey (striped)	Black	Black	Black
	1275GT Clubman Estate 1100 Special	Black	Black	Black	Black
Rose Metallic (BLVC303) CMM	1100 Special (UK)	Savannah Check	Mink	Savannah	Black
Silver Metallic (BLVC202) JMR	1100 Special 1100 Special (UK)	Black Blue Check	Black Black	Black Black	Black Black
Black (BLVC90) PMA	1100 Special 1100 Special	Black Sorrel (striped)	Black Chestnut	Black Sorrel	Black Black
	1100 Special	Beige (striped)	Chestnut	Beige	Black

⑥ Clubs & Specialists

Of course, a good deal of the Mini's attractiveness comes from the pleasure they give to the person sitting in the driver's seat. But the lone pleasure of owning, maintaining, restoring and driving a Mini are multiplied several times over when those pleasures and the experiences of them can be shared with others and when a little more can be learned about the car. The best way of meeting like-minded enthusiasts is by joining the appropriate one-make club which provides meetings, competitions and shows for the enthusiast to attend and which is the best source for all practical, down to earth information on running the car. And not only will there be social and practical benefits from joining the club, there will probably be financial ones, too, saving the membership fee several times over.

Clubs and services are detailed in the following list with, after each one, a brief résumé of what it has to offer. There are, of course, others but those shown below are those which are most well known and which, in the author's opinion, have most to offer the Mini owner.

Clubs

The **Mini Owner's Club** was founded in 1979 by Chris Cheal, who still runs the club and takes a strong personal and friendly interest in the members and their cars. 'For many years', writes Chris, 'there was no club for Minis and according to letters read in car magazines, Mini owners wished to have one formed. The MOC was formed to get people together through club magazines and some social meetings, who had an interest in this great little car.'

The Club offers many benefits to Mini owners: insurance reductions, agreed valuations for cars which are now becoming 'classic', good spares availability, recommended suppliers, technical advice through the magazine and over the 'phone, Club regalia and a national meeting each year. The Club produces a quarterly magazine and members are encouraged to send in articles, hints, tips and photographs for publication.

The national meeting involves a full Concours competition for several different classes including the more recent Metro and there are always many sidestalls selling second-hand and new spares. Everyone agrees that it is a really good, social, friendly day out.

For more details send an SAE to Chris Cheal, MOC, 15 Birchwood Road, Bowley Park, Lichfield, Staffs WS14 9VN, England.

Also formed in 1979, the **Mini Cooper Club** has rapidly grown from its original membership of 40 to 2000. Originally it was intended to cater for Mini Coopers only, but due to the demand of owners of other Minis, the Mini Cooper Club now caters for all variants of Minis including the later GT's, Sprints, Mayfairs and Metro's, etc.

Activities offered by the Club are varied to suit all tastes and cover days out, car shows, summer camps and treasure hunts.

Available to members is a regular magazine, a special insurance scheme, free for sale and wanted ads and free technical advice.

All new members will join a friendly and enthusiastic group of Mini owners. Apply: Mrs M.J. Holman, Secretary, Mini Cooper Club, 9 Walesbeech, Furnace Green, Crawley, West Sussex RH10 6SJ, England.

The **Mini-Sportscar Club** incorporates the following clubs: GTM Owners Club, Hustler Owners Club, McCoy Owners Club, Midas Owners Club, Mini Drivers Club, Mini-Jem Owners Club, Mini Marcos Owners Club, Nomad Owners Club and Status Owners Club.

The MINI-SPORTSCAR CLUB serves as an 'umbrella' organisation for these separate clubs, which each cater for a particular make of car using the BL Mini or Metro power unit. The current ones are listed above and include specialist cars supplied fully assembled, kit cars, and standard-bodied Minis. Further clubs will be created to reflect the vehicles owned by members of the Mini-Sportscar Club.

Members have a tremendous amount in common and there is a very useful interchange of technical help through the club magazine, assistance on the availability of spares, social and competition events, and individuals to give advice on a geographical basis. A single headquarters address for all the individual clubs looks after correspondence and phone calls, and houses a permanent Secretariat available between 9 am and 5 pm on Mondays to Fridays, with a telephone answering machine at all other times.

The Mini-Sportscar Club is RAC-recognised which we hope will encourage members to have an active involvement with motor sport. The membership records, including car histories, is in process of being computerised for easy access. The existing range of Club regalia and components will be expanded to cover each associated club. Attention is being given to trying to have stocks manufactured of any parts which are proven to be difficult to obtain.

Subscriptions can be started, or renewed, by phoning 01-467 6533 (24 hours) with an Access or Barclaycard number. Naturally you can pay with a cheque, postal order or your credit card number, using the post. The membership fee is £6 and this is for 12 months from the date of joining and covers both the Mini-Sportscar Club and one of the associated owners' clubs. There is no joining fee.

The address is: Bank House, Summerhill, Chislehurst, Kent BR7 5RD, England.

The **Mini Moke Club** was formed in April 1983 for Moke owners and enthusiasts whether their Mokes were made in England, Australia or Portugal.

The aim of the club is to provide social contact through meetings, events and a newsletter; also to ensure availability of spares and cheaper insurance.

Membership is not restricted to UK: we have members in Ireland, Italy and have contact with Moke clubs in the USA and Australia.

For details write with S.A.E. to: Mini Moke Club, 7 Oakdene, Hartlebury Park, Stourport, Worcs. DY13 9NF, England. Tel: (02993) 4488.

Specialists

The **Mini Spares Centre** is the only Mini specialist with British Leyland Heritage approval. They offer the widest independent range of Mini spares anywhere in the world as well as the most knowledgeable service (although remember when calling that they can be extremely busy!). With the Mini Spares Discount Club offering worthwhile reductions on parts, the Mini Spares Centre can be a godsend to the Mini restorer, especially for those hard to find parts. (Keith Dodd) Mini Spares Centre Ltd, 29-31 Friern Barnet Rd, Southgate, London N11 1NE, England. Tel: 01-368 6292.

It's easy to forget **Austin-Rover/Unipart** when talking about Mini spares but their spares stock and dealer network are second to none – after all they made the cars in the first place! If you want to find parts, try visiting your local parts dealer during a quiet spell and get the storeman to go through the parts book as well as the mind-blowing microfiche system. You (and the storeman!) will be surprised just how much is available. See your telephone directory for local stockists.

The **Midland Mini Centre** specialise in Mini spares, new and used. 317 Highfield Road, Hall Green, Birmingham B28 0BX, England. Tel: 021-777 1961.

SIP (Industrial Products) Ltd. Manufacture an impressive range of quality workshop equipment: MIG welders, spot and arc-welders, spray guns and compressors in all shapes and sizes. Keen prices, and strongly recommended! SIP (Industrial Products) Ltd., Gelders Hall Rd, Shepshed, Loughborough, Leics LE12 9NH, England. Tel: 0509-503141 – ten lines.

The Welding Centre. Offers a range of DIY-type gas welding sets available at a wide range of prices. The Welding Centre, 165 Netherauldhouse Road, Newlands, Glasgow, Scotland. Tel: 041-649 7536.

Murex Welding Products Ltd. Manufacturers of Porta-Pack portable but professional type welding kits. Used in combination with BOC mini-bottles and obtainable for private use. Regional Sales Office, P.O. Box 32, Oxford Street, Bilston, West Midlands WV14 7EQ, England. Tel: 0902-404811.

Lifesure Ltd. Specialists in providing car insurance for classic cars of all types, especially for Agreed Value policies where the car's value is agreed in advance rather than left to the 'low' book price that normally prevails. Lifesure Ltd. 34 New Street, St. Neots, Huntingdon, Cambs PE19 1NQ, England.

Waxoyl. Rust inhibiting fluid from Finnigan's Speciality Paints Ltd., Eltringham Works, Prudhoe, Northumberland, England.

Spridgebits Ltd. Ideal for 1098cc and 1275cc new and second-hand engine tuning parts. Spridgebits Ltd. (Mailing Address) 54 St. Peter's Road, Handsworth, Birmingham B20, England.

Sykes Pickavant Ltd. Full range of excellent DIY and professional panel beating tools. See local DIY and Accessory shops.

Mini-Mania. Pierre Schmit is continental agent for Mini Spares Centre. 54 Rue Des Champs, L-3442 Dudelange, Luxembourg. Tel: 51-11-44.

Classic Car Restorations, as their name implies, carry out restoration work to all types of Mini (and that has included the author's concours-winning 1959 Austin Mini) as well as other makes of classic car. Leading panel beater, Ken Wright, has restored cars featured in Haynes 'Restoration Guides' as well as *Practical Classics, Sports Car Monthly* and *Classic Cars* magazines. You don't get much better than that! Contact proprietor Gordon Ashford at Chestnut Cottage, Tedstone Wafre, Bromyard, Hereford HR7 4QB, England, or telephone the Green Farm Workshop on 0885 82330, or ring Gordon 'out of hours' on 08867

The Taunton Mini Centre. Specialises in the repair of Minis mechanically and bodily. Real enthusiasts who are ready to offer useful advice based on much experience. The Taunton Mini Centre, Priory Bridge Road, Taunton, Somerset. Tel: 0823-54706.

7 British & American Technical Terms

As this book has been written in England, it uses the appropriate English component names, phrases and spelling. Some of these differ from those used in America. Normally, these cause no difficulty, but to make sure, a glossary is printed below. In ordering spare parts remember the parts list will probably use these words:

English	American	English	American
Accelerator	Gas pedal	Leading shoe (of brake)	Primary shoe
Aerial	Antenna	Locks	Latches
Anti-roll bar	Stabiliser or sway bar	Methylated spirit	Denatured alcohol
Big-end bearing	Rod bearing	Motorway	Freeway, turnpike etc
Bonnet (engine cover)	Hood	Number plate	License plate
Boot (luggage compartment)	Trunk	Paraffin	Kerosene
Bowden cable	Flexible pull cable	Petrol	Gasoline (gas)
Bulkhead	Firewall	Petrol tank	Gas tank
Bush	Bushing	'Pinking'	'Pinging'
Cam follower or tappet	Valve lifter or tappet	Prise (force apart)	Pry
Carburettor	Carburetor	Propeller shaft	Driveshaft
Catch	Latch	Quarterlight	Quarter window
Choke/venturi	Barrel	Retread	Recap
Circlip	Snap-ring	Reverse	Back-up
Clearance	Lash	Rocker cover	Valve cover
Control cable	Flexible pull cable	Saloon	Sedan
Crownwheel	Ring gear (of differential)	Seized	Frozen
Damper	Shock absorber, shock	Sidelight	Parking light
Disc (brake)	Rotor/disk	Silencer	Muffler
Distance piece	Spacer	Sill panel (beneath doors)	Rocker panel
Drop arm	Pitman arm	Small end, little end	Piston pin or wrist pin
Drop head coupe	Convertible	Spanner	Wrench
Dynamo	Generator (DC)	Split cotter (for valve spring cap)	Lock (for valve spring retainer)
Earth (electrical)	Ground	Split pin	Cotter pin
Engineer's blue	Prussian blue	Steering arm	Spindle arm
Estate car	Station wagon	Sump	Oil pan
Exhaust manifold	Header	Swarf	Metal chips or debris
Fault finding/diagnosis	Troubleshooting	Tab washer	Tang or lock
Float chamber	Float bowl	Tappet	Valve lifter
Free-play	Lash	Thrust bearing	Throw-out bearing
Freewheel	Coast	Top gear	High
Gearbox	Transmission	Trackrod (of steering)	Tie-rod (or connecting rod)
Gearchange	Shift	Trailing shoe (of brake)	Secondary shoe
Grub screw	Setscrew, Allen screw	Transmission	Whole drive line
Gudgeon pin	Piston pin or wrist pin	Tyre	Tire
Halfshaft	Axleshaft	Van	Panel wagon/van
Handbrake	Parking brake	Vice	Vise
Hood	Soft top	Wheel nut	Lug nut
Hot spot	Heat riser	Windscreen	Windshield
Indicator	Turn signal	Wing/mudguard	Fender
Interior light	Dome lamp		
Layshaft (of gearbox)	Countershaft		